Marilyn
1991

MAKE ROOM FOR DANNY

Danny Thomas

WITH BILL DAVIDSON

G. P. PUTNAM'S SONS

New York

G. P. Putnam's Sons
Publishers Since 1838
200 Madison Avenue
New York, NY 10016

Library of Congress Cataloging-in-Publication Data

Thomas, Danny.
Make room for Danny / Danny Thomas with Bill Davidson.
p.   cm.
1. Thomas, Danny.   2. Comedians—United States—Biography.
3. Actors—United States—Biography.   4. Television personalities—
United States—Biography.   I. Davidson, Bill, date.
II. Title.
PN2287.T36A3 1991   90-41585 CIP
792.7'028'092—dc20
[B]
ISBN 0-399-13566-9

Printed in the United States of America
1   2   3   4   5   6   7   8   9   10

This book is printed on acid-free paper.
∞

TO MY BELOVED ROSE MARIE,
AND OUR MARLO, TERRE
AND TONY

chapter

1

My real name is Muzyad Yakhoob. At least that's what it was when I was a baby, when everybody called me "Muzzy," for short. When my father later Christianized our names, he became Charles Jacobs, I became Amos Jacobs, and my mother became Margaret Jacobs. My mother was always confused about my name. She was the kind of lady from the Old Country who answered a simple question like "When was I born?" with "Well, it was lightning that knocked down the tree and it was the cow she have calf."

To add to the confusion, Mother was convinced my name was Alphonsus because I was baptized at St. Alphonsus Church in Deerfield, Michigan. So the name Alphonsus Jacobs somehow got onto my early legal papers. That was the name I had to use when I married my wife, Rose Marie, some twenty years later. But my true legal name is Amos Jacobs, and my friends, like Frank Sinatra, always call me "Jake." The only person who addresses me as Amos is Rose Marie. When she says "Amos," instead of "Honey" or "Sweetheart," I know I'm in trouble.

So how did I get the name Danny Thomas? Like all good things that happened to me in my life, it came about by accident. I had been struggling as a saloon entertainer in Detroit to eke out a living for my wife and my daughter, Marlo, when I decided to go to Chicago to try my luck as a character actor—an ambition which I still harbor to this day. I made valuable contacts in Chicago, and I was doing fairly well in radio drama. In truth, though, I worked mostly in commercials where the call was for "a Persian-sounding gentleman." This was 1940, before the advent of television, when radio was still king.

In the midst of this rather modest success, the William Morris Agency recommended me for a one-week job as master of ceremonies and comic at a converted auto show-room called the 5100 Club, on the far North Side of Chicago. The pay was fifty dollars a week—more than I was making in radio—but I was terribly embarrassed about it. What would my Chicago radio contacts think? What would the folks back home think after I had left *their* clubs to start my new career as a character actor? So when the 5100 Club's owner, Harry Eager, asked me how I wanted to be billed, I racked my brain to come up with an assumed name that would keep me anonymous. I thought of my oldest brother Daniel and my youngest brother Tom, and blurted out, "Danny Thomas."

That was August 12, 1940. The name Danny Thomas stuck with me because the one-week engagement at the 5100 Club stretched out to more than three wonderful years. It was the real beginning of my career. I was a thousand times bigger hit as Danny Thomas than I ever had been as Amos Jacobs.

Of course, as Danny Thomas, I had my ups and my downs. As I have always said, the good things happened to me almost by accident, usually when I wasn't looking. A good example is how I stumbled into my big television success—the situation comedy *Make Room for Daddy,* which was on the networks in prime time for eleven years.

I had been doing very well in nightclubs with my act, but I wanted to get into the exciting new medium, television. My biggest booster was Abe Lastfogel, the head of the William Morris Agency. I loved him like my own flesh and blood and called him "Uncle Abe." Even though he passed away a few years ago, I still refer to him as Uncle Abe.

It was 1953 and the newly formed American Broadcasting Company was trying to put together a television network. They desperately wanted the great comedian-dancer Ray Bolger, who was also a client of Uncle Abe's, to do a weekly show for them. Uncle Abe said, "You can have Bolger, but only if you also take Danny Thomas to do *his* own weekly show." The ABC people were a little reluctant. Some of them were *very* reluctant. I guess they figured this puss was not exactly the all-American face at that time. But in order to get Bolger they had to take me. Everyone was so sure I'd flop that they even wrote an escape clause into the contract. If my TV show got canceled, I'd do thirteen weeks on the ABC radio network.

So now came the question: What was I going to do in a half hour on television? The network didn't want me to host a variety show; they wanted a situation comedy. So I sat down in my house with producer Lou Edelman and writer Mel Shavelson to kick around ideas. We started with a concept about a theatrical boarding house and went on from there. Nothing worked.

Finally Shavelson got to his feet and said to Edelman, "You know, Lou, I don't really have the time to come up with a premise. I have other commitments." I went into a panic. I said, "Hey, guys, you gotta come up with something to keep me here in L.A. My God, I'm on the road half the year or more. When I come home, I got the wrong toys for my kids, I got the wrong dresses for the girls. Jeez, my son is now—what?—five years old and I hardly know him. I didn't get much of a crack at raising my two girls. My wife did a good job, but I'd like to be here with my son. The way it is now, I come home after being on the road for weeks and my dog attacks me. The kids call me 'Uncle Daddy.' Last Father's Day, when I was playing someplace in the country, Marlo sent me a telegram and it said, 'Daddy, dear old Daddy, you're more than an uncle to us.'" I collapsed in my chair.

Mel sat down, too. "That's it," he yelled.

"What's it?" I asked.

"The premise for the show," Mel responded. "I'm going home to start writing the pilot script right now."

"But I was only kvetching, complaining," I said.

Edelman said, "No matter. That's the show we're going to do—an entertainer who's on the road all the time and his kids complain he's Uncle Daddy. In fact, that's the title we should use."

My wife, Rose Marie, was listening outside the door. She came in and said, "No. Call it 'Make Room for Daddy.' That's what the kids say when they hear Amos is coming home and they have to move out of my bedroom." And so, that's how the show got on the air—and I was able to stay home with my family in Los Angeles for the next eleven years.

Accidental success? It happens to me all the time. My faith has a lot to do with it, too. For example, when I was so down-and-out in Detroit in my early years that my wife wanted me to give up show business and become a grocery clerk, I accidentally learned about the almost unknown St. Jude Thaddeus. One of the original Twelve Apostles, Jude was all-but-forgotten over the centuries because he was confused with the Apostle and traitor of a similar name, Judas Iscariot. But somehow, he became the patron saint of the hopeless, impossible, and difficult cases.

When I first prayed to St. Jude on that dark day in the Great Depression when my wife was expecting our first child, Marlo, I asked him to show me my way in life, and I vowed to build him a shrine. Soon after that, I had my first big success at the 5100 Club in Chicago, and I set out to fulfill my vow. The shrine became the world-famous St. Jude Children's Research Hospital in Memphis.

My St. Jude experience has led to a lot of friendly teasing on the part of my fellow comics.

Bob Hope says, "Danny Thomas is so religious that he gets stopped by the highway patrol because he has stained-glass windows in his car."

Red Buttons says, "Danny Thomas is the only Catholic in the world who had himself cloned so he could hear his own confession."

Even President Ronald Reagan got into the Danny-teasing act. In 1982, he told the Touchdown Club in Washington: "I was a little embarrassed when I first came to the White House and they played 'Hail to the Chief' when I entered the room—until I found out that when Danny Thomas walks in, they play Handel's *Messiah.*"

Strangely, the biggest kidders have been among my most generous supporters throughout my life.

Looking back on my life as I approach my seventy-sixth year, I'm happy to say that it's always been interesting. Rose Marie and I have produced three brilliant children. I have worked with some of the biggest stars in show business, and have rubbed elbows with kings, queens, and presidents. I have hobnobbed with the top moguls of the movie business—all of whom unsuccessfully tried to get me to have my nose fixed before appearing in their movies.

As is the case with anyone who has worked so many years in nightclubs, I came in close contact with the underworld. Once, in St. Louis in 1952, I did a benefit for an orphanage, on behalf of an Italian women's group. After the show, a guy came over to me in Biggie's Restaurant. I knew who he was, and I was scared to death when he grabbed me by the shoulder. He said, "That was a wonderful thing you did for them ladies."

I said, "No, it was nothing really."

He said, "You're an okay guy. Not much anyone can do for a guy like you, but I'll tell you this . . . (tightening his grip on my shoulder) . . . you got two hits comin' anytime you want them."

And then there are the sports figures. Few people know that I was one of the original principal owners of the Miami

Dolphins and still own a small piece of the pro-football franchise. I have hobnobbed with athletes like Joe Di-Maggio, Bob Griese, Magic Johnson, and Joe Namath. Among my politician friends have been five presidents, Ike Eisenhower, John F. Kennedy, Lyndon Johnson, Gerald Ford, and Ronald Reagan, as well as many members of Congress, many of whom banded together to engineer one of the great honors of my life.

In 1983, Congressman Nick J. Rahall II of West Virginia got up in the House of Representatives and entered a bill proposing me to be a recipient of the Congressional Medal. I had no idea what that was. It certainly couldn't be the Congressional Medal of Honor, which is only given to military super-heroes—and I hadn't even killed a mosquito, let alone five hundred guys in combat. I soon learned that it only had been awarded to civilians about a hundred times since George Washington's day, and that one of the recipients had been Bob Hope for his morale-building work with our troops overseas during our last three wars. Why was *I* being proposed? For my role in helping to found the St. Jude Children's Research Hospital.

I also found out that for me to get the medal, it would take a two-thirds vote of both houses of Congress. That seemed to me to be an almost hopeless long shot, so I promptly forgot about it. But Speaker O'Neill and Majority Leader Jim Wright got behind the measure and the bill passed. The speaker himself told me about the vote. I couldn't believe it. Tip said there had been only one negative vote in the House, and that was cast by a guy my daughter Marlo had campaigned against.

I was asked how I wanted the medal presented. I said, "Could the President give it to me at the White House, so that the St. Jude research program could benefit as much as possible from the publicity?" I started out to say, "Can Ronnie give it to me?" but I thought better of it. (I always called President Reagan "Ronnie," going back to the days when he was president of the Screen Actors Guild. When he was married to Jane Wyman, he used to play basketball in my backyard with the neighborhood kids.) Instead, I said, "Can the President give it to me?"

I then heard from the White House staff. Ronnie's 1984 reelection campaign was then under way, and would I mind waiting until after the election—some time early in 1985? I said I wouldn't mind waiting.

The day finally arrived, April 16, 1985. I flew to Washington with my family, and with the entire Board of Directors of the St. Jude Hospital. We were ushered into a room just off the Oval Office, which was jammed with my people and the press. The President walked in. I was shaking like a leaf. I said, "Ronnie, how do I handle this?"

He said, "Cool it and just hang in there." I said, "I'm trying."

Actually, it was easy. The President made a little speech and hung the gold medal around my neck, while the cameras clicked and whirred. The President kidded me with, "Great performance, Danny," and we all went into an adjoining room for a reception.

After all the congratulations and back-slapping, I went off into a corner by myself to look closely at my medal. It brought tears to my eyes. On one side, engraved in the gold, was a picture of me, holding a sick little girl in my arms. On the other side was a picture of the St. Jude Hospital. Below it was the inscription, *Medal by act of Congress, 1983.*

At this, one of the highest points of my life, I paused to wonder how all this had happened to me. Here I was, a first-generation American, the son of poor immigrants from the rugged mountains of Lebanon, penniless as a boy, with very little formal education.

And yet, here I was, the guest of honor at the White House.

How did it happen?

How did it *all* happen?

chapter

2

I was born on a horse farm in Deerfield, Michigan, over Mrs. Feldman's bakery in Toledo, Ohio.

That's what I like to say when people ask me about my origins. It always gets a laugh, but in truth it condenses a lot of years into one sentence.

Actually, to really understand my origins, you have to go back even farther.

To the village of Becheri, high in the mountains of Lebanon, about fifty miles north of Beirut. That's where my mother and father were born before the turn of the century.

Life was hard in Becheri (pronounced B'Sharri) in the early 1900s. At that time in history, the area was part of the Ottoman Empire and ruled by the Turks. The people of Becheri were fiercely independent and proud of their heritage, with ancestral ties to the ancient Phoenicians and the Thirteenth-Century Crusaders. As an early center of Christianity, Becheri's people still spoke Aramaic, the language of Christ, and even their Arabic was tinged with Aramaic words and cadences, making them the butt of jokes by other

Lebanese. When they couldn't scratch a living out of the rocky soil, many of them emigrated to America, usually to towns and cities where other Lebanese had settled previously. When my mother was ten years old, she and her parents settled in Toledo, Ohio.

In the Lebanese community, those were still the days of the arranged marriage. Back in Becheri, my father, a strapping young bachelor, knew about a fiery redhead with green eyes and milky-white skin (due, perhaps, to some Irish Crusader in her ancestry) who had emigrated to Toledo with her family a couple of years earlier. Her name was Julia Saad. My father carefully negotiated with Julia's relatives in Becheri, and then left by slow boat across the Mediterranean and the Atlantic to claim his bride in Toledo. He arrived and almost immediately found out that the unthinkable had happened.

The day before he reached Toledo, Julia had eloped with another man, Tonoose Simon. It was a love match—almost unheard of in those days.

My father was then nineteen and known by his Arabic first name, Shaheed, which means "The Witness." His father (my paternal grandfather) witnessed quite a bit of Shaheed's anger over the next couple of days. But Shaheed was a bright man (he had graduated from high school in Lebanon; he could read Aramaic, Hebrew, and Arabic, and spoke some English) and he decided, finally, to make the best of the situation. It was some situation. Back in Lebanon, running off with a man's intended bride could result in a blood feud, with one family massacring the other—not unlike the Hatfields and the McCoys.

To head off such fatal gunfire in Becheri—and also in the

streets of Toledo, where it wouldn't look good for the Lebanese immigrants' image—my grandfather advised his son to visit Tonoose's mother in Toledo and assure Mrs. Simon that he was *not* exercising his right to start a feud. Grumbling, my father followed the advice.

While he was discussing the matter with Tonoose's very nervous mother, Tonoose's thirteen-year-old sister walked into the room and asked my father if he wanted a drink of water. My father later told me, "As I watched this girl walk away from me to get the glass of water, I immediately fell in love." The girl was to be my mother, Margaret. Thus her brother Tonoose (by then known as Anthony or Tony) became my uncle, and Julia, the redhead he had snatched from my father, became my aunt. Beloved Aunt Julia and Uncle Tony were to be very important to me later on. Tony, in fact, was the prototype for the character Uncle Tonoose played so brilliantly by Hans Conried in my TV series, *Make Room for Daddy*.

Remember, though, that all these events—bride snatching, possible blood feuds, and such—all took place in 1903, more than ten years before I was born. In the meantime, my father and mother settled down to a struggling but happy marriage. In those days the principal role of the Lebanese woman was to bear sons, and Mother more than lived up to her duties. Four of my brothers came along before I did, the first when Mother was only fifteen. Then came one girl, Emily, and four more boys. In all, Shaheed and Margaret had nine sons and one daughter.

Father, small in stature but strong as a lion, did everything he could to provide for his growing family. He searched the alleys of Toledo for scrap he could sell, he worked in the factories as a laborer, he even tended the garden of the Presbyterian minister down the street. Eventually, Father acquired a horse and wagon and became a peddler of dry goods, kitchenware, and anything else he could get his hands on that he could buy cheap and sell high. His ambition was to accumulate enough money to buy a farm where he could breed dray horses and sell them to farmers for ploughs and wagons.

Father and his wagon became a familiar sight in the villages and hamlets of southern Michigan, north of Toledo, where he went from farm to farm selling his wares. The farmers got to like this powerful-looking man with the thick Middle Eastern accent, who always traveled with his lovely bride at his side. As my four older brothers were born, they were left with relatives in nearby towns, except when they were infants and rode in the wagon. At night, they would camp by the side of the road, with Mother cooking over a wood fire.

Mother later told me how she loved to listen to Father's fascinating stories about life in the mountains of Lebanon, and she would listen for hours to the music he skillfully played on a variety of strange Lebanese and Syrian instruments. His favorite was a weird one called the "mizwiz." It is made of two hollowed bamboo poles with five finger holes in each, and held together by waxed string, with reeds made of smaller bamboo, and sounds like a Scottish bagpipe. To play it, one must master the old Arabian secret of inhaling and exhaling without stopping. It takes prodigious strength, and Father used to play four hours at a time at christenings and weddings until dancers dropped from exhaustion.

The mizwiz was a key factor in a story my mother used to tell me. It seems they were camped in a dry river bed and Father had gone to fetch water while Mother prepared the noonday meal. Sleeping on the grass nearby was my infant brother Thomas, their first born, whose name in Arabic meant "The Tiller," since he had been born while my father's farmer customers were planting their crops.

Anyway, my mother says she looked over to where the baby was sleeping and what she saw made her freeze with shock. A huge snake had coiled itself around little Tommy, not touching him but surrounding him like a barrel hoop!

Mother ran to where Dad was collecting water. His first instinct was to kill the snake on the spot, but Mother pleaded with him not to do so because the baby would be harmed. So he got his mizwiz from the wagon and proceeded to play the instrument. Now you don't have to believe this. *I* do because I took whatever my mother told me as being authentic and final. As she related the story to me, the snake slowly uncoiled itself from around the baby and with head held high, crawled in the direction of the music.

My mother picked up the baby and ran with him to the wagon. A few minutes later, she heard Father calling her and when she returned, she found him standing there with a big smile on his face, hatchet in hand, and a headless snake hanging around his neck—looking like a great hunter back from the big kill.

If it had been me, it would have been a smiling snake with a headless man around his neck.

Anyway, according to Mother, that's what it was like to be on the road in a peddler's wagon in those days. I never cease to admire the courage and persistence of immigrants—the parents and grandparents of so many of us, no matter what their national origin or religious persuasion—who struggled so valiantly to make a go of it when they first came to this country.

In my parents' case, it got more and more complicated as one newborn son after another joined the little family in the wagon. After Thomas, "The Tiller," came William ("The Welder," in Arabic), Frederick ("The Solvent One"), and Raymond ("The Bearer of Good Tidings"). Finally my mother said to Dad, "This wagon is getting too crowded, and you might as well know that it won't be too long before there will be another passenger." She was referring to *my* impending birth. She made it very clear that she wanted to settle down somewhere. We didn't actually live in the wagon. It was Mother's way of telling Dad she was with child again.

As Mother tells the story, Dad took her in his arms and held her tightly. When he let her go, she had the imprint of his fingers on her arms. He had a grip like a vise. He had hurt her, but didn't mean to. She didn't care. She knew he had given in.

The money he had saved immediately went into the purchase of a horse farm in Deerfield, Michigan, which Dad had seen and coveted many times on his rounds. He had loved horses in the Old Country, and now he wanted to breed them for profit, producing draught animals that would be big and strong and could pull heavy wagonloads for miles. He deduced that his next son—me—would be

23

born on that farm he now owned and that the son, like the horses, would be big and strong. He gave me the Arabic name—Muzyad—which means "The Extraordinary One" because of the way I was born.

My birth, a few months later, was indeed extraordinary— but not in the way he envisioned. I came into the world on January 6, 1914. A blinding snowstorm was raging all over Lower Michigan. I started to be born in the birth-sac, completely enshrouded, and my mother was in real trouble. All her previous deliveries had been aided by midwives, but now she desperately needed the help of a doctor. In the blizzard, the local physician could not be reached.

My father jumped on one of his big horses and rode bareback to fetch his veterinarian, who lived nearby. The vet took one look at my mother—and the part of me that was visible—and made the snap decision that he had to perform his first *human* delivery. Thank God for that horse doctor! Without him, isolated as we were in that blizzard, we both could have died. When he delivered me and gave me that first slap, the vet said, "There's going to be a lucky colt." All this, of course, gave rise to another of those religious jokes about me: "born in a stable, of course."

Mother was very, very ill for a long time after that difficult delivery of extraordinary me. She didn't recover anywhere as quickly as she had after the arrivals of my four older brothers. Work on the farm was hard. She tried to cook, and tend the vegetable garden, and help Dad with the horses. But she was in pain and exhausted from the ordeal of bearing me. My father was too proud to ask for help from his family, but finally there was no other way. Whom did

he call? Aunt Julia, the redhead who had spurned him for
Mother's brother, Tonoose. She and Tonoose showed up
a couple of days later, taking the workload off mother for
many months to come.

They were the only ones in the family who could take
that much time off from their daily jobs. Uncle Tony owned
a little coffee shop, a grocery store, and a rooming house
for newly arrived immigrants from Lebanon, Syria, Ar-
menia, Turkey, Greece—anywhere in the Eastern Mediterranean. He was a happy-go-lucky man, a James Thurber
type. He was a great storyteller and rarely took anything
seriously—not even funerals. In fact, he was so funny that
he was barred from funerals because he made everyone
laugh at a time when they were supposed to be crying.
While watching a funeral go by and someone asked him
"Who died?" He said, "The gentleman in the first car." He
always referred to the deceased as being very lucky because
he didn't have to get up to go to work in the morning.

I used a lot of his humor in my act later on. Uncle Tony
would tell the story—and so did I—of the old widower who
wanted a husky young nurse as a wife, to comfort him and
take care of him in his declining years. He found such a
lady, who turned out to be a real shrew. She used to say to
people, "I just can't wait to walk on his grave." Well, the
old man really fixed her clock. He put it in his will that he
should be buried at sea.

Aunt Julia sparkled in her own way. She was a great
helpmate to Tony in his various businesses, but there was
a certain sadness about her. She was physically incapable of
conceiving a child—my people still used the biblical term,

"she was barren"—but when she arrived at the farm to take care of me during my mother's illness, it was as if God had bestowed on her a special blessing. I'm told that she cared for me with great joy, as if I were her own infant. This went on for months, until Julia finally had to leave the farm to go back to her own life with Uncle Tony in Toledo.

With Julia's special care—along with my mother's as she recuperated—I developed into a robust baby. Remember that Mother still had four other growing young boys to worry about. Once, my brother William fell into a creek and nearly drowned. He was saved when a local Irish lad named Amos Hurley jumped into the rushing waters and pulled William out, more dead than alive. That's when my father decided on the name Amos for me when he got around to Americanizing our names. He told my mother, "This little Muzyad is going to be courageous and daring, just like Amos Hurley." So I became Amos. Later, when I went to St. Francis de Sales Catholic School in Toledo, the nuns didn't think Amos was Christian enough for a Catholic boy. They tried to talk my parents into changing it to Ambrose. *That* would have looked great on a nightclub marquee—"the Great Comedian, Ambrose Jacobs." And you will recall that my mother still thought I was Alphonsus. That would have been even worse on the marquee.

With my mother's imprecision about dates as well as names, I don't know how long I lived on the farm as an infant. What I *do* know is that my father lost the farm, just as his horse-breeding business was beginning to pay off. And he lost it in a pretty spectacular fashion.

Dad was a fearless man, who would beat the daylights out

of us if we ever showed cowardice in our dealings with other kids. At the same time he was friendly with everyone, just so long as they didn't make the mistake of picking on him. In Michigan, he got along well with his fellow farmers, whose ancestry was mostly Anglo-Saxon, Scotch, Irish, or German. They liked the outgoing Middle Eastern fellow, who was suddenly plunked down in their midst, and they bore no prejudice toward him. In fact, they almost immediately invited him to play poker with them. Maybe they thought Dad would be a patsy, but he soon showed them he could read cards, bluff, and win with the best of them.

Then came what was known in Deerfield, Michigan, that year as The Big Game. It was held in the huge red barn of the wealthiest farmer in the area. I think Father said this man was Amish, but I don't believe the Amish play cards. Anyway, his name, as Dad recalled it, was Erich.

The game was five-card stud. Dad did very well, and the game boiled down to a single-hand between him and Erich. By that time, everyone else had tapped out. I've heard the story so much over the years that I know the details of every card that was dealt.

Dad began with a queen in the hole and another queen showing.

Erich's hand showed one ace up. He and Dad raised and counterraised.

On the next card, Dad got another queen. Two queens showing, and a third one in the hole. Erich got a king to go with his ace.

More raises.

Dad got a six of spades; Erich got another king. It looked

like a pair of aces and a pair of kings against Dad's three queens.

The last cards were meaningless—a jack of clubs to Dad and a lowly deuce to Erich. Both men kept raising. The barn was bursting with tension. Erich kept heckling Dad, saying he was bluffing, making Dad feel all the more that his three queens was the winning hand.

Before the last raise, when the money ran out, Dad signed a paper, pledging the deed to his farm, against Erich's prize forty acres.

"Call," said Erich.

Dad triumphantly turned over his third queen. The crowd cheered.

But Erich then turned over *his* hole card. It was a third king.

As far as our family was concerned, it was a call heard around the world. The farm was gone, the breeding horses were gone. We had to move back to Toledo, where my father, the almost-entrepreneur, had to take a job as a laborer in a factory to support his wife and six children (by that time, my sister, Emily, had been born). He remained a laborer for the rest of his working life.

Once again, Uncle Tony and Aunt Julia came to the rescue. Tony's Middle Eastern coffee shop was prospering, so he was able to buy a two-family house in an almost-but-not-quite slum area of Toledo. He and Julia moved into the small apartment upstairs; he gave us the much larger lower floor. I was two years old at the time and unaware of the disappearance of the trees and the grass and all those horsies, duckies, and bunnies, which Aunt Julia later told me about.

On the other hand, I was delighted to be back in the warm arms and on the soft bosom of Aunt Julia, who spoiled me as much as my mother did—even more so than Mom, who also had five other kids to worry about. But then came another incident which could have been destructive in my very young life. But it wasn't—probably because of the incredible warmth that existed in the extended immigrant families of the day.

What happened was that Uncle Tony had an opportunity to open a super-duper coffee shop in Detroit, which would mean they'd have to move to that city, about sixty miles away. Because of her love for me, Julia didn't want to go. She said, "I won't go without the boy."

Tony said, "What boy?"

She said, "Amos."

He said, "If you think I'm going to go down there and tell Charlie Jacobs I want to take his son, you're crazy."

After Julia and Tony argued back and forth, a terrific conversation between Julia and my father took place. I always thought it would make a great scene in a play. Julia came down from her upstairs apartment and Dad was sitting in our living room, reading his Arabic paper and smoking a cigarette. He always hand-rolled his cigarettes, two at a time—one to smoke, the other to keep handy, tucked behind his ear. As Julia came into the room, Dad stood up. Arabic men always stand when a woman comes in. It's a custom. And Dad was a perfect gentleman, besides.

"Charlie," Julia said, "life is very peculiar. You came to this country to marry me. And from that marriage, you expected sons. Fortunately for you, that marriage didn't take place, for I never could have given you sons."

Dad just looked at her and said, "Go on."

Aunt Julia looked him right in the eyes—this was one of the things he loved about her—and she said, "Charlie, I couldn't give you a son, but now I want you to give me a son—Amos. I love him and I can't live without him. You have four others and a daughter, and the Lord will bless you with more. I cannot be so blessed. I beg you. Give him to me."

She was crying. Big, sincere tears.

My dad was never one for pathos. He just stepped back and said, "Julia, I've known for a long time that this day was coming. Now that it has, I say to you, 'Take him.' Bring him up in love of God and neighbor. But as his uncle and aunt. He still has a mother and father. He must know that as he grows, you are his uncle and aunt."

And so it was, after Uncle Tony had squared it with his sister, my mom.

I lived with Julia and Tony until I was fifteen years old.

chapter

Not quite.

Because Aunt Julia and Uncle Tony didn't live in Detroit for very long and they came back to Toledo. They then almost always lived in a house or an apartment close to my parents', and there weren't many days when I didn't drift over to Mom and Dad's to play with all those kids I thought of as my cousins at that time.

Why did Uncle Tony decide to return to Toledo so quickly? His coffee shop in Detroit was an enormous success, but after we had lived there less than a year, his youngest sister, Agnes, only nineteen years old, died suddenly of a ruptured appendix—a frequently fatal illness in the days before sulfa drugs and antibiotics were available. I was then nearly five, and one of my earliest memories was Aunt Agnes's wake. It took place in our huge coffee house. I remember the strong scent of cut flowers, especially gardenias. Which probably explains why I still hate the smell of gardenias.

Anyway, we traveled to the funeral in Toledo in two specially chartered railroad cars, and then back to Detroit. Uncle Tony just couldn't stand Detroit after his baby sister had died there. So he sold the business—and back to Toledo we went to live. Such are the workings of the Lebanese soul.

By now, my brother Paul had been born, to be followed in quick succession by Edward, Samuel, and the baby, Daniel. Dad no longer insisted on giving his kids romantic Arabic as well as Christian names. After me, Muzyad the Extraordinary, the children—from Emily on down—had names that were the same in Arabic as in English. A bigger problem was to find enough room for everyone—even with tripling up in the beds.

But I had no such problem. I lived in the comparative luxury of Uncle Tony and Aunt Julia's house, and from time to time I would go to spend the night with my brothers. I especially enjoyed the company of my next oldest brother, Ray, and he and I became very close. I led an interesting double life. It wasn't that Uncle Tony was so wealthy, but Dad was so poor. He had to struggle constantly as a laborer to make enough money to feed eleven mouths.

Occasionally, some amateur psychiatrist asks me if I felt a sense of abandonment at having been given away by my parents. I can honestly say that it never entered my mind. I soon learned that my brothers and Emily were not my cousins, but actually my siblings, and it made no difference to me whatsoever. I felt that I was blessed in having two families instead of one, and I loved Uncle Tony and Aunt Julia equally along with everyone else.

As I got older, I'd look at my father from time to time

as he sat in his chair and savored his sips of booze (later gulps), and I wondered how he was affected by the twin blows he suffered when I was a baby—his losing his farm in the poker game, followed by his giving me away to Julia. He was a complete stoic and never discussed either matter.

But one night I got a clue about the situation involving me. I had forgotten to tell Aunt Julia I was spending the night with my folks, and the poor woman came looking for me in the snow. She had a coat over her nightgown and only her bedroom slippers on her feet. She was hysterical. It was after midnight, and she had awakened from a sound sleep and discovered I wasn't in my bed. I recall that she and Dad had a few heated words. She accused him of trying to lure me back. He wasn't, of course. He finally told Julia that he just couldn't bring himself to tell a young son of his "to go home." He was unaware that I hadn't received Julia's permission "to stay over."

What a difference in the four adults who dominated my young life. Uncle Tony was the bon vivant, the entrepreneur, the teller of outrageous stories. Aunt Julia was his opposite. She didn't have to work, but she always did. When she and Tony had a restaurant, she was buyer, cook, and waitress. When they owned a small hotel, she was room clerk, chambermaid, and janitor. With all her tenderness toward me, she was utterly fearless, like my father. Julia was buxom and strong. When there was an unruly man at her bar, I saw her standing toe-to-toe with him, literally slugging it out at times.

My mom, on the other hand, was the gentlest, kindest, most honest, loving person I have ever known. She couldn't read or write in any language. But she was brilliant—in her plain, everyday, horse-sense way. Also, she had a faith in God I've never seen matched anywhere.

For example, I'll never forget how she reacted when my baby brother Danny—then only six months old—was bitten on the hand by a rat as he lay in his crib. Little Danny's screams awakened everyone, and Mom and Dad rushed him to the hospital. The doctors did all they could with the limited medical techniques available at the time, but poor little Danny was just about given up for dead. I've seen my mother pray, but never like that night. She fell to her knees and screamed aloud, "Please, God, spare him and I will vow to you." (Middle Easterners make a lot of vows.) "I vow," she said, "that I will beg pennies from door to door for a whole year to give to the poor. Spare my baby. Please, God, spare my baby."

Miraculously Danny lived—maybe even with rabies from the rat. We all attributed the miracle to Mom's prayer. *"She* did it," we kept saying.

Anyway, for an entire year after that, Mom used to take the streetcar to the end of the line (to "where the car bends," as they say in Toledo), and she would walk all the way back downtown, begging pennies door to door with that Middle Eastern accent of hers. They can't pronounce the letter "P," you know. So she would say, "Blease give bennies to the boor. I bromise God."

Sometimes, doors were slammed in her face, this lady with the black scarf on her head, but she persevered for the full year. I'm sure that that memory of her was the chief reason why I later kept my own vow to St. Jude when I made it.

What was my father's reaction to the rat incident? He was a proud, stubborn, sometimes kind, sometimes cruel man, who had a strange and savage way of expressing his love. First of all, he, too, dropped to his knees and prayed—the first time I'd ever seen him do that—and he, too, made a vow to God that if He spared little Danny's life, he'd never gamble again. It was a vow that he kept. I never saw him gamble again.

But when Danny lived, the other side of Dad came out. He had to take revenge on the rats. This will be hard for you to believe, but I swear that I saw it with my own eyes.

Dad removed a couple of flattened tin cans he had hammered over two ratholes under the kitchen sink, and he carefully spread a trail of bread and cheese crumbs. The trail led to an old-fashioned portable washtub he had inverted a few feet away. He propped up one edge of the upside-down tub with a wooden potato masher. He tied a long string to the potato masher. Then he sat down in the small dining room, holding the end of the string.

His unique trap didn't take long to work. Two rats came out of the holes and followed the trail of crumbs under the washtub. Dad pulled the string, yanking away the potato-masher support. The tub came down, imprisoning the rats beneath the tub.

I remember Dad smiling the way movie gangsters do just before they knock someone off. He took out his pouch of tobacco and his imported Greek cigarette paper and rolled a cigarette. He put the freshly rolled cigarette behind his ear and slowly walked toward the tub.

He lifted the tub just enough for one rat to get his head

out, then grabbed it by the throat and held it in his vise-like grip. The huge rat vainly tried to bite and scratch my father. He drew the rat closer and closer to him and he said, "If I thought you were the one that bit my kid, I'd bite your damned head off." Then he strangled the rat to death and let it drop to the floor.

Dad went over to the sink, washed his hands, took a few puffs of his cigarette, snuffed it, put the cigarette back behind his ear—and then returned to the tub to dispose of the second rat in the same way. This went on for five nights, at the end of which time there were no rats coming out of the holes under the sink. It was only a symbolic victory, however. There were other rats. There are *always* other rats in slum-type buildings.

My schooling was under the care of the Ursuline nuns at St. Francis de Sales. I went there with my brother Ray, and spent as much time with him as possible after school. By then, my parents were living in a big apartment on Canton Avenue, in Toledo's commercial district. The apartment was cheap because of where it was—upstairs over two storefronts, one a pool hall, the other Mrs. Feldman's bakery. Hence, the second half of my opening line: "I was born on a horse farm in Deerfield, Michigan, over Mrs. Feldman's bakery." Dear, wonderful Mrs. Feldman, another gentle soul, who loved us as if we were her own children. She was a big woman (let's face it, she was fat) who worked like a slave to keep her own life together but who couldn't have been more generous to us.

Widowed several years before we moved in, Mrs. Feldman not only baked and manned the counter in her bakery, but also made deliveries in a beat-up old Ford truck. Every night she'd come home in the old truck and climb the stairs to Mom and Dad's apartment, singing Jewish tunes from the Old Country and carrying two bags filled with the leftovers from her deliveries—broken cookies, scuffed rolls and bread. It supplemented the food my father could bring home—a lamb shoulder, for example, which would last a week. (I, of course, had the luxury of going back to Aunt Julia for more staple fare.)

Mrs. Feldman would sit with us for a while and tell us stories—mostly about her relationships with her in-laws, but sometimes about life in the Polish *shtetl* in which she grew up. The stories were both hilarious and sad. It was my first introduction to the marvelous subtleties of Yiddish humor, which I have used copiously in my own storytelling ever since I began to work as an entertainer.

And Mrs. Feldman's songs. I'll never forget those haunting melodies. The one I remember best was a lullaby, "Sleep, My Little Darling." Years later, Warner Brothers came up with the same Yiddish lullaby for me to sing when I starred in their remake of the Al Jolson film *The Jazz Singer.* All the time while I rehearsed and performed the number, the crew used to tease me: "Go on. You stole it from Mrs. Feldman." I had talked about her that much.

For years, my act was filled with Mrs. Feldman stories. I don't know how much is fact or fiction anymore. But there is considerable truth in one anecdote I used over and over again. It generally got enormous laughs—especially from Jewish audiences.

It seems that Mrs. Feldman used to go and put flowers on

37

her husband's grave a couple of Sundays a month. She went one Sunday and found that the cemetery was under new management. Someone else had bought it. What happened next was typical of Mrs. Feldman. She was witty, faster than greased lightning. Joey Bishop's humor always reminded me of her.

Anyway, Mrs. Feldman had a big armload of flowers. She was going through the big iron gate, and there was a man there taking the names of the people who were visiting their relatives' graves. She didn't know what he was doing, so she pushed on through with her flowers. The man looked up and saw her and said, "Wait a minute, lady. Where do you think you're going?"

Mrs. Feldman said, "To pluck a chicken. What does it look like? I got flowers I want to put on my husband's grave."

The man said, "What's his name?"

She said, "Why. You want to talk with him?"

He said, "Look, lady. The cemetery is under new management and we are taking the names of people visiting graves, and also the names of the graves. Now what's your husband's name so I can conduct you to the grave?"

She said, "I don't need a conductor. I can see the stone from here. I know where I put him."

He said, "Wait a minute. You don't understand. I can't let you in unless you give me a name."

She said, "Oh, for God's sake . . . Seymour. Seymour Feldman."

The man looked in his books and said, "I'm sorry. We can't let you in. We have nothing under Seymour Feldman."

She looked at the man and said, "What happened, he moved to a better location? When he was alive, the dumm-kopf wouldn't move unless I told him. Get out of my way. I can see the stone from here."

The man said again, "We have no Seymour Feldman."

She said, "Wait . . . wait. I just remembered. Look under Sarah Feldman. Everything is in my name."

So dear Mrs. Feldman, in addition to bestowing great love on a little boy, was also a key factor in teaching that little boy to be a storyteller—along with other practitioners of the art like my Uncle Tony and my mother.

chapter

What do I mean when I refer to myself as a storyteller? Well, I don't tell jokes. My forte is not the one-liner, which is done so brilliantly by many of my friends, like Bob Hope, George Burns, and Milton Berle. Rather, I take incidents from real life, which I've seen and heard, and build them up—with exaggeration—into a lengthy funny story, with a plot.

My stories come from everywhere. Recently, for example, I did a series of television commercials in a retirement home, and I got involved in some hilarious conversations with the old folks there. One lady said to me, "You look like my third husband."

I said, "Oh, yes? How many times have you been married?"

"Twice," she said, with a twinkle in her eye.

Another elderly lady told me how she had met her doctor on the street and he had asked, politely, "How are you?" That opened the floodgates as she gave him a long recitation about pains in her chest, her legs, her back, her gall bladder, everywhere.

The doctor said, "Oh, you better come in to see me on Thursday, Mrs. Goldfarb."

Mrs. Goldfarb replied, "I will, doctor—if I feel better."

I can take several authentic conversations like that and construct them into a long routine about the foibles and the humor of the aged.

Sometimes my friends kid me about this technique. Once, for example, Jackie Miles said, "If it's a simple story about two old Jews getting off a bus, Danny Thomas would begin it like this: 'In the year of our Lord, nineteen hundred and fifty-four, two gentlemen of the Jewish persuasion descended from a public conveyance.' "

It has been a good gag for Jackie over the years, but I don't go that far, of course. Nevertheless, I *could* get a good story out of two old geezers getting off a bus—if they were arguing about something ridiculous. This use of my eyes and my ears to dig up material is the cornerstone of my technique.

My school days were a rich source of material.

The St. Francis de Sales School attracted kids of all faiths and creeds because it was centrally located at Superior and Cherry streets in Toledo, and because its Ursuline nun teachers were so outstanding. They also were renowned for their ability to handle the roughest of boys. And were they rough.

Here is a story about the roughest of them, one Red Murphy, who more than anyone seemed destined for the electric chair:

Red came home one day and had a discussion with his mother about the role of his father. It should be explained that Red loved gangster movies and used to steal to get in to see them.

Said Red, "Hey, Ma, is it true that the good Lord gives us our daily bread?"

His mother said, "Yes, dear."

"And is it true that Santa Claus brings the toys?"

"Yes, dear."

"Is it true that the stork brings the babies?"

"Yes, dear."

"Then why don't you let me bump off the old man? We don't need him."

I used to do a lot of Red Murphy stories in my act, but I didn't see him for a long time. And you want to know something? He ended up becoming a priest. How he made it, I'll never know. But he did. There were a lot of us who made it who shouldn't have.

To try to keep up with Murphy and the other boys, I had to give the appearance of being as tough as they were. It was necessary because any kid in the neighborhood who didn't have all his front teeth knocked out was considered a sissy. We used to brag that we played a game called "Spin the Cop" (an exaggeration), and one of our principal extracurricular activities was to go down to the produce market and steal fruit (another exaggeration). Actually, we'd nudge the pushcarts to make the fruit fall off, and then we'd get it from the storekeepers since it became damaged goods, which they couldn't sell.

In truth, the cops were good to us. Sometimes, they'd

steal the fruit *for* us so we wouldn't have to nudge the pushcarts. On other occasions they'd get us (I never knew how) baseball gloves and bats from the sporting-goods stores. The cops had a favorite name for us kids from Cathedral School. They called us "The Raggedy-ass Cadets."

My favorite teacher at the Cathedral School was Sister Mary Ursula. Was she strong! I thought she could have been the lightweight champion of the world. She had the fastest left hook I ever felt in my life. I mean, she could sucker-punch you. She also was the choir teacher. You didn't dare to sing off-key.

My favorite memory of Sister Mary Ursula is of something that happened after I left school. I was a success in television by that time, and I was called to do a benefit to raise money for the Ursuline convent in Toledo. "Those nuns are having a rough time," I was told. "The granite blocks are falling off the walls of their convent." So I went and did the benefit show, which raised quite a bit of money. After the performance the mayor and the superintendent of schools took me out to see the Mother Superior of the convent, to be thanked personally.

I was ushered into her office, and there she sat—Old Ironsides herself. Sister Mary Ursula hadn't aged a minute—peach-pink flesh, steel-blue eyes. She got up, came toward me and said, "You're Amos. I'd know that face anywhere." (Remember, I'd come to town as Danny Thomas.)

She put her hand on my shoulder and her eyes started to well up. So did mine, I'm not ashamed to tell you. Sister Mary Ursula took a deep breath and said, "Glory be to

God, it's really you. I was sure you were executed long ago."

How tough *was* I at the Cathedral School? A lot of it was pretend stuff. I had to act tough because my face, with its big hook nose, made me natural prey for the big, strong kids who might have been tempted to straighten out my honker. I had another weapon against them. If someone threatened mayhem, I'd distract him by launching into a funny anecdote about someone else in the school. It was a small dividend, but even then, my storytelling ability was paying off.

Even outside of school, the world around me was filled with raw story material. Toledo abounded with immigrants of all ethnic varieties—Irish, Italians, Poles, Lebanese, among others, all living in peace and harmony with each other—and I found them all fascinating. I was particularly attracted to the Irish, whose humor and folkways were so different from those of my own people. Thus, I was about ten years old when I first became acquainted with the doings of Crotchy Callahan—one of the mainstays of my nightclub act for years.

I loved Irish wakes as a boy. I often said I wanted to die Irish because they know how to die. They get wished bon voyage. There's no weeping and wailing. Everyone has a good time. I used to peer into the windows and sometimes was invited inside—even though I didn't even know "the stiff," as the deceased invariably was called.

Crotchy Callahan was the neighborhood's most dedicated wake-goer. He'd read the obituaries in the newspapers, and every time he'd see an Irish name, he'd be there for the wake—sometimes even before the arrival of the stiff from the funeral home. The local legend included the time Crotchy read about the demise of one Patrick O'Hara over on Toledo's West Side, Collingwood Avenue to be exact. He got to the O'Hara home, and, as usual, he was the first to arrive—once again before the corpse, who had *not* been among his acquaintances.

No matter. For three days and three nights Crotchy drank more and ate more and told more stories about O'Hara than anyone else in attendance. Pure invention, of course. The only time he saw the stiff was on his way to the bathroom.

I remember Crotchy having a terrible cough, probably from the booze and the cigarettes. Once, on his way to the bathroom, the widow stopped him and said, "That's an awful cough you have, Mr. Callahan." To which Crotchy replied, "Yeah, and wouldn't your husband love to have it."

Then came the morning of the burial and everybody was piling into cars. Everybody but Callahan. He was in the kitchen eating grapes and compounding the effects of the alcohol with the fermentation of the grapes. Mrs. O'Hara came in and said, "Glory be to God, man. You must be a saint. You must have been awful close to me husband since you've been here longer than anybody, including the remains. And since you were so close I was thinkin'. Should I give him the regular burial or that newfangled cremation stuff?"

Lifting himself up to his full height, Crotchy said, "Madame, don't be a damn fool. Stuff him, and keep the party goin'."

True? Some of it was. The storyteller embellishes. I

should say that Crotchy Callahan was not his right name. I changed it out of deference to his son, a classmate of mine at the Cathedral School, who later became a high public official in Ohio.

But I kept picking up one outrageous Crotchy Callahan story after another. He used to go to the saloon every Saturday night, and whenever he heard about a gang fight in town, he'd rush to get into it. One night, Crotchy beat up a policeman. When he was arrested, he told the arresting officers, "Glory be to God, I thought I was beating up a British naval officer." When he got out on bail, he came to see my father, the neighborhood letter-writer, who had a reputation for coming up with good alibis and mitigating circumstances for people in trouble with the law. Dad said to Crotchy, "Tell the judge you were on your way to confession, and you were short of material."

It didn't work, and Crotchy spent some time in the hoosegow.

Another ethnic group in Toledo with which I closely identified was the Jews. Most of the local Jews came from Eastern Europe, but their religious roots, from centuries past, were so similar to those of us Lebanese. After all, they came from the next-door country, and in Becheri, the ancestors of my people spoke the same language, Aramaic, which was the common language of the Jews at the time of Christ. Only the priests spoke Hebrew in ancient Israel. I was always amazed at how much the Jews' religious chants sounded like the wailing melodies my father played on his mizwiz and other Middle Eastern musical instruments.

I hung out with some of the Jewish kids, and one day I

became a proxy Jew myself. One of the guys, the center on the neighborhood basketball team in the Jewish Educational League, came down with some long-term illness. I filled in for him (I was tall for my age and a pretty good athlete), and I played with the team for the rest of the season. Nobody asked any questions. I just happened to look like the center of a Jewish basketball team.

There was an amazing lack of religious prejudice in Toledo in those days. I used to go to the Presbyterian Church with the Jewish kids and my Catholic buddies. Why? Because they served ice cream and cake after their service. I guess it was more a practical matter than a case of non-prejudice. Looking back, any church probably could have converted us; all they had to do was feed us. And speaking of feeding, the dinner tables in our North Side of Toledo had a United Nations flavor—thirty years before the United Nations even existed. On one table it was common to see Irish stew, Italian ravioli, Lebanese meat pies, Hungarian goulash, Polish sausage—and one of the neighbors brought the bicarbonate of soda.

That was a line I used in my storytelling when I was only eleven years old.

chapter

5

Winters in Toledo were rough. My brother Ray and I spent a couple of them selling newspapers as part of the old Newsboys Club, founded by the philanthropist John E. Gunkel to help keep kids from straying into waywardness. It was a pretty successful program and produced many civic leaders in Toledo—judges, lawyers, and even a governor of Ohio.

But Ray and I couldn't stand the bitter cold in January and February, and we decided to seek part-time employment inside, where it was warm. That's how I obliquely got into show business for the first time. Sort of. Ray and I teamed up with our cousins Al Jacobs and Tommy Saad, and we went to see Harry Markwitz, manager of the Empire Burlesque Theater. He hired us, as a group, to sell soda pop and candy in the theater's balcony. He called us "The Four Greeks." Greeks, Turks, Lebanese, Syrians, Armenians; we were all the same.

It was fascinating to me just to be inside a theater every

day. This was the 1920s, and the entertainment world was in a Golden Age, even in a small city like Toledo. Movies were prospering, radio was coming into its own, but the live theater was still at its zenith. Stock companies would pause for a few days' performance on their way to Chicago, with budding young stars like Spencer Tracy and Pat O'Brien. The movie theaters all had "7 Acts of Vaudeville, 7." As in sports, so many immigrants and immigrants' children were doing quite well in show business that it was an inspiration to the rest of us.

At the bottom of the show-business totem pole was the burlesque house. Every city had one or more. There were girls but no stripping. It was not the sleazy burlesque that was to come later. In fact, burlesque was fairly respectable then, especially the so-called "Columbia Wheel," to which the Empire belonged. It was so respectable, in fact, that I didn't fear revealing to Sister Mary Ursula or Sister Mary Eleanor what my place of employment was after school.

I would watch, fascinated, as I sold candy and soda, as one comic after another came out to do his act. To a great extent, they were storytellers, like me. And they were getting *paid* for telling their stories. I saw the same comedians regularly as they came through on the Columbia Wheel, which was designed to shuttle shows around from one town to the next in a designated geographical circuit of theaters.

I quickly developed my favorites among the comics. To my young mind, the best by far was a gentleman named Abe Reynolds—an opinion that was shared by millions of people, including many comedians of my own generation. Abe was considered the best of the so-called Jewish comics.

He wore a derby hat perched over one ear, he had a little goatee beard, and he did his entire act with an exaggerated Yiddish accent. He didn't speak that way at all in real life, but he explained, "We have to make fun of ourselves. We have to present a picture of the Jew in the way that people think all Jews are."

It was kind of sad, but I didn't think of it that way at the time. I'd roar with laughter every time Abe sang the Irish song "Where the River Shannon Flows," with his distinctive Russian-Jewish inflections. It was hilarious. I learned every one of his routines by heart. There's one that I still use to this day, when it fits into my rambling monologues.

It's about three old Jews—about as old as you can get—who are discussing where they'd most like to be laid to rest after they're gone. The first old man said, "I'd like to be buried next to Haym Salomon, the great Jewish patriot. The Revolution would not have been a success without the financial genius, Haym Salomon."

The second man says, "Give me Grant. U. S. Grant. Did you ever see that tomb he's got by the Hudson? Now that's living."

The third old man said, "Boys, you made a good selection. But me, I'd like to be laid down by Becky Rappaport."

And they said, "Wait, Becky's not dead."

And he said, "Neither am I."

Several times, when I have told that story, old ladies came up to me weeping and said, "It's like Abe Reynolds came to life again."

To me Abe was the funniest man I'd ever heard, and I admired how he could take that simple little Becky Rappaport anecdote and stretch it out to a two-minute routine, adding funny details that made the story different every time. And as I watched from the balcony of that shabby little Empire Theater, it became the epicenter of my show-business universe. It was the only show business I knew. It might as well have been the Palace in New York.

So I knew then and there that my lifetime career was to be show business. Where or how, I didn't know.

Ray felt the same way. So we formed a brother act—Ray and Amos Jacobs—Songs, Dances, and Snappy Patter. I was twelve at the time and Ray was thirteen.

Chick Friedman and Davey Berstein, a couple of our co-workers at the burlesque house and freshmen at Woodward High School, were instrumental in putting together the first high school musical revue in Toledo's history. Even though Ray and I were still in the eighth grade, Chick and Davey asked us to join their revue. The show had a not-very-imaginative title—"Hits of the Day"—but for Toledo in 1926, it was pretty hot stuff. Since there were nuns and clergymen in the audience, I had to restrain myself from using the more prurient material from Abe Reynolds and the other comics at the Empire Burlesque.

Because of "Hits of the Day," which became an annual affair, Ray and I went to Woodward High, when the time came, rather than Central Catholic—which caused quite a flap with my parents, even though my older brother Fred was already a star athlete at the secular school.

However, I didn't start at Woodward High right away because of another crisis in my already complicated double family life. Uncle Tony and Aunt Julia moved to Rochester,

New York, and I went with them. So my high school career actually began at East High in Rochester.

It wasn't much of a high school career. I went to classes for a total of nine days in that entire academic year. The rest of the time I was a truant. I missed Ray terribly. Also, I felt an irresistible pull back to the burlesque houses, where I had been so happy selling my soda and candy, and watching the comics. In Rochester, I ended up at the Gaiety Burlesque, where I sold packaged favors and ice-cream bars in the aisles. I wasn't the only one experiencing the same pull. In the next aisle over, the candy butcher was Benny Baker, later to be a fine movie comedian.

I led a life of total deception. Every morning I'd leave with my books, presumably to go to school. Aunt Julia would give me twenty-five cents for lunch. I'd spend ten cents to pass the time in an early movie, then I'd buy a couple of slices of bologna, a bun, and a half-pint of milk. That cost fifteen cents. I'd hang around the movie house until 1 P.M., when it was safe to walk the streets because many high school kids had work permits and would have been out of school by then and on their way to their jobs. I was above suspicion as I walked to my own job at the Gaiety Burlesque.

Then, after about five months, there was a knock on the door at home one day, and Aunt Julia found herself face-to-face with a Genesee County truant officer. Poor Aunt Julia. I knew she wanted to thrash me good, but she was afraid I'd hitchhike back to Toledo, and she couldn't bear the thought of my being away from her.

I must say she really saved my butt in court. She told the

judge she was a very sickly woman, couldn't afford a nurse, and kept me home to look after her. As robust-looking as she was, she somehow convinced the judge, who let me go with the understanding that I would return to school as soon as possible. The alternative would have been a stretch for me in reform school.

Society would say that I *should* have been sentenced to reform school, and Uncle Tony agreed with society. He certainly didn't agree with Aunt Julia's tactic of lying for me in court. They had quite an argument about it. At the height of the argument, it looked like he was going to slap her. The old-fashioned Lebanese guys, they did that once in a while. I jumped in between them and I yelled at Uncle Tony, "You touch her and I'll clip you right on the chin."

Both Aunt Julia and Uncle Tony were stunned. A terrible silence fell over the room. This was the first and only disrespect I ever showed to either of them. They looked at one another and Aunt Julia went out to the kitchen.

Uncle Tony took out one of his Turkish cigarettes and slowly proceeded to round it from its original oval shape. Then he beckoned me to come over to where he was sitting in his favorite chair. He motioned for me to climb up into his lap, which I used to do all the time when I was a much smaller kid. Still no words were spoken. He kissed me on the back of the neck, as he always had done. Then he turned me around until we were face-to-face. And he said:

"You know, you're not my real son, but I love you as much or more. I love you as much as God rains rain. But if you ever lay a hand on me, I'll break every bone in your body. Now go out and play."

53

He was dismissing me as if I were still six years old. He was right and I was wrong, and I never felt so small in my life.

I should have learned a lesson from that series of incidents—but I didn't. I went back to East High for only four days, and then I resumed my practice of fooling Aunt Julia by taking her lunch money for school, and instead going to work again at the Gaiety Burlesque. I was spoiled and I was dumb. I came up with a lot of rationalizations about why I did this. First, I thought to myself that I had fallen so far behind in school that I would never catch up. Secondly, I truly felt that going to school without my brother Ray was something that I could never enjoy.

That wise woman, Aunt Julia, apparently sensed how much I missed Ray. She sent for him to come from Toledo to spend the summer vacation with me in Rochester, and I cried with joy. It was a great summer. We kept rehearsing our act, and we even put on a show at the Baptist church in my neighborhood. Aunt Julia and Uncle Tony came to see the show, and they must have realized how happy I was with Ray around. Because when school time rolled around again, they suggested that I go back to Toledo with Ray, live with Mom and Dad, and take up my studies with Ray at Woodward High. I was too selfish to think of how this would affect Aunt Julia, and I went.

But my life of deception continued. Ray was a sophomore and I wanted to be in his class. Never mind that I only had nine days of freshman credits from Rochester's East High, I registered as a sophomore. I was happy and I figured, childishly, that the Rochester transcripts would never catch up with me.

I finished my sophomore year, getting good grades in subjects like Algebra Three and Four when I never had taken Algebra One and Two. I guess I was a pretty good student, though a devious one. Ray and I put on our "Hits of the Day" show again, and we were rehearsing it for our junior year at Woodward—when the ax fell.

The principal called me in. He had the Rochester East High transcripts in his hand. He was so angry he was almost apoplectic. He chewed me out for a full hour. I remember hoping he'd get tongue-tied, but he didn't. He ended with the flat statement that if I didn't drop out of the junior class and become a freshman again immediately, I'd be expelled.

Ray and my friends in "Hits of the Day" begged me to be a freshman again for a few days—just long enough to finish the show—and *then* drop out of school entirely. That's what I did. And it was a decision that I regretted for the rest of my life. I blew my chance for any education, maybe college, maybe even an advanced degree. When I set my mind to it, learning actually came easily to me. But in many immigrant families, there wasn't enough guidance from the elders to stress the importance of an education. At age sixteen, my mind was solely focused on show business. Who needed book learning? Today I know better, and I made sure all three of my children received good educations.

Of course, this particular story has an ironic ending. Twenty years later, I was on my way to perform before the queen of England at the London Palladium, when I got a telegram from the authorities at Woodward High School. They asked me to stop off in Toledo en route to London to receive an honorary high school diploma before the entire student body. I didn't think it was an official award. How low a degree can you get with only nine days of official credits? But I accepted the invitation.

I'll never forget that day. I addressed the school, the whole school, and I got a tremendous laugh by beginning, "Fellow students, as valedictorian of my class . . ." I took it from there and went on to do routines and tell them one story after another. It was one of the best performances of my life.

By the way, it *did* turn out to be an official diploma. The principal and the entire faculty made it so.

chapter

Ray went on to his senior year at Woodward High and graduated. I was living with Aunt Julia and Uncle Tony again in Toledo. They had moved back after Julia had come to Toledo for the funeral of her ninety-eight-year-old mother and realized how much happier I was than I had been in Rochester. She had written Uncle Tony a letter telling him that Toledo was where she wanted to live, and that he was going to be a very lonely man without her and the lad he had raised—unless, of course, he decided to re-relocate to Toledo, too. I know what was in Aunt Julia's letter because I wrote it for her.

Tony worshipped Julia. In the Arabic way of speaking, she was his sun, his moon, his stars. So Tony gave up his business in Rochester and re-relocated. We were all together again and I was happy with my two families.

I was putting in all my time now with Ray, polishing our Ray and Amos Jacobs act. We had big plans. We felt we were good enough now to get a booking in burlesque, which we both knew so well. Just a little seasoning before heading up to the big time. At seventeen and eighteen, you have a lot of confidence in yourself. It was 1931 and the Great Depression was under way, but so what? We kept reading about how Irving Berlin, George Gershwin, Will Rogers, and others were still making it big in New York. What egos we had!

There was one thing that I forgot to include in my calculations. A little fellow named Cupid entered into the picture with his nasty little arrow—to break up our act before it got started.

Ray was a brilliant tap dancer, which made him so good in the act. He was also a brilliant ballroom dancer. This was his hobby, his avocation. In the month before we were planning to unveil our act to the paying public, he relaxed every night after our rehearsals by frequenting his favorite dance hall—the old Recreation Dance Palace. There he met Mary, a little blue-eyed Bulgarian girl. As he whirled her around in tangos, rhumbas, and waltzes, Ray fell in love.

Mary was raised on the East Side of Toledo. It was the area of the iron-ore docks, where many of the Eastern European immigrants worked. Nearly everyone carried a lunch pail and put in a respectable eight hours of hard labor for a day's pay. Show business, with its built-in instabilities and travel requirements, was something Mary would not put up with, and she let us know in no uncertain terms. But Ray was in love, and he and Mary got married before the month was up. Ray grabbed a lunch pail—and that was the end of our act.

I was on my own. I had to grab a lunch pail myself for a little while, because I needed clothes and I didn't want to look too shabby as I looked for work as an entertainer. Without Ray, all my Toledo plans had fallen through, so I knew I'd have to go to the nearest metropolitan area, Detroit. I went to work as a punch-press operator's assistant at the Autolite factory in Toledo. That sounds like a pretty fancy job, but what it meant was: I swept the floors of scraps and shavings from the punch press.

I stayed at Autolite just long enough to be able to buy a nice new suit and a couple of shirts. I had enough money left over for bus fare to Detroit, and I took off as soon as I could. One of the great things about being from an extended immigrant family was that you could always get help from a relative in a strange city. In Detroit, there was my Uncle David Azar, my mother's brother-in-law, and he took me in as if I were his own son.

At first, I didn't want to impose on Uncle David too much, so I commuted back and forth from Toledo to Detroit every day. How does a penniless young guy commute? I hitchhiked, and one morning I was picked up by a trucker, to whom I blurted out my ambitions to be an entertainer. That wonderful man then made arrangements with me to provide me with gratis transportation until I found a job in show business. Every morning, I'd wait for him outside the Toledo truck terminal. He'd get me to Detroit by noon, and then, by waiting for him outside the Detroit truck terminal, he'd get me back to Toledo on his return trip in the evening. I tried to repay him by telling him my funniest stories as we rode along. He was a very good audience.

Years later, I tried to repay the man with something more substantial. When I gave interviews, I always told how kind he had been to me and asked him to get in touch with me. I never heard from him.

Back in 1931, my two months of unorthodox commuting eventually paid off. The payoff was not in dollars. This is not one of those romantic suddenly-I-was-discovered stories that press agents love. It simply was that I auditioned for an amateur hour on a Detroit radio station, and I was accepted—to show what I could do.

The show was called "The Happy Hour Club," and it aired every afternoon on radio station WMBC. The host was a man named Chuck Stanley. He had played in vaudeville and burlesque, and his accumulated expertise had made his "Happy Hour Club" do better in the ratings than the competing shows of all the network radio stations in the southern Michigan area. When I auditioned for Chuck, his eyes went up when I did some of the material I had learned at the Empire and the Gaiety burlesque houses (he apparently knew it well from his own burlesque experience) and he gave me a one-shot appearance on "The Happy Hour Club." If you were no good you were dropped. If you showed any promise, you were moved up to two shows a week, then three. I'm proud to say that I reached that plateau after a couple of weeks. No money, of course. Remember, we were amateurs.

I still couldn't pay rent to my Uncle David Azar, but he wouldn't have taken it anyway. Actually, I spent most of my time next door in the home of his daughter, Annie. What a woman! I called her Saint Annie. By now, Chuck Stanley had put me on *five* times a week and had made me his assistant. He got around the amateur rules by slipping me carfare and lunch money under the table. Six dollars a week.

By this point, I had learned there were ways of making an extra buck. Prohibition was on its way out and 3.2 beer had become legal—and beer gardens were springing up like mushrooms. To compete with the speakeasies which sold real booze, the beer gardens had to come up with some kind of entertainment. So I got jobs in these sawdust joints, telling my ethnic stories to mostly ethnic audiences. They *loved* Crotchy Callahan. I got the magnificent sum of two dollars a night.

Still, it was tough going. I ate a lot of bologna sandwiches when I couldn't get home to Saint Annie for regular meals. It was tough going for everyone then. The Depression had really settled in since the Stock Market Crash of 1929. I passed breadlines on my way to work and sometimes stopped in for a bowl of soup myself.

But the worst was yet to come for me in those rough times of the 1930s. The blow I suffered was emotional, not monetary. I got word that dear Aunt Julia had been struck by a car in the street in front of our house in Toledo.

She had been talking with friends and didn't notice the oncoming car. It swerved, but a hinge protruding from the side of the car struck her on the temple. She never regained consciousness.

Heartbroken, I rushed back to Toledo and sat helplessly at her bedside in the hospital with Uncle Tony. We both kept crying and hugging each other. Aunt Julia died seventy-two hours after the accident.

Uncle Tony never got over it. He gave Aunt Julia the

most magnificent funeral, but had to sell everything to pay for it—including all the wonderful jewelry he had given her, and his own priceless gold watch and chain. I couldn't contribute anything.

After the funeral, no one ever heard Tony laugh or tell jokes again. He wasted away. About a year later, he was diagnosed as having a serious liver condition, which I now think was cancer. He was hospitalized and began looking more shriveled up every day. He kept saying, "I want to be with Julia." And soon, he was.

Just before he died, he gave me his ring—a present from Julia, which was the only piece of jewelry he had left. He said, "I always wanted to leave you so much, but now this is all I have. Don't cry. I'm going to Julia." I didn't want to take the ring, a cameo set in gold, but he insisted. I've never been able to bear wearing it. Perhaps I'll leave it to my son.

Anyway, I went back to Detroit with a heavy heart. It's always been my theory that when something terrible happens, something wonderful comes along to counterbalance it. And it did in this case, too. Because into my life came Rose Marie, who was to be my wife of many, many years. I can't say *how* many, because Rosie has an aversion to age. She says, "You don't have to tell people. We don't look as old as we are." But FDR was about to begin his second term in the White House, so you can figure it out for yourself.

How did we meet? It was on "The Happy Hour Club," to which I returned after Aunt Julia's death. One of the first things I noticed when I got back was that a new "regular" had been added to the show. Here was this beautiful little girl—only five-feet-two, with olive skin and burning black eyes—who sang like an angel. She used the name Rose Marie Mantel, because Mantel had been her mother's professional name when she once sang in a local opera company. Rosie's real last name was Cassaniti. She was Italian through and through.

I discovered that this beautiful little thing lived on Meldrum Avenue, a mile west of Uncle David's house, and that we both took the same streetcar, the Grand Belt Line. I made sure that we got on the streetcar together every day after the show. Soon I found myself walking a mile down Meldrum Avenue so we'd be on the same streetcar going *to* the show. A streetcar is not the most romantic setting for falling in love—but that's where it happened.

One day, I was scheduled for the show, but Rosie wasn't. I couldn't face not seeing her for a whole day—especially not on the streetcar—so I figured out a strategy just to get to her for a few minutes. To give you some idea of how poor I was at the time, I had only six cents in my pocket. I knew how much she liked Milky Way candy bars, so I bought her one—for a nickel. That left me only a penny— not enough for the streetcar. I walked the mile to Rosie's house, gave her the Milky Way, and then I walked the six miles to the studio.

That's love.

When I later told Rosie about the long hike I made just to present her with the Milky Way, she cried. That began a pattern in our relationship which has existed over the decades. I give Rosie gifts and she cries.

It took a long time for her parents to accept me as a future son-in-law. Actually, Rosie's mother was very sweet. She was of Sicilian descent but had been born in Baltimore. Her father came from the Old Country and tried to act very tough, as if he had influence with the Mafia. He used to look at me out of the corner of his eye and say things like, "You go with my daughter, and if you fool around with another woman . . ." He'd pause and run his finger across his throat, adding ominously, "It takes just one phone call, y'know."

Later, I heard those same words from Rosie whenever I went off on a trip without her, and might be exposed to other women: "It takes just one phone call, y'know." It was a running gag between us. I don't think she was serious. Or was she?

In any event, we finally decided to get married. I hadn't quite won over Rosie's dad yet. When she told him of our intentions, he said, "If you marry that Turk, you're gonna end up in a tent."

He finally gave in, however, and Rosie and I were married in a Belgian church on Mack Avenue in Detroit. I called her "Velvet," because of the marvelous texture of her skin. I called her father "Pa," because that's what Rosie called him. On Pa's insistence, the ceremony was performed by an Italian priest, who said, at the conclusion of the ceremony, "And God bless you kids. You gonna be together until death do you part." Pa looked over, drew his finger across his throat, staring directly at me, and said, "Atsa right."

Pa and I got along well after that, but I couldn't help getting back at him a quarter of a century later. It was the twenty-fifth anniversary party for Rosie and me, and it took place at our house in Beverly Hills. There were so many guests that the caterers had to erect a tent over our swimming pool and paddle tennis court to accommodate the crowd. Everything was decorated with beautiful red roses and bright-green ferns. A gorgeous chandelier hung from the middle of the tent's roof.

The guest list was a Who's Who of show business. Jack Haley was the M.C. and he called on everybody to make a toast. Finally he got to me. I lifted my glass of champagne and I turned to my father-in-law.

I said, "Pa, do you remember when you said to Rosie twenty-five years ago, 'If you marry that Turk, you'll wind up in a tent'?"

I paused meaningfully and said:

"Well, here we are."

chapter

7

Rosie was seventeen when we got married. At least that's what I thought she was, because even then she was averse to telling her right age. When I first met her, she had a younger brother named Vincent. Now she has an *older* brother named Vincent.

In the months before our wedding, Rosie (hardly anyone called her by her full name, Rose Marie) had become a very successful performer—by the standards of that day in Detroit. She had moved on from "The Happy Hour Club," and had her own fifteen-minute radio show, billed as "The Sweet Singer of Sweet Songs." She worked with a piano accompanist and sometimes a guitarist. Most important of all, The Sweet Singer of Sweet Songs was earning the magnificent sum of twenty-five dollars a week. My own salary was still only six dollars a week. I was afraid that I'd be accused of wanting to marry her for her money. So I waited to propose until the beer garden where I worked at night gave me a full-time job at thirty-five dollars a week. I felt

like a millionaire. It was more money than I had ever
earned in my life.

But I soon found that thirty-five-a-week was barely
enough to support a family of two, even in those distressed
times. Rosie's radio show got canceled, so we didn't have
the windfall income we had expected from the both of us.
She picked up a few bucks by singing from time to time in
dance halls, but basically we had to live on what I made.

At first Rosie shared my room at Uncle David Azar's
house. Then we moved into a boarding house run by a
Lebanese couple on Adelaide Street. The rent was five
dollars a week. When we had company, we were allowed
to use the living room of the house. For that privilege,
however, Rosie had to clean all the boarders' rooms.
God, I'll never forget what she went through there, clean-
ing and scrubbing, just to use the living room from time
to time.

Then Rosie broke the news to me that she was going to
have a baby. I was delirious with joy, but I worried even
more about our finances. I wanted her to give up work and
take care of herself. She hasn't sung professionally since that
day.

I had to get more money somewhere. I was working at
night at the Ambassador Club for thirty-five dollars a
week—M.C.'ing the show, telling my stories, doing a little
singing and dancing—which gave me time to look for work
in the daylight hours. Radio drama was very big then, so
I auditioned for every radio producer in town. I picked up
work here and there. On a "Lone Ranger" show, I was
hired to make the sound of horses' hooves by beating my

chest with two toilet plungers. My only speaking line was to whinny like a horse.

On a big show in Detroit, WJR's "The News Comes to Life," they needed someone to impersonate Al Jolson on the day George Gershwin died. I sang "Swanee." I was much better at imitating Jolson's singing than his speaking voice, but it was good enough. I got five dollars for that shot, and was included in the show's cast. My fee: five dollars for the one show a week that I did, sometimes ten dollars.

Do you want to hear about the really *big* money I made then? Horace Heidt came to town with his Alemite radio show. He did four shots from Detroit on the CBS network. I was hired to be "the Alemite Voice" in the commercials—a gravelly sounding fellow who was wasting money by not buying Alemite products. My financial reward for being on a national network for the first time was thirty-five dollars per show, for a total of a hundred and forty dollars. That's what performers were getting paid on big-time radio in those days. Of course, I wasn't doing much big-time performing, but the regular actors in the shows I worked in weren't getting much more, either. I became friendly with them and watched them closely—and I developed an ambition which I still harbor to this day. I was determined to become a character actor.

I kept getting slightly better radio acting jobs and finally built up a savings account of six hundred dollars, which I thought would get me through the expenses of the birth of our baby.

Then, another disaster. I was suckered out of the six

hundred dollars in a way that reminded me of how my father lost his farm in the Big Poker Game in Deerfield, Michigan.

What happened was that the Ambassador Club—my main source of income—hit a slump, and the proprietor decided to remodel, to attract a better class of clientele. He put all his savings into the remodeling and talked me into lending him *my* six hundred dollars, making me a partner, and assuring me that I'd get back many times my investment in future profits.

Well, you can guess what happened. My money went down the drain, and I didn't even get my salary for two months. I continued working and borrowed ten dollars every week from customers at the club, just so Rosie could buy groceries. Finally, I had to go back to the "Happy Hour" show at WMBC radio. I got paid seven dollars a day, seven days a week, and used nearly all the money to pay off my debts. A week before the baby was born, I had the grand total of seven dollars and eighty-five cents to my name. What was I going to do? My despair led me to my first exposure to the powers of faith.

It didn't start out that way. It was Sunday, so I went to Mass. I put my usual one dollar in the collection box, but then there was an appeal for the propagation of the faith. In other words, they needed money for missionaries. The priest was very good in explaining the need. I got carried away and ended up giving my six dollars for a year's membership, with all that spiritual good.

Then reality hit me. I walked up to the altar rail, got on my knees and prayed. I said aloud, "Look, I've given my last seven bucks. I need it back tenfold because I've got a kid on the way and I have to pay a hospital bill." Then I went home with my remaining eighty-five cents.

You won't believe this, but the next morning the phone rang in the rooming-house hall. Someone yelled, "Amos, it's for you." I picked up the receiver and a man's voice said, "We have a picture of you here at the Jam Handy Commercial Motion Picture Studio. We need a fellow to portray a Persian. You look the type. Think you can do it?"

I was stunned. "What's the job?" I asked.

The man said, "Oh, it's not a movie or anything. It's a little demonstration skit for the Maytag washing-machine sales convention."

My heart sank. Just another two-bit job?

The man said, "But the pay is pretty good. Seventy-five dollars."

I literally dropped the telephone receiver. First I whooped with joy; then an eerie feeling came over me. What had I said at the church altar the day before? That I had given my last seven dollars and I needed it back ten-fold, in order to pay the hospital bill for the birth of my baby. The seventy-five-dollar fee—unheard of for me at that time—was almost exactly ten times the amount of money I had donated to the church.

I told Rosie about the call and she was skeptical about it. Someone must be pulling my leg. But I did the Maytag convention show on Wednesday; I got paid the seventy-five dollars on Friday; and on Sunday, Rosie gave birth to a beautiful little dark-haired baby girl. The bill at Grace Memorial Hospital was exactly seventy-four dollars and eighty cents, which I was able to pay in cash. My friends kid me about my fervor for religion, but after that, how could I ever again doubt the power of prayer?

But I wasn't out of the woods yet. The delivery was a difficult breech birth and the bill of the obstetrician, Dr. Lawrence Adler, came to a fairly modest fifty dollars. But I didn't have any money left and I couldn't pay him. He never dunned me.

Some time later, however, Dr. Adler wrote and kiddingly reminded me that I owed him fifty dollars. I immediately sent him a check and apologized profusely for having forgotten it all those years.

The check came back with a note saying, "No way. Marlo was *my* baby and I have her show business pictures all over my office. Besides, I want to tell everybody that Danny Thomas, the great performer, owes me fifty bucks."

chapter

The name Marlo came about in a complicated way. Like all Lebanese men, I had expected a son and I was prepared to name him Charles Anthony, after my Dad and my Uncle Tony. But as soon as I saw the little girl—and fell immediately in love with her—I named her Margaret Julia, after my mother and Aunt Julia. Knowing how I felt about my two sets of parents, Rose Marie enthusiastically went along with the idea.

So we began to call the infant Margaret, then "Margo," which we thought would be easier for her to say as she began to speak. It wasn't easier. The closest she could come to Margo was "Marlo," as in "Me Marlo." And that's how another soon-to-be-well-known stage name was created.

I've never ceased to marvel at how much key attitudes can change in a single generation in immigrant society. My father and my uncle only spoke of "having sons"—to help them till the fields in the Old Country, I suppose. Daughters were only to be future providers of sons for someone else's sons. One look at little Margaret/Margo/Marlo (whatever her name was at the time), and that theory went out the window. I just wanted her to grow up healthy and beautiful and an *achiever*—which I knew was possible in the United States of America.

In order to help her fulfill those objectives—and with another small mouth to feed—I had to continue my struggle to make ends meet in the months and years after she was born. More than anything, I wanted to be a character actor in radio, but the chances of that happening in Detroit were slim, as casting was concentrated in New York, Chicago, and Los Angeles. So I had to continue to make most of my living as an entertainer in saloons. As much as I loved that type of work later, I grew to hate it at the time. I couldn't get out of the rut of being known around Detroit as "a pretty fair fifty-dollar-a-week M.C." That's what one club owner said when he opened a bigger, fancier club downtown, and I thought I could make it a showcase of my talents for agents and casting directors coming through Detroit. The club owner made it very clear that his new place was not for a fifty-dollar-a-week M.C.

Hearing that, I was never more depressed—at least to that point in my life. It was like the chord you hear in the movies when the body is found. Well that's what I heard—and the body was mine. I was dead and finished. I walked out of the place in a daze. I must have walked for hours, because when I finally came to, I was standing on the bank of the Detroit River, crying like a baby. The only thing that saved me from doing something drastic was the thought of home and Rosie, who would smile at me as if we didn't have a care in the world. Then I'd look down into the crib of little Marlo, who was smiling, too. And for that moment at least, I *didn't* have a care in the world.

The worst thing for me was that I loved Rosie so much, but I couldn't buy her pretty clothes. Once, while window-shopping, she looked at a black cloth coat with a strip of fur down the front, and I knew how much she wanted it. But it would have cost eighty-eight dollars, with payments, on time, of four dollars a week. I just couldn't see my way clear to add that expense to the others, so the best I could do was a fifty-dollar coat with a little wolf collar. Payments: two dollars a week.

I went to work at the Palm Beach Cafe. I no longer was a fifty-dollar-a-week M.C. I had slipped back to forty dollars. I got a booking to replace a man with a fine singing voice, who had been there for a year. The main attraction at the Palm Beach Cafe was a dance orchestra, but there were a few acts. My predecessor sang, introduced the acts, but never told jokes.

My booking was for a two-week tryout. When I got onstage and poured on the comedy, I caught sight of the boss scowling at me. At first I thought he was smiling at me, but it was a scowl, all right. After the show, he sent for me and said, "Hey, kid, who told you you was a funny?"

I said, "Nobody. I just thought . . . that is . . ."

"Look," he said, "I hired you to introduce the acts. Do that. And, if you think you can, sing one song and get off. You're here two weeks. Be a nice fella. Don't give me no trouble. I got good customers—and I don't wanna lose 'em."

So I held back on the jokes for the rest of the week, and we didn't lose any customers.

At the beginning of Week Two, the boss called me in again, and this time his attitude had changed. "Hey, kid," he said, "I got a good orchestra, Don Pablo's coming in next week for an indefinite stay. I been tryin' for a long time to get a radio station to broadcast the orchestra remote from my joint. Now I'll make a deal with ya. I understand that sometimes you do radio shows, so you must know people in the business. If you can talk 'em into putting a remote wire in here for Don Pablo's Orchestra, you can keep your emcee job here, and I'll give ya a raise—fifteen dollars for one of the small radio stations, twenty-five dollars for one of the two big ones. And you can tell jokes if you want to—but not too many."

It so happened that in my radio dramatic work, I had become friendly with Ty Tyson, then a great sports announcer at WWJ. I told Ty about my predicament, and he swung the deal for me. WWJ put a remote wire into the Palm Beach Cafe for Don Pablo's Orchestra, for live broadcasts at least once a week. And that's how I got out of the fifty-dollar-a-week M.C. mold. Overnight, I rocketed up to sixty-five dollars a week.

But that still wasn't enough to sustain my little family the way I wanted to—even in a boarding house.

Nor was the eighty-five dollars a week I got for my next job at the Morocco Club—which, ominously enough, had taken over the location of the Ambassador Club, where I had been suckered into losing all my money. I was hired for eight weeks, mainly because they thought I had been responsible for the pickup of business at the Palm Beach Cafe. I was, in a way, but I couldn't dare to explain why. The people were flocking into the Palm Beach, not because of the big-nosed M.C.-comedian, but because of Don Pablo and his remote dance-orchestra broadcasts.

I knew I wasn't going to be extended beyond the eight weeks, but I worked as hard as I could and tried to save the extra twenty bucks a week. I took heart when Bob Hope came through Detroit and dropped in at the Morocco Club—the first time I'd ever met him. As the M.C., I called on Bob to take a bow, and I witnessed firsthand how a real pro can captivate an audience. It had been raining that day and Bob looked down at the mud spots on his pants, and he said, "Boy, those Detroit cab drivers come awful close." That was all. The audience cracked up, and he could have recited the telephone book after that and gotten laughs. It taught me a big lesson about grabbing a crowd with my opening remarks.

That was the highlight of my run at the Morocco Club. I continued to tell my best stories, but the audiences dropped steadily from the night Bob Hope was there. Business was bad and I knew the club was going to close. I'd be out of work again. I grew more and more depressed.

That's what my mood was when something weird happened right there in the Morocco Club. It was a something that changed my life.

It was on the second or third day of the seventh week of my eight-week run. I was sitting at the bar after my performance, when a customer came up to me. He was really having a celebration. He was, politely, intoxicated.

During our mostly unintelligible conversation, he kept drooling out the words, "St. Jude Thaddeus." I thought to myself, "Holy smoke, I not only have a drunk on my hands, but a religious nut!" I started to get up and he said, "Sit down. I've been listening to you for an hour. You can listen to me for five minutes. You think I'm drunk?" I didn't answer. "Well, I *am* drunk," he said, "but I know what I'm saying. It's just that I'm not saying it so good right now, but I'll tell anybody who's listening."

I listened, and in a few seconds, I became fascinated. The drunk told me that his wife was in the hospital, suffering from terminal cancer of the uterus, when, just two days before, the man had fallen to his knees in the hospital and had prayed to St. Jude, the patron of hopeless cases, begging the saint to spare his wife's life. He said he didn't know how long he was on his knees, but he had begun his praying in the early evening.

At about four in the morning, he felt a tap on his shoulder. It was his wife's doctor, a Jewish man. The doctor said, "Charley, I don't know who you're talking to, but tell him, 'A good Jew says thanks.' Come on upstairs. Something good is happening." What was happening was almost inconceivable. The entire tumor had passed from her body. She now was cancer-free, and as I learned later, she lived to be eighty-nine years old.

That was some story. Why was the drunk telling it to me? "Because that was part of my bargain with St. Jude. If he answered my prayers, I would tell everyone I could about this forgotten saint." The drunk staggered off, but I couldn't get him and his story out of my mind.

The next day, I went to the Church of Saints Peter and Paul across the street. It was a Wednesday. I never go to church in the middle of the week, except for Holy Days. I had never before heard of St. Jude, but I fell to my knees and prayed specifically to him. If he was supposed to be the saint of the hopeless, that certainly included me. If ever a guy felt hopeless in his work, I did—and I told him so. That's when my wife was saying to me, "Get a job in a grocery. Get a job in a shoe store. Get a job somewhere, nine to five, so we can raise a family."

Well, naturally I wanted to stay in show business, but I wanted the Forgotten Saint to tell me if I should remain in the business or get a job somewhere else. I was a little embarrassed because it wasn't a life-or-death situation. But I blurted out those words, "Help me to find my way in life, and I'll build you a shrine." I went home, feeling a little better. I said nothing about my visit to the church to my wife, or anyone else.

The Morocco Club closed. Since I had no other work, Rosie, the baby, and I left on a short vacation to visit my folks in Toledo. It was July 7, 1940. We gave Mom and Dad a chance to fuss over their new grandchild, and then we went over to spend the night with my brother Ray and his wife, Mary. They now had a son, Ronald, who was to become very important to me in my work later on.

That night was a very restless one for me. I couldn't sleep. I tossed and turned, with all sorts of thoughts running through my head. Something kept saying to me, over and over again, "Chicago . . . Chicago . . . Chicago." In the morning, Rosie said, "Dear, what's in Chicago?" I was startled. I said, "How did you know I was thinking about Chicago?" She said, *"Thinking?* You were saying it all night in your sleep."

I then told her what had come into my mind in the wee hours before I finally had fallen asleep. I said, "Honey, I'm going to drive to Chicago and take a look at what's going on there. Something tells me to do that. Maybe I can get a job, and we'll be able to move out of Detroit. I don't seem to be getting anywhere in that town."

Rosie said, "But my folks are in Detroit, we were married in Detroit. Everyone we know is in Detroit. Who do you know in Chicago?"

"No one," I said, "but I think I should go, anyway."

So I went the next morning, in our beat-up little 1935 Ford. I gave Rosie one hundred and fifty dollars to help pay the grocery bills while she and the baby stayed at Ray's house. I promised to be back in three weeks, if nothing happened to get me employed in Chicago in the meantime.

I realize now what *chutzpah* I had in making that trip. My faith in my faith got the better of me. I began to have second thoughts long before I reached America's Second City. I had shown a lot of bravado before I left, telling everyone that my career as a saloon comic was over, and now I was going to be what I always wanted to be—a character actor in radio. But how? The only person I really knew in Chicago was Earl Ebi, who produced radio dramas at WMAQ, the NBC station there. I had done a few dramatic roles for him in Detroit, but come to think of it—I now told myself—Earl must be having a tough time in his own right, just doing unsponsored, sustaining radio shows at probably seventy-five dollars a week. And he might not even remember me.

I was filled with dread as I approached the city at twilight, its towers and skyscrapers gleaming orange in the setting sun. This was no honky-tonk town; this was the big time. I got more and more scared. My heart was thumping wildly. I must have slowed my car so much in the thirty-five-mile-per-hour Outer Drive, that the autos behind me started honking furiously. I pulled off the drive and sat there thinking for a long time.

Finally I decided that this was a crazy idea and that I should go home. I made a U-turn and headed back in the general direction of Toledo. I wanted to find a phone to call Rosie and tell her about my change of heart, and to expect me home in a few hours.

I parked across the street from a drugstore and had to walk directly in front of a Catholic church. I stopped to make the sign of the cross, as I usually do, and at the moment, I felt a sudden surge of something I can't explain. It wasn't mystical or supernatural. But my brain became filled with the overwhelming thought: "Oh, ye of little faith!" I never made the phone call. I got in my car, made my second U-turn of the day, and headed back downtown to the Loop in Chicago. I spent the night in a cheap hotel.

In the morning, I still had misgivings, but nowhere near as many as I had experienced the night before. As I walked to the Merchandise Mart building, where NBC had its offices, I simply worried about what kind of reception I'd get from Earl Ebi. I talked to myself and people must have thought I was crazy: "Hmm. Big shot Earl. Who does he think he is, anyway? Maybe he'll tell me to get lost. Maybe he'll say, 'Why are you bothering me, you little punk from the sticks?' If Earl gets snooty with me, I'll tell him to take his damn radio job and shove it . . ."

If you're familiar with my act, and this rings a bell with you, it was part of the genesis of one of the routines I'm most famous for: The Jack Story, about a guy walking down a lonely country road to borrow a jack to fix his flat tire. But more about the evolution of The Jack Story later.

Anyway, I finally got to Ebi's office at the Merchandise Mart. I *was* about to tell him to take his job and shove it, when he came rushing out of his office to greet me. He yelled, "Amos, you old son-of-a-gun, you're a sight for sore eyes. What the hell are you doing in town?"

Before I could answer, he turned to the three other producers who shared his office and said, "Hey, everybody, I want you to meet a pal of mine from Detroit—a fine character actor. He can do more voices than you can shake a stick at." To which one of the guys said, "If he can do a Russian, I can use him right now."

This producer's name was Clint Stanley. He handed me a script and I did a reading for him on the spot—in front of all the others. I read the part of a renegade Russian, a penal colony guard on an island somewhere in South America. Stanley said, "You got the part." The other producers in the room then asked me what other dialects I did, and I put on a little show for them, doing snatches of Crotchy Callahan and others of my stock characters. When I finished my little presentation, one of the other producers gave me the part of a gangster in a drama he was doing later that week.

I could hardly believe it. Two acting jobs in less than an

hour. And I had come into the office expecting to have to tell Ebi to shove it . . .

Not only that, but Ebi must have sensed how broke I was, because he offered to let me bunk in his apartment, where I could sleep on the couch and get fed regularly by his wife, "until you can get rolling." Wonderful man.

I did the Russian and the gangster, both local Chicago shows. I wrote an excited letter to Rosie telling her everything that had happened, and I said I would call her as soon as I did a part on a network show, so that she and all my family and friends could hear me in Toledo.

That opportunity came up pretty soon. Earl Ebi told me that Charley Penman was in town producing a CBS network show for Colgate called "Stepmother." Earl and I had both worked for Penman in Detroit, where he had been director of "The News Comes to Life," on which, if you remember, I had impersonated Al Jolson. Earl called Penman, who said, "Yeah, I got a job for the kid in a show we're doing tomorrow night." I couldn't wait to phone Rosie to tell her to listen to me tomorrow night. She, in turn, couldn't wait to call everyone I knew in Toledo— including Mitch Woodberry, the radio critic for the Toledo *Blade*. It sounds like an age-old newspaper cliché, but Mitch actually ran a column about me with the headline, "Hometown Boy Makes Good."

I did the show. It was a fifteen-minute program. After about eleven minutes, my part came up. I was in the Colgate commercial. Using a deep, guttural voice, I played tough Mr. Hard Bristle Toothbrush. In a sweet, highpitched female voice, Miss Soft Bristle Toothbrush argued back and forth with me until we both decided that hard or soft bristles, Colgate toothpaste was the best for our masters' teeth.

In Toledo, at least, the show's ratings never had been as high. I never had the heart to tell the folks at home which part I played. Actors were rarely announced by name in those days, and since I had so many different voices, I could have been playing any of the male lead roles in the drama itself. No one ever asked, and I didn't enlighten them.

I got twenty-two dollars and fifty cents for the Colgate job—seventeen fifty for the original broadcast and five dollars for the repeat to the West Coast. That's what actors' fees were like in 1940. But some were higher, according to the length and importance of the role, and with three or four jobs a week, I was equaling or surpassing my eighty-five-dollar-a-week peak in Detroit.

I thought I had it made—that my prayer to St. Jude was paying off. Still living with the Ebis, I was saving a little money. And every weekend, I'd drive the 234 miles to Toledo to see Rosie and the baby, and, of course, Mom and Dad and my sister and brothers. I'd drive back to Chicago on Sunday night. I was sure I'd soon be able to bring Rosie and Marlo to live with me in Chicago.

It happened—but not in the way I expected.

As I learned a long time ago, life sure does take some strange twists.

And St. Jude, apparently, was not yet finished with his part of our bargain.

chapter

During the fourth week of my career as a radio character actor in Chicago, I didn't work at all. In the fifth week, my only job was in Nashville, playing a Southern tobacco auctioneer in a cigarette commercial on a program called "The Uncle Ezra Camel Show."

Even before I went to Nashville, I decided I'd better insure myself against such lapses by going to see all the booking agents in Chicago. I offered myself to entertain at so-called club dates—weddings, private parties, conventions, bar mitzvahs. I was a fairly successful character actor in radio by now, and such non-public appearances as club dates would not be seen by enough people to diminish my radio-actor image. And it would bring in a few bucks to tide me over during the periods of inactivity.

One of the people I saw in my search for club dates was at the Chicago office of the William Morris Agency—then and now one of the most prestigious agencies for entertainment talent in the United States. When I got home from the

Nashville trip, I found a message from Leo Salkin of the local William Morris office. I called Salkin back, and he said, "I can get a booking for you in a nightclub on the far North Side."

I said, "No. I'm a radio actor now. I don't want to work in saloons anymore. Private parties—club dates are different. Don't you have any of those?"

Salkin said, "No, but I'll have plenty of them in the fall. That's why I want you to take *this* job, so I can come and see you work and decide if you're suitable for club dates. Besides, it's only a one-week booking."

I thought about it for a minute and reasoned that if it led to William Morris booking me into club dates, it was worth the one week. I finally said, "Okay."

I went up to the place, called the 5100 Club, and I wasn't too impressed. It was near the very fancy Edgewater Beach Hotel, but it was obvious that not too long ago the club had been a Studebaker automobile agency. Some Studebaker signs were still plastered around what had been the showroom. I met the boss. His name was Harry Eager. He was a gruff, no-nonsense guy. A bartender told me I'd be lucky to last the week because Eager had a tendency to fire his M.C.'s left and right. I didn't care. I just wanted to last until Friday, when Salkin was scheduled to come to see me.

I showed up for rehearsal the next day, and nobody was there but me. Eager said, "By the way, what's your name, kid? I want to put it up on a poster outside."

I already had told him it was Amos Jacobs, but he had forgotten. I said to myself, "With all the hoopla back in Toledo about my new career as a radio actor, how could I let them find out I'm working in saloons again?'' There was only one answer. I had to come up with a pseudonym so they'd never know about my regression—no matter how brief it was. As previously mentioned, that's how I pulled a new name for myself out of the air: Danny, my youngest brother's name, and Thomas, my oldest brother's. That was August 12, 1940.

"Danny Thomas" went up on the billboard outside, I rehearsed briefly with the piano player, Wally Popp, and I was ready for the first show. We had a five-piece band, a girl singer, a dance team—and me, the M.C. and comic. If you add in six waiters, a cook, three bartenders, and a dishwasher, we outnumbered the audience. There were only eighteen patrons in the joint. Maybe I was so loose because I didn't really want the job and Leo Salkin wasn't coming to see me until Friday, but I never had such an instant rapport with an audience. There was an air of excitement in the whole place—if eighteen people can create an air of excitement. The waiters were all standing around, watching and listening, and even the cook came out of the kitchen to see what was going on.

Sensing the makeup of the audience, I told a lot of my Yiddish stories, starting with my classics about Mrs. Feldman. I didn't know it at the time, but in the audience there was a wealthy diamond appraiser, Max Finkelman, who was staying at the nearby Edgewater Beach Hotel and had stopped by with his wife for a cold beer on that warm night. This man became my biggest booster. There were two big Jewish private clubs in Chicago, the Covenant and the Standard. The diamond appraiser spread the word around these two clubs, and people soon came flocking to see "this great new Yiddish comic." I never said I was or wasn't Jewish. After all, an Irishman, Jimmy Hussey, was a great Yiddish comic in New York, so why not a Lebanese-Yiddish comic in Chicago?

But after that first show—with only eighteen people in the audience—I figured I had had it and could just go back to waiting for radio acting jobs. There were another two shows scheduled for later that night, and I didn't know what to expect from the hard-bitten boss, Harry Eager. I had found out, in the meantime, that Eager had been shot in the leg by a former girlfriend, and that he was now married to Thelma, who was the head nurse at Weiss Memorial Hospital, where he had recovered from his wounds. The word was that he had proposed to her between backrubs and dressing changes. There were other graphic stories about how tough Eager was in the very tough nightclub business, especially in a Chicago dominated by Al Capone's gangland heirs.

The first thing Eager said to me after my first performance was: "Your pimp told me that if I didn't like you, I should pay you seven bucks and let you go." To him, agents were pimps.

I said, "Should I leave now, or should I do the other two shows?"

"Not so fast," he said. "The contract says I can fire you, but you can't quit."

I said, "Look, I'd like to stay until Friday so the agent—er, the pimp—can see me. Then let me go, if you want."

He took off his glasses, wiped them, took his cigar out of

his mouth, wiped the glasses again—never once looking at me. Finally he spoke: "You like Jewish food, kid?"

I allowed as how I did, and he took me to a delicatessen a couple of blocks away. I ordered steamed Hungarian hot salami, which I had learned about in Rochester; Eager had lox and bagels. As he munched his food, this hard-as-rocks man suddenly looked up and said something I had never heard before. He said, "Boy, you're going to be a big star in the entertainment business. You're going to make a lot of money."

I mumbled my thanks, hardly letting myself believe he had really said that—especially after that first-show audience of only eighteen people. I mostly took it as an oblique answer to my question about whether he'd let me stay on until Friday, when Leo Salkin was due.

The audiences at the 5100 Club picked up considerably on Tuesday, Wednesday, and Thursday. I continued to get that great response from the people as I told my stories and sang my little songs. I don't know, somehow it was different from all the nightclubs I had worked in before, experiences which had been discouraging enough to make me decide not to continue in the field. It doesn't happen to me anymore, but nightclub audiences can be cruel. They have no idea how much heartbreak and work goes into pleasing people in what essentially is a saloon. Some are interested in pickups, others are cheating on their mates. Some are loudmouthed drunks, who distract the people in the audience who are interested in what is going on in the show. Others are alcoholics who pass out and sleep directly in your vision, making it difficult for you, the performer, to concentrate.

It was better at the 5100 Club, but not enough to dissuade me to depart from my original objective—to concentrate on radio acting, with private parties on the side if Leo Salkin thought I was good enough.

All that changed when Salkin finally showed up on Friday night. I went all out for him, and I could see he was impressed, though agents traditionally try to keep a poker face. Most important of all, his lovely wife, Hazel, was laughing until the tears rolled down her cheeks.

Afterwards, we talked. The boss, Harry Eager, apparently had told Salkin his estimate that I was going to be a big star in show business, and Salkin apparently wanted to get Eager out of his hair because he had kept hiring and firing his clients in the M.C. job. Eager, in short, had been a big headache to him. Salkin told me how bad the private-party club date business was and that I could have steady work at the 5100 Club while still taking on radio acting jobs that did not conflict with my hours. My head was reeling.

Eager wanted to sign me to a two-year contract on the spot, but I was turned off by that number I hated—fifty dollars a week. Salkin came back with a better set of figures—a four-week contract, to begin, at sixty dollars a week, with a ten-dollar raise every week. That meant that at the end of the four weeks, I'd be earning the grand sum of one hundred dollars, plus whatever I could get in radio acting. We all shook hands on the deal.

I couldn't wait to phone Rose Marie to tell her what had happened. I began with my name-change to Danny Thomas and went on to my discussions with Salkin and Eager. I also said I couldn't stand being without her and the baby anymore.

On Sunday morning, I received a special delivery letter from Rosie. She was anguished. "Everybody knows you as Amos Jacobs," she wrote, "so why do you suddenly become someone named Danny Thomas?" Poor Rosie. After all my bragging about my radio work, little did she know that everybody who knew me in Chicago as Amos Jacobs consisted of a handful of directors and producers, who wouldn't care if my name was Benedict Arnold. As far as her coming with the baby to live with me in Chicago was concerned, she wrote, "Whatever you decide."

I decided that a family should be together. On Sunday night, I asked Mr. Eager if I could take Monday off to drive to Toledo to pick up my family. He said, "What's the matter? The train's not running? She should get on a train and come here."

I said, "Please, my wife's never been out of Detroit without me, and I would feel much better driving her and the baby."

"Okay," he grumbled, and I took off at 4 A.M. on Sunday night, after the last show. I drove so fast that it's a wonder I didn't get tickets from all the police in Indiana and Ohio. I made the trip in four hours and thirty-five minutes. Rosie was still in a state of shock and filled with misgivings. We packed up all of our earthly possessions—which didn't take much packing—and the three of us (Margaret/Margo/Marlo was then two and a half) were back in Chicago late Monday afternoon. Earl Ebi took us in for the night, and I went to work at the club.

The next day, we rented a little walk-up apartment on the third floor of a building at Clark and Deming Place. That marked the beginning of some of the happiest years of my life.

Because Chicago truly *is* a wonderful town—and gruff old Harry Eager kept renewing my contract over and over again.

I didn't exactly forget my contract with St. Jude, though I wasn't able to keep my share of it for some time to come.

Old St. Clement's Church was just down the street from our apartment, and I went over and lit a candle there the very night we arrived. That was my thanks for what had happened to me.

And I've arranged to have a candle burning in that church ever since.

chapter

10

I don't know why I did so well as a live entertainer in
Chicago, after having floundered so badly in Detroit. I can
only say that Detroit was like high school to me, and when
I got to Chicago, I was in college. I had learned how to
study and concentrate better.

As I said before, studying was the key to my entire act.
Not studying books, but studying human beings and listening to what they had to say, so that I could come up with
funny story material. And there never was a source of such
riches like Chicago. And never a more varied ethnic mix for
me to draw from.

Our next-door neighbors were Sam and Ruth Wolfe,
who had emigrated from Poland a few years before. With
the Wolfes living across the hall, we never needed a baby-
sitter. They were always there to be with Marlo when I was
at work and Rosie wanted to go out. Sam was a tailor, who
took care of my clothes, and Ruth was a seamstress, who
took care of Rosie's and the baby's. All free of charge.

They were also very funny. I was often grumpy, having worked until four in the morning the night before. Shortly after we got to know them, Ruth said to Rosie, "What does your husband do, Mrs. Jacobs?".

Rosie replied, "He's a nightclub entertainer—a comedian."

"Comedian?" said Ruth. "I thought he was an undertaker."

Another good self-deprecating story for my act.

I used to walk to work along Broadway, all the way from Clark to Carmen—a good four miles. I got to know many of the people along the way, and they were all wonderful. There was Sam the delicatessen owner, who always had a free sandwich for me to nosh on my way to work. There was Joe the bootblack, who made me stop for a free shine. There was Antonio the barber, who trimmed my locks gratis. There was Dennis the bookie, who threatened to break my hands if he ever caught me gambling. They all had stories to tell me, many of which I refined to use in my act—as I had done on a much smaller scale as a kid in Toledo.

For example, at the delicatessen I heard about Mrs. Lefkowitz, who came in and said to the clerk, "I would like to have some lox."

The clerk said, "How much lox would you like, Mrs. Lefkowitz?"

She said, "Just cut, cut."

After a few slices, the clerk said, "This will make a nice lunch for you and your husband."

She said, "Go ahead. Cut, cut."

Finally, after he had sliced through about half of the smoked salmon, the clerk stopped and said, "Mrs. Lefkowitz, you want all that lox?"

She said, "Nah. Just the next two slices."

That story still gets a big laugh when I tell it.

Some of my best story material came from the Irish. Two of my good friends got to be Luke Caniff and Bill Flynn, who worked for the local Alderman, Frank Keenan. They were always bubbling with Irish humor, which I was able to add to my Crotchy Callahan collection. Maybe the anecdote was about Casey or Murphy, but when I used it, I changed the name to Crotchy Callahan (so named, by the way, because his stomach was so big that he had to wear his belt below it).

Here's one that I picked up on the street on my way to work:

This old Irish woman goes to confession and for penance, she is told by the priest to say three "Our Fathers" and three "Hail Marys." On the way out, she figures that that's not enough, so she kneels down and decides to say her Our Fathers and Hail Marys on every step of the front of the church—about twelve steps.

Out of the church comes Crotchy Callahan, who has just done his own confession. He sees the old lady on the steps and figures this is a new procedure in the church. There's always something new. So he kneels down behind her.

At about the fifth step, the old lady's heel gets caught in the hem of her skirt. She can't move. The more she struggles, the worse it gets. Finally, she turns to Crotchy and says, "Would you kindly lift my skirt."

"I will not," says Crotchy. "It's for doin' *that,* that I'm doin' *this.*"

I can amplify that little story to two or three minutes on the stage. And Harry Eager kept wondering how I was able to come up with fresh material every night at the 5100 Club.

As I walked along Broadway in Chicago, I also got friendly with clergymen of all denominations. One of them told me about a preacher—not of *his* denomination, of course—who was asked to address the International Rotary convention. The Reverend Johnson, as my informant called him, chose what he thought was one of the most pressing subjects of the day—sex. He made a stirring speech to the Rotarians, leaving out none of the pertinent components— promiscuity, adultery, teenage pregnancies, the spread of venereal disease. The sex-lecture was very well received by the Rotarians.

When the Reverend Johnson got home, his wife, Martha, asked him what was the subject of his speech. Now Martha was a very straitlaced woman, the epitome of Puritanism, who habitually wore long, black crinoline gowns with white lace collars and cuffs. The Reverend didn't *dare* tell her he had talked about sex, so after hemming and hawing for a moment, he said, "The subject was boating and yachting, dear."

The next day, Martha met a member of the local Rotary, who said, "Oh, my dear, the Reverend gave the greatest speech in the history of Rotary. It was wonderful."

She said, "Yes, but I was surprised at his subject matter.

He's only tried it twice. The first time he threw up. And the second time, his hat blew off."

The Catholic clergy, too, was an excellent source of material for me. A bishop told me a story about a stubborn old Irish priest who had given *his* bishop fits over the years. This Irish priest was so anti-British that he constantly embarrassed the diocese by using his sermons to attack the Royal Family, the British armed forces, even the whiskey that came from England.

Finally, the bishop called the priest in and said, "Look here, Father Harrigan, if you make one more anti-British utterance from your pulpit, I'm going to have to relieve you of your duties in your parish and replace you with some other priest."

That scared Harrigan for a while, and he said nothing at all about the Brits. Then came the Easter season and he prepared his usual account of the Last Supper. He got to the point where Jesus said to the twelve disciples, "One among you is going to betray me." Then Father Harrigan couldn't control himself. He had Judas Iscariot answering in an unmistakable English cockney accent: "I say, Guv'nor, you wouldn't be meanin' *me* now?"

The local rabbis, too, were good for occasional story material. Walking along the street with me one day, one distinguished member of the local rabbinate told me an anecdote that I couldn't believe would be coming from him. It was about a priest and a rabbi who had just attended an interfaith rally downtown in Chicago. They stopped off for a drink at one of the Rush Street bars. Today, it would be called a gay bar. As soon as they walked in, the priest

(Left)
Here I am at eighteen months.

(Below)
That's Mother and Dad with their
five eldest sons. I'm the little guy
on Dad's knee.

(Above)
That's me at about age seven. I was living with Uncle Tony and Aunt Julia at the time.

(Left)
That's Uncle Tony in native Lebanese mountain costume.

(Right)
Me with my beloved Aunt Julia.

(Above)
Trying to look tough in
Toledo. That's me in the rear
of this group of ferocious
youngsters.

(Left)
I was the center on my Lewis
Street Center basketball
team—and I was only five
foot ten.

(Right)
The day after we were
married, Rosie and I were
photographed in front of
WMBC, the Detroit radio
station where we both
worked as amateur
entertainers.

(*Above*)
The great Fanny Brice gave me my
start in big-time radio.

(*Left*)
Telling my "Jack Story" in the early
days at the 5100 Club in Chicago.

(*Right*)
As a starving young comic at the
Ambassador Club in Detroit.

(Right)
With my boss, Harry Eager, at the 5100 Club in Chicago, scene of my first big success.

(Below)
My WWII interlude consisted of my U.S.O. tour with Marlene Dietrich, shown here with her arm linked with mine.

(Above)
That's me with Danny
Kaye and Eve Arden.

(Left)
With my partner
Sheldon Leonard on the
set of *Make Room for
Daddy.*

(Above) Both Jimmy Durante and I made movies at MGM at the same time. Here we are trying to coax a laugh out of producer Joe Pasternak.

(Left) Working in television gave me more time to spend with my kids. Above, that's me with Terre and Marlo, and below, with Tony.

I've worked with many stars in my day, including *(left)* Jane Russell, Marilyn Monroe, and Lou Costello of the great comedy team Abbott and Costello. *(Above)* I'm teaming up with Jackie Gleason and Rose Marie (the entertainer, not my wife) at the famed Copacabana in New York City.

(Photo courtesy Jaffe Studios)

(Above) Both Jimmy Durante and I made movies at MGM at the same time. Here we are trying to coax a laugh out of producer Joe Pasternak.

(Left) Working in television gave me more time to spend with my kids. Above, that's me with Terre and Marlo, and below, with Tony.

I've worked with many stars in my day, including *(left)* Jane Russell, Marilyn Monroe, and Lou Costello of the great comedy team Abbott and Costello. *(Above)* I'm teaming up with Jackie Gleason and Rose Marie (the entertainer, not my wife) at the famed Copacabana in New York City.

(Photo courtesy Jaffe Studios)

(Above)
With Doris Day in the movie
I'll See You in My Dreams.

(Left)
With Marilyn Monroe
at a benefit at the
Hollywood Bowl.

My littlest co-star was Margaret O'Brien, in the movie
The Unfinished Dance.

was beset by one gay young man who insisted that they dance together ("Everyone does it here.") The priest kept insisting that he was a man of the cloth but that didn't deter the young man.

Finally the rabbi said to the priest, "Let me handle this." The rabbi took the young man aside and a minute later, the youth mumbled his apologies and sidled away.

"What did you say?" the priest asked.

"I told him we were on our honeymoon," the rabbi said.

In recent years, I get into these religious stories after telling the audience how other comedians tease me for being too religious—such as Bob Hope's famous line, "Danny Thomas is so religious that he thinks the *Happy Hooker* is a book about needlepoint." I tell the stories as a group, and the way I stretch them out, they can eat up a good ten or fifteen minutes of my act.

Back in the 5100 Club days, I did the religious stories willy-nilly, wherever I thought they could legitimately fit in with whatever subject I was rambling on about. For example, if I had been at the racetrack that day, I'd tell about two rabbis who were at the track (a true story), and one said to the other, "I bet on this horse, and prayed to the prophet Elijah, and the horse ran last in the field." To which the other rabbi replied, "Elijah's no good for flat races. He's for trotters."

The most important thing I learned to do during my days at the 5100 Club was to coalesce various pieces of material I had heard or experienced over the years. A good example, as I mentioned before, was the evolution of my Jack Story, which people still call for whenever I perform.

George Burns flatters me by saying The Jack Story has become part of the English language.

The root of The Jack Story actually was a Lawn Mower Story from Ireland. Predating that, I'm sure, was a sleigh-hauling Coal Story from Ireland. Both versions were told to me in 1939 when I was a thirty-five-dollar-a-week comic at a saloon called The Bowery in Hamtramck, outside of Detroit. Between shows, I'd sit in front of The Bowery, my feet dangling from the rumble seat of a car, and I'd exchange views with some other local comics.

One of the comics told me the story. It's about a guy who had to walk down the road to borrow a lawn mower from his brother-in-law, Mike. On the way, this man thought of all the grievances between him and the brother-in-law and became more and more incensed. Now he was sure Mike wouldn't lend him the lawn mower. When he finally arrived, he was so furious that when he knocked on the door and the brother-in-law came out and pleasantly said, "Well, Pat. What can I do for you?" Pat yelled, "You can take your stinkin' lawn mower and shove it up your ass."

The next step was from my own experience, when I first came to Chicago to ask Earl Ebi about a job, and similarly got so upset in my fantasies about what Ebi might say in rejecting me, that I was ready to tell *him* to take the job and shove it.

That made me think back to the Irish lawn mower story, when I got to the 5100 Club. Since many people in my audience were Jews, I wanted to convert it into a story in which I could ramble on in a Yiddish accent. But in those days, not many Jews lived in houses where there were lawns, and they didn't use lawn mowers. But there were a lot of Jewish traveling salesmen, and—aha!—if one of them got stuck on a lonely country road at night with a flat tire and no jack, he might have to borrow or rent a jack.

So my story developed into this:

The salesman starts walking toward a service station about a mile away. He's talking to himself as he walks. "How much can he charge me for renting a jack? One dollar, maybe two. But it's the middle of the night, so maybe there's an after-hours fee. Probably another five dollars. If he's anything like my brother-in-law, he'll figure I got no place else to go for the jack, so he's cornered the market and has me at his mercy. Ten dollars more." I go on and on like this for seven minutes or more, dragging in all sorts of extraneous things to make him more angry.

Finally he gets to the service station, whose owner greets him affably with, "What can I do for you, sir?"

The salesman explodes. "You got the nerve to talk to me, you robber. You can take your stinkin' jack and shove it up your . . ."

Believe it or not, but in all the years I've done that story, I never once completed the sentence. The orchestra hits a chord, and the audience, which generally knows the story almost by heart, already is howling so loudly that they wouldn't have heard the dirty word, anyway.

That's why I like to say, "My act is so clean that even nuns can come to see it."

And plenty of them did during that happy time when I was at the 5100 Club in Chicago.

chapter

>>11<<

And it *was* a happy time.

For the first time in my life, I was financially secure. As gruff as he seemed, the club's owner, Harry Eager, was a real softie underneath—at least so far as I was concerned. He had told me in the beginning, "If I make, you make," and he lived up to his word. He kept renewing my contract for twenty-six weeks, with periodic raises, so that I ended up making over three hundred dollars a week. From my original audience of eighteen people, we now had crowds of a hundred or more pushing to get in. Harry even had to put up curtains on the windows of the old auto showroom. Originally, he had just darkened the lower half of the windows with black paint. But that made the show visible to people on the Broadway streetcar line, which ran past the club. They would look through the upper unpainted half of the windows, and as the show became more and more popular, the streetcar motorman would tarry for lengthy periods outside. Hence the curtains, to block out the freeloaders.

We still lived in the third-floor walk-up apartment, but there was plenty of money now to put food on the table, and, at last, for me to buy pretty things for Rosie and little baby Marlo. I also was able to send money regularly to Mom and Dad back in Toledo.

But even more than the money, I finally had something that was tremendously important—self esteem. It was something that had eluded me in Toledo and Detroit. The wonderful people of Chicago made me into a local celebrity. I was asked to entertain at fund-raising functions for various charities. Irv Kupcinet, later the famous columnist of the *Chicago Sun-Times,* then was a young reporter, but he came to see my show whenever he could and wrote about it, whenever his editors would allow it. Even though I had no academic education whatever, I was asked to speak at educational functions, even at the colleges.

Then came Pearl Harbor, and the nation was at war. I signed up for the draft, but they weren't taking married fathers. In February 1942, I got a call from Clint Stanley, one of the producers for whom I had done my earlier radio acting. Clint was now Lieutenant Stanley at the Great Lakes Naval Training Station. He asked me to M.C. a variety show that would be done for the naval trainees and broadcast over the NBC Blue Radio Network. I was delighted to do it, not only out of patriotic duty, but, frankly, because I was flattered to join the ranks of people like Bob Hope and Jack Benny. Little local-boy me! I couldn't believe it when NBC labeled the program, "The Danny Thomas Show." It was my first opportunity to be a network comic.

I kept doing these performances for the Navy, squeezing them in between the first and second shows at the 5100

Club. The night we premiered, Chicago had its first war-time blackout and I had to grope my way back to the club in the darkness. When I arrived, the second show already was under way. Fortunately, by that time we had acquired the fine singer Mark Fisher, and he was filling in quite capably for me as M.C. When I walked in, a blinding spotlight caught me and I fell to the floor in a mock faint. I had been trying for a year to get Eager to install a spotlight, but he had protested that he didn't want to pay an operator to man it. Now, he had given the spotlight to me as a gift, but he had saved it as a surprise for when I returned from my patriotic Great Lakes stint. That's the kind of man tough Harry Eager was.

As it turned out, we *needed* the spotlight because more and more celebrities kept making the long trip up to 5100 Broadway to see our show—and the light had to be turned onto them when I introduced them. Among those who dropped in were comedians Harry Richman, the Marx Brothers, Lou Holtz, Joe E. Lewis; bandleaders Russ Morgan and Charlie Spivak; the Andrews Sisters; and Buddy Ebsen, then a big Broadway musical star. Some of them came back time and time again. I couldn't believe that such luminaries were so anxious to catch my act.

One of my biggest fans turned out to be Ben Bernie, a funnyman on radio and also a famous orchestra leader, known as "The Old Maestro." Ben came up to me one day and offered me sixty-five thousand dollars in exchange for one-third of all my future earnings. I turned him down. As much as I liked him, I didn't want to be owned by anyone—even though his faith in my potential boosted my morale considerably.

A short time later, Ben said to me, "A couple of friends of mine in New York have just written a musical, and there's a great part in it for you—a Persian rug peddler. I've arranged for you to have a reading." I said no. A few days later, he said, "You don't have to go in for a reading. Just say that you want to do it, and you have the part." I thanked Ben but said, "I appreciate it, but I just don't want to uproot my family again and move to New York."

I don't know whether to regret having made that decision or not. Who were Ben's two friends in New York? Richard Rodgers and Oscar Hammerstein II. The name of their new musical which I turned down so cavalierly? *Oklahoma!*

But what did I know in those days about Broadway musicals that had the capability of breaking all existing box-office records?

My mind really was in a state of turmoil in those days. I still wanted to be a character actor more than anything else, but the offers from radio producers were few and far between. Short of fulfilling this ambition, I was happy where I was at the 5100 Club. Harry Eager couldn't be nicer. We now had only a handshake deal; I only had to give him two weeks notice if something better came along. Rosie was happy with my steady income, but she still had her doubts as to whether it would last. One day she said to me, "Now that you've proved you can make it in show business, how about settling down to something nice and reliable in the grocery business?" Again with the groceries! I don't know why she thought that was the safest field for anyone to be in.

To tell you the truth, I was interested in safety, too—but

not in a grocery store. I especially felt that way when I found out that Rosie was pregnant again. Other offers came in, but this was no time to make a move. Joey Jacobson, one of the owners of the Chez Paree, came to see me and offered me a seven-week contract to move to his club, one of the most prestigious in Chicago. Also, the Martinique in New York City wanted me, but it was a deal at so-called "showing date prices," which meant that I wouldn't get a decent salary until I proved myself with the tough New York audiences. Harry Eager was getting jittery. He raised my pay to meet the incoming offers.

This was all very exasperating to Leo Salkin, my agent at the William Morris office, who was handling me on good faith because I had never agreed to sign a formal contract with him. I am one of the great procrastinators, so I decided to put it all aside until the birth of our second baby.

My mother came out from Toledo to be with Rosie in the last days of her pregnancy. Mom and I had long talks, during which she told me most of what I know about her early days in this country with Dad—about how I was born on the horse farm in Michigan, etc. She went to church every day, and I asked her which saint in particular she prayed to. She said, "St. Theresa. And when the baby girl is born I think that's what you and Rosie should name her—Theresa."

I said, "But Mom, I'm expecting a boy this time. My friends have given me all kinds of athletic equipment for him." Once again, I was going to name the boy Charles Anthony, for my father and for Uncle Tonoose. Mom said, "We'll see."

I had to rush Rosie to Edgewater Hospital at 4 A.M. on November 9, 1942. The baby was delivered at about eight in the morning. Mom looked smug when we found out it was a baby girl. The newborn infant looked like a Pueblo Indian, with long black hair and black eyes, but I knew even then that she'd grow up to be an olive-skinned beauty (which she did). Her name? Theresa, of course.

Totally exhausted, I didn't go to work at the 5100 Club that night, which precipitated my first and only quarrel with Harry Eager. He actually fired me, as of the following week. We didn't speak for three days. After the last show on the third night, he said, "Come here, you black-eyed Syrian, I want to talk to you." I walked over and he said, "Now that your family is bigger, you'd better start thinking about the future."

I said, "What future? I'm leaving you next week. You fired me, didn't you?"

He said, "Don't be a wise guy. Listen to what I've gotta say."

I listened. "Danny," he went on, "I guess you know I never had any use for actors, and I should have my head examined for what I'm going to propose. But I've got confidence in you, so I want to make you a proposition."

The proposition made my head swim. Without going into technical details, he was offering me one half of the business, lock, stock, and barrel. And it would cost me nothing. I'd be an equal-share owner of the thriving 5100 Club, paying Harry back with a percentage of my profits to come. What an offer!

I told Harry I'd talk it over with Rosie, and I rushed

home to tell her. She was ecstatic. It was her dream come true. Maybe not a grocery store or a shoe store, but I'd be the owner of *something.* As for me, I could keep working at my profession, and make money from the business besides. I could finally settle down to raise my family in one town, maybe own a house, and live as a respectable citizen of a community.

It seemed all set. Rosie kissed me, and I said I'd tell Harry the next day.

It didn't work out that way.

The next day was Sunday and I went to church. It was an early morning Mass, and there were very few people there. As I knelt down to pray, I noticed a little pamphlet in the pew in front of me. I picked up the pamphlet and it was the announcement of a novena to St. Jude Thaddeus, to be conducted by the Claretian Fathers at the National Shrine of St. Jude in Chicago, Illinois.

I was in a state of shock. Quite frankly, I'd pretty much forgotten about my promise to St. Jude that I'd build him a shrine if he showed me my way in life. Now he had showed me the way, and I'm suddenly finding out that he already *had* a shrine in the very city to which Fate had taken me. Or, rather, to which St. Jude had taken me. I learned that St. Jude's national shrine in Chicago was just a wooden side-altar in a church on the West Side. Was this another sign from him that he wanted me to build a more imposing shrine?

It struck me that I couldn't make enough money to do it if I settled down to a nice comfortable life as half-owner of the 5100 Club.

So I prayed again to St. Jude to show me the way, so I could indeed build him the shrine he deserved.

When I told her all this, Rosie was beside herself. She said, "Ah, holier than thou. St. Jude talks to you personally?"

Probably not. But a short time later, while I kept Harry Eager waiting for my answer, a man came into my life who was to shape my destiny for decades to come: Abe Lastfogel, the all-powerful chief of the all-powerful William Morris Agency in New York.

How did he come to a little Chicago pisher like me? That *is* somewhat of a miracle.

chapter
12

The head of the William Morris Agency rarely came to Chicago. He was too busy with major Hollywood stars and big Broadway names, I guess, to spend much time with lesser actors in the cities in between. But on this particular day in 1943, he had a few hours between trains in Chicago and he dropped in at his agency's Chicago office. In those days, the deluxe way to travel coast-to-coast was to take the Twentieth-Century Limited from New York and then switch to the Super Chief in Chicago. It was all very luxurious, but it always involved a wait, from the arrival of one train to the departure of the other.

I didn't know any of this, of course, my only experience with trains being the hard coach seats in the inter-urban lines. I also didn't know, until later, what had transpired when Mr. Lastfogel dropped into his Chicago office during the four hours before he could board the Super Chief.

Apparently, he had discussed a variety of matters with his Chicago people, among them Leo Salkin, who had originally booked me into the 5100 Club. He said to Salkin, "What's with this Danny Thomas kid? How come you can't sign him to a William Morris contract? Does he have any talent?" I guess Salkin told him I *did* have talent, but that I probably was going into the saloon business with a half-interest in the 5100 Club. Mr. Lastfogel had never heard of the 5100 Club, but Salkin's response must have piqued his interest. He said, "Get the kid down here to see me. Maybe *I* can get him to sign with the agency."

The first I knew of all this was when Salkin phoned me and invited me to rush down to his office, posthaste, to meet the Big Boss from New York. I got very excited because every performer in the country knew the name Abe Lastfogel. He was to the entertainment world what Franklin D. Roosevelt was to politics.

When I got to the Chicago office of William Morris, I was ushered into a conference room, and there sat a little man with the brightest, most intelligent eyes I'd ever seen. He was introduced to me as "the greatest mind in show business," and I said, "It's an honor to meet you, sir."

He looked amused at all this protocol swirling around him, and said, "Hello, my boy. Sit down and let's talk."

I sat down, and prodded by his sharp questioning, I told him all about myself—from my beginnings in Toledo to the 5100 Club. After about a half hour, Mr. Lastfogel said to Salkin, "Have my train reservations changed. I want to stay over tonight to see this young man's act at this 5100 Club."

He showed up that night with Salkin, Wally Jordan, the head of his radio department, and with Joey Jacobson of the Chez Paree, the fancy downtown nightclub. With him, too, was Lastfogel's charming wife, Frances, who once was a top vaudeville performer. Harry Eager went crazy. He served the drinks personally and whispered to me how glad he was that he had put the curtains on the windows.

When it came time for my act, I was scared to death. But something strange always happens to me in times when I have to be my best. An inner spirit seems to come up from inside me and takes over my body and my brain, something inside me that surfaces and comes to the rescue—almost like another person altogether, who has no fear or anxiety. That's what happened to me that night. I was onstage for an hour and five minutes, doing every dialect known to man. I had previously taken to inserting little preachments into my act about how I felt about the fellowship of man regardless of race, creed, or ethnic background—lightened by a little joke at the end. Sometimes these inserts were a little stiff, but this night they flowed like fresh spring water.

When I finished, I joined the William Morris group at their table. Mr. Lastfogel was deep in thought. Everybody was waiting for him to speak. Finally, his wife, Frances, broke the ice. She said, "You've sure got a lot of talent for a Lebanese from Toledo. Are you sure you're not a Jew from New York?" Everyone laughed. Then Mr. Lastfogel said, "How is it that a boy with the talent you have can possibly think of going into the saloon business? There are so many facets in the theater in which you're sure to succeed." Almost as if I weren't there, he said to the others, "If this kid is properly handled he could be a combination of Al Jolson and Will Rogers. And I think I'm going to handle him myself."

I couldn't believe what I had heard. Neither could Mrs. Lastfogel. She said, "Abe, you know you haven't got time to take on any newcomer right now."

Mr. Lastfogel said, "Oh, yes I do. Funny, but for the last few days, I had a sort of feeling that something exciting was going going to happen, and Frances, I think this is it."

He turned to Joey Jacobson, who was sitting beside him. "Joey," he said, "someday this boy will work for you."

Jacobson said, "I already offered him a job. I'll take him right away."

"No, not now," Mr. Lastfogel replied, "He's got to get a lot of polish, and when he does, you'll get him. By the way, you'll pay for the polish, too."

This was my first experience with how the big minds of show business worked, with their parrying and thrusting. I was dizzy from what I had heard. But not so dizzy that I didn't agree to sign with William Morris and Abe Lastfogel. From that moment on—and until the day he died—he became my Uncle Abe. That's what I always called him. He *was* like an uncle to me. And Frances Lastfogel was always Aunt Frances to me.

I went back to finish out my last seven weeks for Harry Eager at the 5100 Club. Harry knew what was happening to me, and was sad and happy at the same time. A few days after I had met Uncle Abe, I got my first example of the skill and clout which he exerted in the entertainment world. Leo Salkin called to tell me I had my first theater booking, at the Oriental Theater in downtown Chicago. It was a movie house, but it had live acts between each showing of the film. The original offer was seven hundred and fifty dollars for the week, but Uncle Abe got on the phone and told Salkin to phone a Mr. Hogan at the Oriental and tell him that I was to get one thousand two hundred and fifty—and that Hogan wouldn't quarrel with it. Hogan didn't. He told Salkin, "If Lastfogel thinks he's worth it, he must be."

I opened at the Oriental and did well. The theater was jammed with all the loyal people who had seen me at the 5100 Club. They screamed and hollered so much that I was moved up from the next-to-closing act to the final act, just before the movie went on. Working before a huge crowd like that, I had to change my act to some extent. Uncle Abe had told me to cut down on the Yiddish humor, and I did. He called to say, "My boy, you're acquiring polish."

All this was just five days after I had finished my last show for Harry Eager at the 5100 Club, and I had a heavy heart. Tough guy Harry had come up to me before I left and handed me something wrapped carelessly in a piece of plain tissue paper. It was a ring inscribed "H.E. to D.T. 7/4/43," and its centerpiece was a two-carat, fifteen-point diamond. "I got you this, kid," he said, "because it'll look good on the stage at the Oriental when the spotlight hits it." I still wear that ring. Harry's last words to me were, "With you gone, I don't want to stay in this business. Six months from today—mark it on your calendar—I'm selling out."

And he did.

With all that's happened to me since, that time at the 5100 Club remains my most unforgettable experience. Not only because of Harry, but because of the club's fans who kept following me all over the country—just as they did when I opened for that one week at the Oriental Theater.

All over the world, in fact. For example, years later, at the London Palladium, an elderly gentleman came up to me and said, "I'm a guy who used to see you at the 5100 Club. Do The Jack Story for us tonight, Danny."

chapter

13

Uncle Abe sure was working on my case. Shortly after I said goodbye to Harry Eager and did my stint at the Oriental Theater, he phoned, saying he wanted me to come in for what he called my "invasion of New York." All expenses would be paid by the William Morris Agency.

I took the 20th-Century Limited and checked into the St. Moritz Hotel on Central Park South. The first phase of my invasion was to sit around in a meeting with Uncle Abe and all his top agents. I didn't talk at the meeting. I just sat and listened while I was discussed and analyzed by these people, who were the movers and shakers of show business. After a while, I felt like a prize pig at a state fair, but I didn't mind. I kept thinking back to when my only dealings with agents were to hear them say to a saloon-keeper, "Try the kid out, and if you don't like him, pay him for the night and let him go."

The second phase of my invasion, as arranged by Uncle Abe, was to go with him to all the famous night spots in

New York. He said, "Take a good look, my boy, and when you see the place where you want to open in September, just give me a nudge."

Visiting those fabulous places I'd only read about was like a trip to Fairyland for me. You must remember that nightclubs, in those days, were the acme of the entertainment world, second only to the Hollywood movie studios. Uncle Abe and I shuttled from one club to the next. I finally nudged him when we got to La Martinique, that glittering showplace on 57th Street west of Fifth Avenue. The headliner was the singer Frances Faye; the comic was a young, very funny guy, Jan Murray. Most important of all, the entire place exuded *class,* as a young entertainer from the sticks would dream about it. When the Martinique show was over, Uncle Abe said, "Let's go. Be at my office at nine o'clock sharp tomorrow morning."

I was so nervous that I got there at 8:45 and had to wait for Mr. Lastfogel to show up. He ushered me into his office and pulled out a piece of paper with the note on it, "Martinique—Best for Danny Thomas." The note apparently had been there long before I nudged him at the club the night before. We were thinking alike.

I went back to my hotel, quivering with excitement, and then I got a phone call from Uncle Abe. He said, "Go home, my boy, and have a nice vacation. You won't be having another one for some time."

So back I went to Chicago, to a still-skeptical Rose Marie. Knowing her as I did, I knew the main reason for her discontent was that she finally had settled in, in Chicago, and now she was facing another move. Rosie has always hated moving. But her enthusiasm began to pick up as we packed our things, loaded the two little girls into the car, and headed off to Toledo to spend a little time with my parents.

It's funny, but every time there was an impending change in my life, I was always irresistibly drawn back to Toledo. It was the place of my roots, my home base. In my act, I've always gotten a laugh—and credit—for singing a song about much-maligned Toledo with the same fervor that Tony Bennett exhibits when he sings about leaving his heart in San Francisco. As a matter of fact, I have the band use the same introductory music, leading the audience to think that I'm going to sing about San Francisco. Instead, I launch into the fight song, "We're Strong for Toledo." The audience usually breaks up. But I genuinely love the grimy old city.

On my many visits back home, I spent a lot of time with my brothers. Time and again, one or two of them would accompany us on side trips (to Florida, for example), which always began in Toledo. I even organized a golf tournament in Toledo for all the Jacobs boys, which my older brother, Bill, usually won. Mom and Dad treated me as if I had never been away. It saddened me to see how my lovely mother was aging. The hard work and all the child-bearing were taking their toll. She was to die soon, at the relatively young age of sixty-two.

On this trip back to Toledo in 1943, I was determined to do something to lighten my parents' later years. My brothers and I had been contributing to their support for some time, but the folks still had the same crummy living quarters. My father refused to move away from his old cronies and the environment in which he was most comfortable.

By now I had saved up what seemed like a lot of money at the time, and I had bright prospects for making more. So I said to Dad, "If you won't let me buy you a new house, at least let me fix up this one." He reluctantly said, "Okay." So I put Rose Marie to work planning the redecoration. Over a period of time, the floors were scraped and restained, the walls were repainted, in came new draperies and furniture. We covered the entire place with wall-to-wall carpeting.

Later, when it was finished, how did my father react to all this comparative splendor? Like the tough old Lebanese mountain man he always was. I came back to see him and I was amazed at what Rosie had done. There even was a dainty new powder room off the living room. But the living room was filled with Dad's old Lebanese, Syrian, and Turkish pals, and they were sitting around with Dad, schmoozing and smoking their Turkish pipes and cigarettes. They used to drop the ashes on the bare floor, which Mom would sweep afterwards, but now there was expensive wall-to-wall carpeting.

I figured I was a big man now, so I tried to lay down a few ground rules. I said, "Dad, it's nice for you to have these old-timers here, but tell them they shouldn't be dropping ashes in the corner, and they shouldn't . . ." I went on and on. Dad listened. Then he looked at me and he said, "You finished?"

I said, "Yes, sir."

He said, "Let me ask you something. You built this house for your mother and me, right?"

I said, "Yes, sir."

He said, "You gonna live here?"

I said, "No."

"Then finish your coffee and get the hell outta here."

I loved him for it. He was still the proud, stubborn man I had known as a child, and, in a way, I was glad to see that nothing was going to change my cherished image of him— not even a son who was making his mark in show business.

But back in 1943, when the remodeling idea first began, I was still sitting around in Toledo, enjoying this time with my parents and my brothers and sister, and wondering what would be the next step in making my mark. When would Uncle Abe call me and tell me to start back to New York?

He called unexpectedly, but it wasn't to summon me immediately to the Big Stem. In fact, the call was a little disappointing. Remember how I mentioned the club in Hamtramck, The Bowery, where the evolution of my Jack Story began? Well, Frank Barberro, the owner of the club (who had paid me thirty-five dollars a week) had called the William Morris office in a panic. Harry Richman, a legendary vaudeville headliner, had been booked in The Bowery, but had to back out of the engagement because of illness. Uncle Abe said to me, "I know you're resting, but if you feel up to it, go to Detroit and fill in for Richman. It can't hurt you."

I said, "But Uncle Abe. The last time I worked there it was for thirty-five dollars a week."

"Don't worry," he said, "this time I'm asking twelve-fifty for you."

He transmitted that information to Barberro, who, when he picked himself up off the floor, finally settled for eleven hundred dollars a week.

In a way, it turned out to be fun returning to the Detroit area in triumph for this brief period. Word had filtered in about my success at the 5100 Club in Chicago, and critic Hershel Hart wrote glowingly about me in his newspaper, the *Detroit News.* I was a conquering hero coming back to the site of earlier failures, and (Hart wrote) I was now "considerably improved."

I was pretty cocky, refining my act further for the Detroit audiences—"gaining polish," as Uncle Abe put it. But then I learned a valuable lesson, which, I hope, also added to my polish.

A performer is the most insecure person in the world. As he gets up before an audience every night, he keeps asking himself, "What if I flop this evening? What if I flop altogether? What if I can't please them?" Jerry Lewis had a sign on his dressing-room door: I CAN GIVE YOU THE FORMULA FOR FAILURE: TRY PLEASING *everybody*.

Despite the inner spirit I told you about, which seems to take over my mind and body when I'm on a stage, my fear of failure was as pronounced as anybody's—especially in those early days. Sometimes this insecurity is justified; more frequently it isn't.

While I was doing my vacation-stint at The Bowery, I got word that a big New York impresario was coming to see my act. He arrived with George Woods of the William Morris Agency. The impresario was involved with the famous Copacabana Club in New York and also produced Broadway musicals. He arrived at The Bowery at 9:45 and was told I'd be onstage at 10:15. But the show dragged on, with the very capable M.C. Charley Carlyle singing and dancing and telling one story after another before he introduced me.

When I finally got on, I looked over at the impresario. He was fast asleep. He slept through the entire act. He only woke up once, while I was doing my Ode to a Wailing Syrian routine, in which I wear a sheet over my head and tell stories from the Old Country. I'm sure that the only time the man saw me was when all there was to see was my big hook nose sticking out of the sheet.

When I finished the act, I was ashamed to walk out into the club for fear that I'd run into the man, so I left by the back way. I couldn't sleep. If my act wasn't good enough to keep the impresario awake, this could be an indication of what could happen to me in New York. The thought sent a chill down my spine. Not only had I blown a chance to eventually get to play the Copacabana, but now the word might get around New York that my act was a sleep-inducer.

In the morning, I got a phone call from George Woods. He hastened to explain what had happened. He knew from experience with the impresario that he was a man who could not sleep without sleeping pills. It was his habit to take them about an hour before he got back to his hotel, when he was on the road. The night he came to see me, he swallowed the pills just as Charley Carlyle began to introduce me, figuring I'd then be on for an hour and the pills would take effect about the time he'd be ready for bed. As it was, Charley took so long in introducing me, that the impresario was fast asleep before I got on the stage.

"He was so out of it," said Woods, "that I had to lug his dead weight to a cab, and into the hotel, and he never woke up until we had to catch our plane in the morning."

Then Mr. Lastfogel got on the phone. He said, "Don't let it throw you, my boy. This guy can't hurt you."

I still wasn't quite sure.

But when I got back to Toledo after The Bowery engagement, there was a telegram from Uncle Abe.

I was to open at La Martinique in New York on September 8th.

chapter

Rosie and I left for New York on September 5th, leaving our two small daughters in the care of my brother Bill and his lovely wife, Bea, who makes the best oatmeal cookies in the world. I was edgy and irritable on the drive, like a prizefighter waiting for the bell of a championship fight.

And talk about a reversion to insecurity! The Martinique had placed an ad about me under the headline, GALES OF LAUGHTER FROM THE WINDY CITY. That was the kiss of death, I thought. New Yorkers hate anything that comes from Chicago. I was doomed. Should I call Abe Lastfogel and tell him, "It's been nice knowing you—but goodbye?" Should I call Harry Eager and tell him I was coming back to be his partner after all? I don't know how Rosie put up with me on that trip—but, calm and reasonable as ever, she did.

So frantic was I in my insecurities, that when we checked in at the St. Moritz Hotel on September 6th, I registered us under our legal names, Mr. and Mrs. Amos Jacobs. I didn't use the name Danny Thomas because when I failed at La Martinique, I could check out without the embarrassment of people knowing who we were.

Actually, the way my Martinique deal was written, I couldn't fail as quickly as I thought I would. The contract called for a four-week engagement (during which, good or bad, they had to keep me) followed by three four-week options (if I were good) with a hundred-dollar-a-week raise in salary for each option renewal. But I thought I'd never get through the first night.

That's where my dear Rosie's great skill in handling my turbulent emotions came into play. When we were settled in our hotel room, she came over to where I was sulking in a chair, kissed me, put her arms around me and said, "You're going to kill the people, honey. You can do it. Do it for Marlo and Terre and especially for me, because I love you." And this from a woman who, all through our married life, had been urging me to go into the grocery business. Rosie kept up this kind of much-needed support for the next two days, while we waited for the Martinique opening. Rather than let me brood, she insisted on our going to shows and taking walks in Central Park.

The night before the opening, Uncle Abe took us to see the Ziegfeld Follies. One of the stars of the show was Milton Berle, and I was taken backstage to meet him. We got to talking about my upcoming New York debut, and somewhere along the line, I said, "I'm scared to death that professional hecklers might pick on me, because I don't know anything about heckling. I'm a storyteller, and if they start heckling, I'm dead."

Berle said, "You really mean that, don't you, kid?"

I said, "I certainly do, Mr. Berle."

He said, "Well . . . Look, I'll be there for your opening. If anybody picks on you, just come down to me with the microphone, hand it to me, and say, 'I got a fella here who handles my small fights,' then you just go sit on the piano."

This not only gave me a laugh, but it made me feel better—because as you know, Milton Berle is one of the great heckler-handlers of all time, and no one would dare to take him on.

Finally the big night arrived, September 8, 1943. There were huge headlines in the newspapers that day: Italy had surrendered to the Allies. When I got to the Martinique, everyone backstage was listening to the news reports on the radio. I did, too. It took my mind off what was coming up for me. I put on my tuxedo. Then I fell to my knees and prayed in my dressing room.

On the stage, the featured singer, Adrianne, was finishing a beautiful rendition of "Falling in Love with Love Is Falling for Make-believe." I peeked out through the curtains and the place was filled. "Yeah," I said bitterly to myself, "they've come to hear 'Gales of Laughter from the Windy City,' like it said in that dumb ad."

Then came the booming voice of Dario Borzani, one of the Martinique's bosses, from a concealed microphone somewhere: "Ladies and gentleman, La Martinique, maker of stars, presents now a young man whose name we sincerely hope will one day be added to the list of stars born here. Here he is—Danny Thomas!"

I could barely make it out onto the stage. But suddenly

I became aware of a huge burst of applause. There were shouts of "Go get 'em, Danny . . . We're with you kid . . . Atta boy, Danny!" For me? In New York? I peered out into the audience, and my heart filled up. The back rows were jammed with people who had come to see me in the 5100 Club in Chicago. I later learned that nearly two hundred of them had come in for a jewelry convention and a furniture show and they had booked tables for my performance weeks before.

I stood there at the microphone, not knowing how to begin. I could see Milton Berle in the audience, silently mouthing, "What are you doing, kid? Make a joke already." I could see Uncle Abe, and Rosie—with tears of pride streaming down her cheeks. Suddenly, I knew what to do. No jokes. I said:

> "There's great gaiety here tonight, and this festive air cannot be credited to the opening of 'Great Gales of Laughter from the Windy City.' There's a much greater reason for rejoicing. Today Italy surrendered and that's the real cause for celebration. But as we celebrate, let us remember that our country still has a lot to do to finish this job . . ."

Dead silence in the house. I could see Milton Berle saying, "Stop with the gab, already. Where are you going with this, kid?" But I kept on with a few words about God Almighty blessing our boys overseas, and that we may someday live in peace, people of all races and creeds.

Then came the joke, and it was totally unexpected after my opening spiel. Thank God the orchestra was ready for it because we hadn't rehearsed it that way:

"I would also like to pay tribute to our allies, the fighting Russians. There's a song they sing, which has inspired them as they fight from city block to city block through Stalingrad. And here's the song:"

The band struck up a boogie beat, and they were playing "Chattanooga Choo Choo," a very hip number of the day. I joined in with the words, a parody I'd written: "Berchtesgaden Choo Choo."

The crowd whooped, and it was not only the Chicagoans. I knew I had them. The inner spirit came over me and I sailed on now, with more and more confidence. I did my old standards: Ode to a Wailing Syrian, The Jack Story, Crotchy Callahan, "We're Strong for Toledo," and others I haven't mentioned. When I finished, there was a tremendous ovation. The next day, Earl Wilson headed his column in the *New York Post* with A STAR IS BORN. Me—a star!

I found out that the Chicago *Daily News* had sent its critic, Sam Lester, all the way to New York to cover my opening. He always had been a booster of mine, and he, too, raved. But as usual with me, there was a fly in the ointment. Ed Sullivan, then the maven of New York columnists, wrote about me, "Too dirty. Clean up your act."

I couldn't understand that because I never used what is referred to in the business as "blue material." I said to Martinique owner Dario Borzani, "What's this all about? When was Mr. Sullivan here?"

Dario said, "He wasn't. It's more against me than it is against you." He then gave me a lesson in how columnist journalism was conducted in New York. Many of their items came not from personal observation, but from press agents who fed the columnists material, in exchange for favorable mentions about their clients. The Martinique's press agent, a regular feeder to Sullivan, had just recently been fired by Borzani for some misdeed or another. To get back at Borzani, this press agent had planted the item with Sullivan about the Martinique's new comic being "too dirty." When I confronted Sullivan himself with this later, he honestly didn't know—and I believed him—that the item even had run. I guess Ed didn't read his own columns all of the time.

Notwithstanding the item, the Martinique was filled to capacity for the rest of my first week there. As I started my second week, Dario Borzani came up to me and said, "Have you brought heavy winter clothes?" I said I had not because I expected to be home by the middle of October. Dario said, "We sent you a registered letter this afternoon, which you obviously haven't received yet. We officially notified you that we've taken up all three of your options simultaneously. You'll be here for sixteen weeks, kid, which will take you well into the winter."

I couldn't wait to get to a phone to tell Rosie the astounding news. She had left after the first weekend to go back to Toledo to be with the kids. I must have sounded a bit downcast at being away from them for nearly four months, but Rosie came up with an easy solution. "I'll come into New York to spend a couple of days with you every week, and sometimes I'll bring the children." Practical Rosie already had figured out that I would be making more than enough money to be able to afford it.

So I was a happy man—in all respects except one. I was

still rankled by that item in Ed Sullivan's column. Everyone told me not to let it bother me, especially Uncle Abe, but I couldn't get it out of my mind. I was still insecure enough to want everyone to like me, especially someone as powerful as Ed. I tried every avenue I knew to get Sullivan to have dinner with me, to discuss his misconception that I was a dirty comic. No go. None of my avenues worked.

Then I heard about a benefit luncheon for a prominent New York judge, the money to go to the judge's most important charity, a local hospital. I was sure Ed Sullivan would be there. I told the charity I wanted to attend, and I was given a chair on the dais. As luck would have it, I found Ed Sullivan in the very next seat when I showed up.

He smiled at me and said, "Hello. How's it going over there at the Martinique? I understand you're really breaking it up." In his way of speaking, he meant that he heard I was a smash. He didn't sound anything like a man who disliked me.

We chatted for a while. Then I decided to take the bull by the horns. I knew there was nothing offensive in my act, but maybe if he had been led to believe there *was,* and his column had got me to change it, that would make him feel like a big man. I said, "By the way, Mr. Sullivan, that material that offended you has been deleted from my act." He looked at me as if to say, *"What* material?" Then he caught himself and said, "I understand. Don't let it bother you. I'll make it up to you."

The next morning, his *Daily News* column carried an item stating simply that I had deleted the *one* offensive piece of material from my act. Not the whole act now, just one piece.

Sullivan continued to make it up to me. He personally invited me to participate in his "The Night of Stars" extravaganza at the twenty-thousand-seat Madison Square Garden—probably the biggest show business event of the year. It was another heart-stopping moment for me. Nearly all the top entertainers in the land would be performing before a huge crowd that night.

I rehearsed at the Garden that afternoon, went back to the Martinique for my first show, then returned to the Garden at about 9:45 P.M. I waited and waited and they didn't call on me. I went over to one of the producers to ask when I'd be going on. He said, "Who are you?" A big confidence builder.

I got more and more nervous about getting back to the Martinique for my midnight show. Finally, Ed Sullivan himself came over and said, "Listen, kid, it's my guess you'll accomplish more here tonight than in a month at that club. Your boss'll understand if you're late. Just sit tight."

I sat tight through one act after another. Then came Kate Smith, ending her act singing "God Bless America," with the entire U.S. Marine Corps Band backing her up with sixty or seventy voices. It was a closing act to end all closing acts. The applause was deafening—and there was I, still standing in the wings.

I saw Ed Sullivan gesticulating wildly and yelling something at Bert Lytell, the evening's sixth M.C. Lytell grabbed the microphone and yelled, "And now, from the famous La Martinique, we bring you . . . Danny Kaye!" My heart dropped to the soles of my shoes. First of all, how could I top a closing act like Kate Smith and the Marines singing "God Bless America"? Secondly, the continuing applause was for Danny Kaye, and when I got on the stage instead of him, they'd boo me out of the joint.

With a lot of prodding from the wings, master of ceremonies Lytell finally corrected his error: "Wait a minute . . . I made a mistake . . . It's not Danny Kaye. It's another Danny, who is enjoying the kind of success at the place that launched Danny Kaye. And his name is Danny Thomas."

Did you ever hear a collective groan go up from twenty thousand people? I was ready to run out of the place. Sullivan tried to calm me down with reassuring words and practically pushed me out on the stage. I was aware of nearly total silence, with only some sporadic hand clapping. My legs were shaking so much that I began to jump up and down to cover up the trembling. I used that as a device to get into my first story, in which I allegedly was jumping up and down with excitement about making a bus trip to California from New York. The story got me to Chicago, where I was able to slide into my Crotchy Callahan stories—and I had regained my composure. I used my best material and from the friendly reaction of the crowd, I knew in my heart that I had done well.

I didn't know *how* well until people started calling me in the morning about Ed Sullivan's column. I ran out to get the *Daily News.* Sullivan had devoted about a quarter of his column to me. Nothing about my material being dirty this time. He wrote, in part:

> At the Tenth Annual "Night of Stars," the 12:30 nightmare assignment was handed to youthful Danny Thomas, Chicagoan now appearing at La Martinique . . . If the youngster's face paled at the prospect, that

was understandable, because he had to follow four solid hours of sock entertainment to which every great name of the profession had contributed talent and prestige . . . But Thomas, receiving only perfunctory applause when he was introduced, made one of the great hits of the night, his fable of the little man seeking an automobile jack convulsing 20,000.

That capped my "Invasion of New York," as Uncle Abe still called it. I guess it was a pretty good invasion because few people make it in their opening assault on the Big Apple. You tell *me* how a scared newcomer could possibly make good his first time up in the Blue Chip League. I can only attribute it to faith, which caused Fate to place me in the right place at the right time.

It took a lot of willpower, as well as faith, to get me through the last couple of weeks of my contract at the Martinique. I had developed arthritic pain and was running a fever, which turned out to be the flu. It was the dead of winter and the basement showroom was cold and damp. Nevertheless, I didn't miss a show, and the crowds kept pouring in. In addition to the regular nightclub crowd, there were a lot of Lebanese and Syrians, mostly from the Bay Ridge section of Brooklyn. I had caught on as something of an idol with the people of my own heritage. They helped make my closing night a triumph, with the entire audience—led by actor Victor Jory—rising to its feet in a standing ovation and singing "For He's a Jolly Good Fellow." The boss gave me a gold Dunhill cigar lighter, wrapped in a thousand-dollar bill. (Incidentally, at the end of my second engagement at La Martinique some time later,

I was given a Packard car with a sign in the trunk: HA, HA.
NO JACK.)

It was a nice climax to my four-month Invasion of New
York. But I was tired and ill, and Uncle Abe sent me home
to Toledo to rest up. My brother Bill had come in for the
closing and drove me home. Rosie immediately put me to
bed, and it took more than a week for me recover from the
flu. And also the exhaustion.

As soon as I began to feel like myself again, I got edgy.
It was marvelous being with Rosie and the children. But
why had I walked out of New York when I was so hot?
Shouldn't I be back there to keep the ball rolling? Despite
all that had happened, it was another crazy manifestation of
lack of self-confidence. If I didn't follow through on my
new-found status, it might never happen again. I held out
as long as I could, and then I phoned Uncle Abe.

I tried to reach him at his William Morris office, but they
transferred me to a new number. When I got Uncle Abe,
I told him I was coming back to New York sooner than
expected. He said he was glad, "because I have a real big
job for you."

I couldn't wait to hear what the real big job was, but
Uncle Abe said he wouldn't tell me until I got to New
York. When I arrived, he said, "I just got an offer from the
Roxy Theater for you, for four weeks at thirty-two-fifty a
week."

I said, "Wow!" It wasn't long before that when I hadn't
made that much money in a full year. Even though it wasn't
Madison Square Garden, I immediately worried about playing *regularly* in a house that size. "The Roxy's a big theater," I said.

Uncle Abe said, "It certainly is, but I want you to play in an even bigger one."

I said, "Bigger than the Roxy? You don't mean the Radio City Music Hall? They don't put on comics, do they?"

"Bigger than that."

"Bigger than the Radio City Music Hall?"

He said, "Yeah, but you'll have to take a slight cut."

"How much of a cut?" I asked.

He replied, "About thirty-one hundred dollars less than you'd be getting at the Roxy."

"You gotta be kidding," I said. "You mean you want me to go back to working for a hundred and fifty a week?"

"Yup," he said, "President Roosevelt has put me in charge of putting together shows for the U.S.O., and right now Marlene Dietrich needs an M.C. for a show she's taking overseas to entertain the troops. You're *it,* my boy. I'll send your hundred and fifty to Rosie every week for all the time you're gone. There's a war on, and you've earned your last dollar until it's over. But don't worry about it. You're no fly-by-night entertainer. All of this will be here for you when you get back. Now go and get your shots."

I went to an army medical facility downtown and obediently got my shots.

chapter

»»» 15 ««

I was inoculated, oriented, and uniformed. Like most entertainers, the army gave me the simulated rank of Captain, so
I'd be treated like an officer in the event I was captured and
became a prisoner-of-war. Marlene Dietrich outranked me.
She was made a simulated Major.

I didn't brood much about the one-fifty a week I now was
making. In fact, I was relieved that I had officially become
part of the war effort. It had always bothered me that I was
only thirty years old and, but for the grace of my deferment
as a married father, could have been drafted into the Army
as a thirty-dollar-a-month private, like everyone else. Now,
I could help bolster those men overseas and contribute to
the war effort.

In my capacity as a U.S.O. entertainer, I certainly was no
Bob Hope. Who *could* be? Bob was to entertaining-the-
troops what Babe Ruth was to baseball. But I put in a good
part of a year overseas and I brought a few laughs and some
solace to a lot of brave guys in uniform. And there was one

thing that I don't believe even happened to Bob Hope. I saw Marlene Dietrich naked. I'll explain that later.

In addition to Marlene and me, our troupe consisted of comedienne Lynne Mayberry, straight man Milton Frome, and accompanist Jack Snyder, who played the piano when one was available, a guitar at other times. Before we left, there was so much secrecy that no one knew where we were going—or when. I was awakened by the Army at my hotel at 4 A.M. one morning, and told to come down to the lobby—not to check out, because someone else would be doing that for me later. By 7:45, we were at LaGuardia Airport and hustled aboard an Army Air Force C-54 transport plane. It wasn't until we were airborne for some time, that we were allowed to open our instruction envelopes. In them, was a notice printed in capital letters: YOUR DESTINATION—ALGIERS, NORTH AFRICA.

We flew to the Azores, refueled, and then went on to Casablanca in Morocco. It was the first time I had flown in an airplane, and I was so airsick that I didn't care if we were flying to Outer Mongolia. The trip took twenty-two hours. When we got there, and with my feet on terra firma, I immediately felt better because the baggage handlers unloading the plane were speaking Arabic. To me, it was a strange kind of Arabic—they were Berbers—but I could understand them and they could understand me, and they treated me as if I were a visiting dignitary from the Middle East.

They immediately got me into trouble with our Army escort officers, because the baggage handlers invited me to visit the Medina with them that night, and I accepted. The

Medina is the native quarter, similar to the Casbah, and it was off-limits to the GIs. The baggage men took me down ominous winding streets and wined and dined me. When thugs or hookers approached me, they pointed to my nose and said, "He is one of us. He is an American who speaks our language." When I got back to our hotel, I told Marlene about my adventure. She was jealous and said she wanted to go to the Medina, too. But the Army wouldn't let her, despite her rank of simulated Major. The army did a good job of chewing out this simulated Captain.

The next morning, we flew to Algiers, where Marlene was greeted at the airstrip by the French actor Jean Gabin, who was then attached to the French Navy. He and Marlene must have been lovers because they attached themselves to each other so amorously that the GIs cheered for at least five minutes while they clutched and kissed in full view of everyone. I began to think this was going to be an interesting trip.

That night, we did our premiere show—the first of hundreds we were going to do in that Theater of War. It was at the Algiers Opera House. Before the show, Captain Mike Cullen of Army Special Services came up to me and said nervously, "Look, Danny, most of the guys in the audience tonight are fighting men back from the front. They do things like throwing paper airplanes at the stage— and they heckle. Please, just ignore the hecklers, and in time, they'll stop."

I said to myself, "Oh, boy, how am I going to deal with these guys when they see someone up on the stage as young as they are and not in the army?" Again, that inner spirit came up from inside me and came to my rescue. I don't know where the idea came from, but when I got up at the microphone, I said, "Fellas, before we start, I know you've been hearing a lot about those Dear John letters from your girls back home, who've taken up with some civilian. So I want you to know why I came overseas. I came here to show you what kind of man is left in the States." Then, turning my hook-nose profile sideways, I said, "Now tell the truth. Could anyone with a puss like this steal your girl or your wife?"

It tore the house down. Even the paper airplanes stopped flying, and my act proceeded smooth as silk. I had won them over with that one joke. I used it as the opening of my act at every soldier show thereafter.

I don't have to tell you too much about what these soldier shows were like—as we made our way to Naples, Anzio, and finally Rome itself, after the Fifth Army took it from the Germans. You've seen the formula a hundred times in all those Bob Hope television shows, as he entertains the troops in war zones. There are hundreds of kids, sitting around on gun mounts, tanks, crude benches—just aching for some contact with home. They laugh at all the jokes, whoop and holler at any mention of screwed-up things in their outfits, but mostly they are hungry to ogle the girls.

In that respect, there was no question about who was the star of our show. Marlene Dietrich was magnificent. Invariable called "Legs Dietrich" in the army newspaper, *Stars and Stripes,* she totally lived up to her screen image. She flirted outrageously with enlisted men and officers alike, she grabbed a mess kit and ate with the men, she slunk around on the stage in a form-fitting gold lamé gown (no under-wear, I'm sure) looking like a Golden Panther, which, as a matter of fact, is what I called her.

An incident that occurred a few nights before Anzio fell was typical of the effect she had on the troops. I was doing a skit with Marlene and Milton Frome. They were supposed to be comparing lovemaking techniques on the screen as opposed to the stage. I was the hanger-on, watching them go at it. For example, while Milton was kissing her, I'd be chewing on her fingers over his shoulder. The guys in the audience kept yelling things like, "Hey, Joe, let me up there."

Finally Marlene said to me, "Would *you* like to try?" I put on the shy act and began to run away from her. I ran all over the stage until I fell from exhaustion, hiding under a helmet and calling for air support, which got a big laugh. Marlene said, "You come here, or I will come after you." I buried my head in my coat and she started for me. This was the sexiest possible Marlene, in her skin-tight gown, walking her famous walk, pawing her thighs with each stride. From the crowd there came a moan, reaching a howled crescendo that shook the ground. Can you imag-ine—twenty-two thousand men screaming simultaneously?

We never finished the skit. The MPs were afraid the men would storm the stage and try to carry her off. They blocked off the crowd, with submachine guns at the ready. Fortu-nately, the skit was supposed to close the show, anyway, but that was the end of our performance for that evening.

Marlene and I got along famously. She listened to my stories about immigrant life in Toledo, and she told me about show-business life in Germany and Hollywood. Only one thing marred our relationship. A magazine photographer was trailing her, recording on film everything Marlene did. A lot of it was pure publicity stuff, and I kept refusing to pose with La Dietrich in her offstage activities. She kept asking for me whenever the photographer would come around, but I'd always disappear. I had worked out a deal with a Master Sergeant buddy, who'd pop me in his jeep and whisk me away whenever I asked him to. He knew that I felt uncomfortable about gaining any publicity for myself—that I didn't want to make myself a big man at the expense of the soldiers, who were doing so much more for our country than I was.

Well, this led to the inevitable showdown with Marlene. One day, Lynne Mayberry, our darling little comedienne/harmonica player, came up to me and said, "The boss wants to see you." We were staying at a hotel in Naples at the time. I went to her room and knocked on the door. "Come in," Marlene said. I went in, and there she was, stark naked, sunning herself on her balcony.

I averted my eyes. Marlene said, "Come on, now. Don't be such a baby." But she grabbed a towel and dangled it in front of her, not really doing much to cover her luscious body.

"You don't like me," she said.

"That's not true. I love you," I said.

"Then why don't you want to have pictures taken with me?"

I explained my reticence about doing anything to cash in on the war with personal publicity. She looked at me with amazement, but walked over and kissed me on both cheeks. "You are a very unusual young man," she said.

And so I was—because I got out of there as fast as I could. Alone in a room with a nude Marlene, and I just took off. I know you don't believe that. And come to think of it, neither would I. But that's what I did.

Nudity never entered into our relationship again. We had been to Bari, Foggia, Sicily, Sardinia, Naples, and Anzio; and on May 11, 1944, the Big Push to Rome began. We followed closely behind the troops, always within the sound of nearby artillery. We skirted mine fields marked by stakes. We'd entertain troops on their way into combat, and sometimes would see the same men, now wounded, in an evacuation hospital on the other side of the same mountain. In one of these evac hospitals, we met up with Irving Berlin and did a show with him that was broadcast back to the United States.

After the fall of Rome, our tour of duty was over and we headed back home via the same Azores route. I thought I was finished with entertaining the troops, but Uncle Abe Lastfogel said, "Wait, there's a war in the Pacific, too. But that'll come a little later. In the meantime, I want you to go to the West Coast to play a part in Fanny Brice's radio show."

I said, "Fanny Brice? Has she ever seen my act?"

Abe said, "No, but my wife, Frances, does your material all the time to amuse her, and she loves it. So she's hired you sight unseen." (For those who don't remember the great comedienne, she was the woman later played by Barbra Streisand on stage and in the film *Funny Girl*.)

I went to Los Angeles filled with awe for the famous Fanny Brice, and I guess it showed when I met her. Uncle Abe introduced me to her at her house in Beverly Hills. I thought I was wearing the proper attire for California—a blue serge suit with white-buck shoes. The first thing she said to me was, "Where'd you get those ooglie-booglie shoes?" This was a lady who really spoke her mind.

I launched into my prepared speech, which I guess was a little pompous: "Miss Brice, it is a great thrill and honor to meet you. I've been a great admirer of yours most of my life. When I worked in burlesque theater as a kid, I used to see a lot of impressions of you, especially the French lady leaning against a lamppost, singing 'My Man.' I never dreamed the day would come when I would share the same stage with you."

Miss Brice cut me down, but good. She said, "Don't give me that shit, kid. You better be funny."

I picked my head off the floor and screwed it back on.

Then came the question of what she was going to do with me in her show. She and her writers decided we would all go to the Hollywood Canteen, where they would watch me do my act for the soldiers, sailors, and marines on leave. I went through my whole routine, including The Jack Story. When I finished, Miss Brice wryly said, "Abe's wife, Frances, does it better."

So I sat down with the show's writers, including Artie Stander, who would work for me later on in my career. We came up with the concept of Jerry Dingle, the mailman who walks along, constantly talking to himself. Everett Freeman, the head writer, didn't like the idea and nearly fired young

Artie Stander because of it. But Freeman went to see Miss Brice and came back with a momentous decision. "It won't be Jerry Dingle, the mailman," he said. "It'll be Jerry Dingle, the postman." Such were the decisions that were made in radio sitcom in those days, and, in fact, are still being made in television sitcom today.

Anyway, I was Dingle the Postman for the rest of that season, and I couldn't have been too bad because both *Billboard* and *Variety* named me Best Newcomer in Radio. But I was fired, anyway.

That didn't seem to bother Uncle Abe because he said, "Now, my boy, you're going to the South Pacific until the war ends. This time I'm giving you your own troupe. You'll be the boss."

The troupe was a male singer, an accompanist, and two pretty girls who sang, danced, and did skits with me. They got almost—but not quite—as many wolf whistles as Marlene Dietrich did. On the whole, the experience was much like it had been in Italy—except that there were more palm trees.

And there was more trouble getting home.

When the war ended in August 1945, all the military planes were going the other way—toward Okinawa and Japan. There wasn't a chance of getting on a U.S.-bound plane, most of which were reserved for the wounded. I was desperate to get home. There was a transportation officer who had been among my fans at the 5100 Club, but not even he could get me on a plane. "I'm sorry, Danny," he said, "but it's hopeless."

"Hopeless . . . hopeless?" I said to myself. I wondered

if this could be a task for St. Jude, the Patron Saint of Hopeless Causes, but decided it wasn't important enough to bother him with. Besides, I felt a little guilty about having taken so long to fulfill my vow about building him a shrine.

Maybe he heard me, anyway. I was called to General MacArthur's headquarters, where the two girls from my show had been given plane seats, because they were women, I suppose. One of them, Penny Piper, told the colonel in charge that she was willing to give up her seat for me. The colonel gave me my travel orders, swearing me to secrecy about where I had got them. He apparently was touched by Penny's offer, because eventually he let both girls on the aircraft, too.

I couldn't help looking up and saying to St. Jude, "Using girls now, huh?"

chapter

The first thing I heard from Uncle Abe when I got back was that he had booked me into the Chez Paree, which, if you recall, had been after me for three years—since my 5100 Club days.

Uncle Abe had called Joey Jacobson at the Chicago night-club and said, *"Now* you can have him."

Jacobson said, "It's about time."

Uncle Abe said, "The only thing is, now it's going to cost you double—three thousand dollars a week." Jacobson nearly fainted, but when he regained his composure, he said okay.

Now that I was on a steady postwar course, I did something I had wanted to do for a long time. Through the Musicians Union, I got the telephone number of Wally Popp, the piano player who had been so kind to me when I was first breaking in at the 5100 Club. I had told Wally then, "When the Lord smiles on me and I need a regular accompanist, I'll be calling on you." Wally's bitter reply to that was, "Oh, *sure.* How many times have I heard that before."

So now I got Wally on the phone and I said, "The Lord hath smiled."

He said, "And you're *calling* me?" He remembered my long-ago promise.

"Yes," I said. "How would you like to be my conductor and accompanist at the Chez Paree in October?"

He literally dropped the phone, but then came back and said, "I'd love it." Wally Popp was with me for thirty-five years. He was like a brother—with me all the way. In all the benefits for St. Jude, Wally was there conducting the music—and never took any money.

Wally was with me for my seventeen weeks at the Chez Paree, where my opening was a duplicate of what had happened in New York at La Martinique—even more so. My rooting contingent from the 5100 Club once again showed up en masse and provided impetus for what turned out to be a long run.

After that, he was with me as I played every major night-club in the United States. I played The Sands in Las Vegas, I played Bill Miller's Riviera across the river from New York in New Jersey, I even played several engagements at the Copacabana, which, you might remember, seemed to have blackballed me forever after their impresario over-dosed on sleeping pills when he came to see my act at The Bowery in Hamtramck.

There's an interesting story about my ending up at the Copa, which involves one of the nation's most famous organized crime figures. But first, let's examine the structure of most of the nightclub business in those days in America. The Senate Kefauver Committee hearings in 1951 and 1952 revealed much about so-called "mob ownership" or "involvement" with many of the clubs, and I cannot deny that I was aware of the shadowy nature of some of the people for whom I worked. Sometimes they scared me, but mostly they couldn't have been nicer. And sometimes my dealings with them were like scenes out of *The Godfather* movies.

My whole first experience with the Copacabana was a good example of life imitating art. The William Morris Agency had a man on its staff who was informally known as the Ambassador to the Mob, though I think he was just a good agent with good contacts. He was George Woods, the man who had brought the Copacabana representative to see me at The Bowery. After my success at the Chez Paree in Chicago, George got word that the Copa would like to discuss a deal with me for the next time I played New York. I distractedly said, "Oh, yeah. Fine," and promptly forgot about it. A few months later, Uncle Abe's people booked me into Bill Miller's Riviera, across the Hudson River but still considered part of the New York area.

During my engagement there, I dropped in at the Copacabana just to pay my respects and to say "Hi" to people I knew. Jules Podell, the Copa's owner, saw me and I realized he was getting very hot. I began to worry when Jack Entratter, a very large man who was the bouncer, came over and stood behind me. Later, Jack was president of The Sands Hotel in Las Vegas and became a very good friend of mine, but on that night his only function was to protect Jules Podell. From whom? Me?

A very agitated Podell rushed over to my table and sat down. He started screaming and I suddenly understood why Jack Entratter was there. Jack was just doing his job. He figured that Podell would get so irritated that he'd hit me and I'd take a swing at him, and Jack would have to cold-cock me. The interesting thing is that before Podell started screaming, he hit the table with his ring—as he always did—and told the waiter, "Gimme a brandy and get some for my friends." *Then* came the screaming.

The gist of his screaming was, "How could you go back on your word that you'd play the Copa the next time you came to New York?" Before I could answer that there *was* no word, he became physical. He began aggressively wagging his finger at me—just *missing* my face—saying, over and over again, "Is that your mouth or your asshole?" He must have said that a hundred times. I finally managed to get up and leave.

About a year later, I was back at the Chez Paree. The first night, the club's new owner, David Halper, came over to me and said, "You're wanted on the phone. Long distance."

I said, "Who is it?"

He said, "F.C."

Those were a set of initials that commanded immediate attention in the hearts of anyone in the know. "F.C." was Frank Costello, who later testified at the Kefauver hearings with only his hands showing.

I answered the phone and a very nice-sounding voice said, "Hello, young man."

I said, "Good evening, sir."

He said, "Do you know to whom you are speaking?"

I said, "Yes, sir. I do."

He said, "I am sitting here with a person named Jules Podell, who just bet me a thousand dollars that you would never play the Copacabana. I bet him you would."

I said, "Tell him you win."

He said, "Thank you very much young man." And that was the end of the conversation. Two months later, I played the Copacabana.

While I was there, I went to Lindy's restaurant for breakfast one afternoon at about 2 P.M. That's when I usually have breakfast when I'm working late at night. I was eating away, focusing on my eggs and bacon, when I became aware of a pair of legs standing beside me. The legs were in beautiful oxford-gray pants. I looked up and saw a beautiful oxford-gray suit. I looked up some more and there was Frank Costello.

He said, "I don't want to disturb your breakfast, young man. I just want you to know that I appreciate very much what you did with the Jules Podell incident. And I also want you to know that if ever there is anything I can do for you, you know where to find me. Good afternoon, young man." And he walked away.

These were strange, fascinating people. For example, they never looked at you when they talked. And they never wanted us civilians, as they called us, to get too buddy-buddy with them. There was always the chance we'd be called in for questioning, and it was better for us to be able to say, "I don't know anything." That's what happened when Frank Sinatra was summoned to testify at a hearing about the underworld in New Jersey. He didn't know anything, and they let him go in about ten minutes. It didn't hurt that just before that, Frank sang—at my request—before the nation's top politicians at an event in Washington to benefit the Everett Dirksen Library, named after the great senator from Illinois.

The closest I came to getting buddy-buddy with the background people in my business was with the Fischetti brothers in Chicago—Charlie, Rocky, and Young Joe. Just as Frank Costello was known as F.C., Charlie Fischetti was simply called "Mr. Fish," and his brother Rocky was "the Rock." Among other things, they ran the gambling room for V.I.P.'s in the key club back of the Chez Paree.

A strange thing happened between me and the Fischettis. Their sister had been engaged to a young man who went overseas in World War II and lost a leg in combat. When he came back, he wouldn't even see the Fischetti girl. It was a sad story. His shame at being an amputee, I guess. The Fischettis' sister kept following him from Veterans Hospital to Veterans Hospital, however, and finally they worked it out and agreed to get married. She convinced him she didn't care he had lost a leg. The ceremony was to take place in Brooklyn. I was appearing at La Martinique at the time.

Out of the blue, I got a phone call from Charlie Fischetti in Chicago. He told me about his sister's wedding and he said, "Would you take your girl singer and go over there to the wedding, between shows, and do a little something. We'll pick you up in a limo and get you back for your next show." So the girl singer, Gail Meredith, went with me to the wedding and we entertained for about an hour.

The next night, at about three in the morning, there was a knock on the door of my room at the St. Moritz Hotel. A voice yelled, "Open up. Mr. Fish sent me." I opened up—in a hurry.

A guy came in and said, "I'm Sal. Mr. Fish wants I should be with you for the rest of your trip in New York. I'm not goin' to bother you. You look over your right shoulder and I'll be there. Reuben's, Lindy's, wherever." The guy stuck to me like glue. In effect, he was a bodyguard, though he also kept buying me expensive cigars. After a while, I said to him, "Go away, I don't *need* a bodyguard."

He said, "What are you tryin' to do? Knock me out of a job? I got orders." So Sal and I were kind of welded together.

The next time I played the Chez Paree in Chicago, a man came up to me and said, "The Rock wants to see you." I went to the back of the room (these guys never sit at ring-side; always in the rear), and there was Rocky Fischetti. He said, "That was a nice thing you did for my sister and my family."

I said, "It was nothing."

He said, "Don't say that. It was something. Now I know you're a big success and God bless you for that. But you can never tell. Even the biggest people get into a jackpot. If that ever happens to you, you call Rocky Fischetti. Now get outta here." He didn't want me to be seen with him.

In underworld parlance "getting into a jackpot" means "getting into trouble." In different words, it was the same offer Frank Costello made. This is the only way these people know how to repay you. Like providing a free bodyguard. What else can they do with a man like me? They pick up a tab once in a while, or buy me expensive cigars, four boxes at a time.

Occasionally, they go a little further—like the Fischettis did. And all because of that one trip I made to Brooklyn for their sister's wedding. When I was in Chicago and couldn't get home for Christmas, they brought Rosie and the kids into town and set them up in a luxurious suite at the Congress Hotel, with a Christmas tree and holiday decorations all over the suite. Like I said, strange and fascinating people.

Fortunately, I never "got into a jackpot," and I never had to call for extraordinary help from the Fischettis, Frank Costello, or anyone else. Especially the man in St. Louis I told you about, who promised me two gratis "hits," if I ever needed them.

Years later, I was at dinner with my television partner, the very funny Sheldon Leonard, and his wife, Frankie. I told them the St. Louis story, and a startled Frankie turned to Leonard and said, "Shelley, does he really know those kinds of people?"

Shelley said, "Shut up! I could be one of the hits."

chapter

17

In 1945, we moved to the West Coast. I bought a nice house on Elm Drive in Beverly Hills, and we settled in there comfortably. On December 7, 1948, Rosie gave birth to our third child, a boy. I finally was able to use the name Charles Anthony, in honor of my father and my uncle. This little boy grew up to be Tony Thomas, a name which is as familiar as mine in show business—but in the production field, not in entertaining or acting.

Why did we move to the Los Angeles area? For three reasons. First, to get away from the cold in the East and Midwest. Second, because Uncle Abe Lastfogel transferred his base of operations to Beverly Hills and I wanted to be near my mentor. And third, because I became a movie star—of sorts.

Yes, I finally became a character actor. True, my film career was comparatively brief, and it may not ring a bell with you, but I made five pictures between 1947 and 1951—squeezed in among my continuing nightclub appearances.

The first one came about when the distinguished MGM producer Joe Pasternak saw me performing at the Chez Paree and told owner Joey Jacobson, "I've got to have that face in my next movie." As it turned out, that face did me in. Three studio heads tried to get me to have my nose fixed.

When Uncle Abe told me about Pasternak's comment, and the offer which followed, all I could say was, "Wow! In the movies? I'm going to be in the movies now." So I signed the contract and rushed out to Hollywood. Pasternak's picture was called *The Unfinished Dance,* and it starred little Margaret O'Brien and Cyd Charisse. I played the part of an old Greek clock-maker—not really old, but defeated by life. Mr. Pasternak took a liking to me. He let me make suggestions about building up my role, and he even included a song I wrote, "Minor Melody," which I sang to a distraught Margaret O'Brien on a rooftop, while playing a concertina. Actually, the song was written by my brother Ray and me. Ray had finally gotten back into show business, calling himself Buddy Thomas, more or less following in my footsteps. He did a lot of the same material, in many of the clubs in which I had once played. He was very good.

When *The Unfinished Dance* ended filming after twenty weeks of production, I was called into the office of Louis B. Mayer, the Boss of Bosses of Metro-Goldwyn-Mayer. Mr. Mayer said, "My boy, you have a great future in the motion-picture business, but you know, the motion-picture business is a fairyland, where the handsome prince always wins the beautiful princess. People who are unattractive and ugly come into our theaters to see our films, and they imagine themselves to be the prince or the princess. We're selling them fantasy. Now let me ask you this. If you had a huge unsightly wart on the side of your face, wouldn't you have it removed?"

I said, "I know what you're talking about and it's not on the side of my face. It's in the middle of my face, and I breathe through it."

He said, "Don't be facetious."

I said, "I'm not being funny, Mr. Mayer. I've got eight brothers and they all look like me. Can you imagine my going home—looking different. Besides, I talk about my nose a lot in the nightclubs. That's one of the keys to the success of my act. I'm no threat to guys in the audience who come in with beautiful women."

By now, Mayer was getting exasperated with me. He said, "Look, we've got you signed to a five-year contract, which is only good if we pick up the option. I'm afraid that if you don't have your nose fixed, no pickup on the option. You *do* have a great future here—but only if you have the nose surgery. Go home and think about it."

I called Uncle Abe as soon as I left the studio. He said, "This is one decision you're going to have to make for yourself." I went home, threw myself across the bed and boo-hooed like a baby. Rose Marie said, "We'll be all right, Daddy. Don't worry about it." Then the phone rang. It was Uncle Abe again. He said, "Sweetheart, I was wrong. I *can* advise you. My advice is, frig'em. Who needs them?"

It seems that Uncle Abe had called his good friend Louis K. Sidney, one of the top executives at MGM, and Sidney had tried to patch things up by offering me a contract to be their toastmaster at MGM's V.I.P. functions. Uncle Abe had turned that down, "even at the risk of my getting barred from your lot." Sidney nervously said, "Who said anything about your being barred from the lot? I'll tell you what. If a big-nosed part comes along in any of our pictures, we'll give it to your boy, Danny. Not under long-term contract, though." That's what had caused Uncle Abe to say, "Frig'em."

So I went back to the clubs, and wonder of wonders, a big-nose part came up at MGM the following year. It was *The Big City,* and it starred a lot of good people, including Robert Preston, Edward Arnold, George Murphy, Betty Garrett, and, once again, Margaret O'Brien. My part was a Jewish cantor. I guess they thought that all Jewish cantors had big hook noses. Actually, I've known several who have little button noses, like Mickey Rooney's. To me, a nose is a nose is a nose.

But Uncle Abe advised me to accept the role, and I did. It was a crazy experience. I wanted to learn more about the Hebrew liturgical chants so I went to Chicago, to my dear friend Cantor Moses Silverman of the Anshe Emmet Synagogue. I marveled again at how much the music resembled the Arabic melodies sung by my father. I also marveled at why Cantor Silverman had never done any acting himself, since he was an extremely handsome man. I asked the MGM people why they didn't have Silverman himself play my part. I got no answer. I guess it was because Silverman didn't have a big nose.

To give you some idea of how crazy the movie business was in those days, they tried to *un*hook my nose after hiring me for that very quality. Every day, I'd go into makeup and sit for an hour or so while they lifted the tip of my schnoz with spirit gum and plastic, anchoring it to a point somewhere between the eyebrows. I looked terrible, more like a punchy prizefighter than a Jewish religious figure. But what did I know? The picture came out and made money.

I wasn't exactly the star of the film, however, and it didn't create much demand for my movie-actor services. So it was another three years for me in the nightclubs, that backbreaking back-and-forth traveling around the country. The only film-role inquiry during this period came from Harry Cohn, the head of Columbia Pictures. He was the second movie mogul to ask me to fix my nose—and again I said no.

After that three-year gap, I did a picture for 20th Century-Fox, *Call Me Mister.* I didn't like the script going in, but Uncle Abe thought I should keep my finger in the movie pie. The picture was a weak version of the stage hit about GIs returning from the war, and it was mostly a romance between Betty Grable and Dan Dailey. I was supposed to be the comic relief. I would have hated making the movie a lot, if it hadn't been for Betty Grable. What a dear, dear lady. We had a lot of fun together, improvising a lot. My best scene was "Ode to the Pots and Pans," which writer Jerry Seelen said was inspired by my nightclub routine, "Ode to a Wailing Syrian."

In this scene, I visualized Betty inside one of my shining pots, and then she materialized in person. Mostly, the camera was on her, shooting across my large honker as I kept staring into the pot. When we saw the raw film at the daily rushes, Betty's response was typical of all actors and actresses. She only focused on what the camera had picked up about *her*—makeup, hair, the way she moved, how she said her lines. When it was over, I said to her, "How could they have done that shot with my great big hook nose sticking out in the middle of the whole scene.

She said, "Nose? What nose?"

My fourth picture came later that year. Director Michael Curtiz had a commitment for a Warner Brothers film, *I'll See You in My Dreams,* a Doris Day musical—and he wanted me as the leading man to play opposite Doris. This was beyond my wildest imagination. Me? A romantic leading man? But then I calmed down. My nose would surely get in the way again. And it nearly did.

I went in to see the head of the studio, Jack Warner. With me were Curtiz and the producer, Lou Edelman, who also wanted me for the male lead in the picture. Curtiz and Edelman made their pitch on my behalf. Warner nodded absentmindedly, then said, "Of course, you'll have your beak fixed." As I had done twice before, I said no, I wouldn't have my nose altered. Warner looked at Curtiz and Edelman and said, "Okay, then. Make a screen test with him and we'll take a look at it." It was the typical Hollywood brush-off.

I said, "I don't want to make any test, Mr. Warner."

He said, "You *don't?*" I guess not many people had told him that before, and he seemed genuinely startled.

"Certainly not," I said. "If you see a couple of hundred feet of film with me, with my big nose sticking out in black-and-white, you'll run out of the projection room screaming, 'Get that aardvark off my sound stage.' "

Said Warner, "And knowing all that, you still want me to give you the part?"

I said, "Yes, sir."

He said, "Predicated on what, may I ask?"

I said, "Well, sir, did you read the script?"

He said, "Of course I read the script. Don't be a smart ass."

I wasn't sure that he *had* read the script, which was a screen biography of the songwriter Gus Kahn. "I'm not being a smart ass, Mr. Warner. I read the script twice, and I'll tell you something, sir. If you put a good-looking man in that part, you've got no picture. This man, Gus Kahn, wrote hundreds and hundreds of 'I Love You' songs, but could never say 'I love you'—not even to his wife except once when she was under ether and couldn't hear him. I'll tell you why, Mr. Warner. It's because he was shy, but more important, because he was not handsome. He didn't believe a face like his could say 'I love you' to a face like hers and get away with it."

Curtiz and Edeleman were sweating. No one talked to Jack Warner like this and got away with it. Warner just stared at me for a long time. Then he said to Curtiz and Edelman, "Would you two gentlemen step into the next room with me?" I was left sitting alone in Warner's office. Curiously, I wasn't nervous. I had spoken my piece and so be it. I knew I was right.

A few minutes later, Michael Curtiz stuck his head out of the next room and gave me the okay sign. I had gotten the part of the not very handsome Gus Kahn.

The picture was a very pleasant experience for me. Most of my scenes were with Doris Day, and she couldn't have been nicer to a comparative newcomer like me. Also, I could sit for hours listening to her rehearse her musical numbers. She sang like an angel. I learned a tremendous amount from director Curtiz, one of the best in Hollywood, and I became good friends with producer Edelman—which was to prove important later on in my life.

When the picture was finished, I knew it was going to be a success, which is just what happened when it was released. It was the typical Warner Brothers musical of that day—not Shakespeare or Ibsen—and audiences flocked to see nearly all Warner musicals, especially when Doris Day warbled very popular tunes, like the title song, Gus Kahn's "I'll See You in My Dreams."

Having thus taken part in a Warner Brothers' success, I found myself wanted again by the studio—and pretty soon. This time, the part would be natural for me. Warner Brothers wanted to do a remake of its classic Al Jolson film, *The Jazz Singer,* with which they had introduced sound movies in 1927. They planned the remake to commemorate the twenty-fifth anniversary of that event. It was to be the same story, slightly updated, about a young man who broke his father's heart by becoming a popular singer instead of a synagogue cantor.

Once again, I was to work with director Michael Curtiz and producer Lou Edelman. Once again, it was they who wanted me for the role. Because of the success of *I'll See You in My Dreams*, the nose didn't matter to Jack Warner in this case.

In preparing myself for the part, I learned some interesting history about the original *The Jazz Singer.* George Burns told me that Warner Brothers' first choice for the role was George Jessel, not Al Jolson, because Jessel had played it on Broadway. But then a hitch developed in the studio's negotiations with Jessel. Spurred on by his friend Jolson, Jessel made an outrageous demand. He wanted stock in Warner Brothers, in lieu of pay. Of course he was turned down. And Jolson got the role. They didn't speak for the rest of their lives.

In *my* version of *The Jazz Singer,* Peggy Lee was my girlfriend; Eduard Franz and Mildred Dunnock played my father and mother. Not a Jew in the bunch. But then again, Sir Laurence Olivier, of all people, played Neil Diamond's father in the *latest* version of *The Jazz Singer* about ten years ago.

People in the industry think that our version, which came out in 1953, was the best of all *The Jazz Singers*. They point out that my chanting of the Hebrew liturgy was authentic, whereas Jolson had skipped most of the words and filled in with a lot of "voy, voy, voys." I heard that from the cantor who was our technical adviser, who had also been the technical adviser on the Jolson version. But no matter the "voy, voys," the great Jolson was the great Jolson, and his picture remains a film milestone. As for the Neil Diamond version, it was mostly a showcase for his modern popular music and he was superb. So I am neutral.

Our film did very well at the box office, but somehow I knew this was the end of my brief movie career. How many parts like this were there for me? I'd lie if I said I didn't care, but it didn't bother me *that* much. Too many other good things were happening.

chapter

When I first got to know him, George Burns told me, "You really haven't made it, kid, until you've played the Palladium in London, England." When I made *I'll See You in My Dreams,* the writer, Mel Shavelson, also talked about the Palladium in glowing terms. "The most appreciative audiences in the world," said Mel. "Not like here in the United States, where they would ask William Shakespeare, 'What have you written *lately,* Bill?' "

The Palladium was furthest from my mind, however, when, in 1950, I was on my usual stint of cross-country nightclub appearances between films. The Palladium, with its famous Royal Box for King George VI and his family, was only for American superstar entertainers, like Red Skelton and Burns and Allen. The biggest repeat American hit at the Palladium was Danny Kaye. The British loved him. He was princely, he was elflike, he had beautiful hands. He'd play an imaginary harp. He'd invite the audience to sing with him. He'd toy with them with his delicate humor. No drawn-out stories. No belly-laugh monologues. He was one of a kind. How could I hope to compete in that league?

When the impossible did come about, it happened at the most unlikely of places. I was doing my act at La Boheme, a club in Hollywood, Florida. The principle attraction there was the gambling—in the back, of course. It was run by Jack Lansky, the brother of the notorious Meyer Lansky, reputedly the mastermind of all the gambling operations of the national crime syndicate. Under a different name, the Meyer Lansky character was portrayed quite faithfully in *The Godfather* movies.

It was one of my brushes with the more shadowy side of show business. Another famous gangster, Joe Adonis, also was involved with La Boheme. I remember Adonis came up to me one day and said, "I hear you're married to a guinea." (Of course, Adonis himself was Italian.) I said, "Yes, my wife, Rose Marie, is Italian."

Adonis said, "You been in the casino in the back?"

I said, "No."

He said, "Come with me." He took me into the locked and closely guarded gambling room, and acted like an effusive tour guide: "Here's the craps table, this is the chemin de fer, and here's the twenty-one tables where you can play blackjack." He paused threateningly and said, "Take a good look at all this, because if I catch you in here again, I'll break your arms and legs. The money you make in the showroom, you take home to your guinea wife." Strange people, protective in their offbeat way. I recalled how Dennis, the neighborhood bookie back in Chicago, had said almost the same thing to me.

Anyway, I was filling out my engagement there at La Boheme, when Uncle Abe showed up with a distinctively British gentleman in tow. "Danny," said Uncle Abe, "meet Val Parnell. He runs the Palladium in London." I had been told Parnell was coming, but it was inconceivable that he would want *me* for his opening night. Which is what he wanted.

Insecure me. I immediately deduced that he only wanted me because he couldn't book Danny Kaye for that year, and that he might be trying to fool the people with someone with a similar name. But it was a genuine offer, and I excitedly said yes.

But then Parnell dampened me down a little more. He started talking about what *not* to do in my forthcoming act at the Palladium. He said, "I note that you are making a lot of fun of American radio commercials. That's out for England. We don't have adverts on the BBC, so the people won't know what you're talking about. Then, of course, you can't do your turn about the wailing Syrian. The British public won't understand that. Or the little Jewish chap trying to fetch a motorcar jack to repair his flat tire. That wouldn't be understood, either."

Talk about being deflated. Parnell had just practically thrown out my whole act. But I said I'd do my best to comply with his wishes.

I went back home to Beverly Hills. I saw Jack Benny at the Hillcrest Country Club and put on a *real* wailing Syrian act for him about my conversation with Parnell. What was I going to do with all my material on the forbidden list?

Jack, a good friend, said, "Look, Danny, I've been there, and I think I know more than Parnell does about his Palladium audiences. They're the nicest, most appreciative people. They're hungry for comedy because they have a great tradition of it over there. You're a fine storyteller. Stick to your own stuff and don't let anyone dissuade you."

I said, "But their humor is so different from ours. What *if* they don't understand me?"

I'll never forget what that wonderful man, said next: "You're going to do your act in English, aren't you?"

"Yeah," I said.

"Well, the language was born there," he said. "They'll understand you."

So I went to England. I took an ocean liner, because I still didn't like flying. It turned out to be my last ocean voyage, because I was seasick for the entire six days of the trip. When we arrived in Southampton harbor, a launch came alongside the liner and twenty-two news reporters clambered aboard to interview me. The press conference didn't help my confidence any. The principal question was, "What is your similarity to Mr. Kaye?" I weakly answered, "Our Christian names are the same. Outside of that, I wouldn't know." But the reporters were kind to me. The thirty-six-point headline on the back page of the next day's London *Daily Mirror* read: "The other Danny arrives." It scared the hell out of me.

So they were comparing me to Danny Kaye, their idol, and no two people could be more different in style.

I carried that thought with me to the theater the night of the performance. Opening night. I marveled at the magnificence of the Palladium, with its huge, polished mahogany proscenium arch. Then, like a little kid, I sat in King

George's box, just to see what it was like. To keep from being too nervous, I moved to another box to watch the first half of the show.

It was great. There were variety acts, including some of Britain's best comics, in the old music-hall tradition. The accents ranged from cockney to Scottish, but I understood everything that was going on. A lot of it was similar to what I had watched as a boy in the Empire Burlesque in Toledo—only much better. Then came one of the best magic acts I'd ever seen. The magician was a big heavy-set fellow who was very funny. The tricks happened when he wasn't looking, and he seemed just as surprised as the audience. Everyone was hysterical, including me. It helped get my mind off my own impending problem.

The problem soon no longer was impending, because I was the second act after the intermission, following a chorus-line number. There was a timpani drumroll and the orchestra conductor dryly announced, "Ladies and gentlemen, in America there are two Dannys. You met one, now meet the other. Ladies and gentlemen, from America, Danny Thomas." Talk about perfunctory introductions. It was like the one I got at Madison Square Garden. When would people stop calling me "the other Danny"?

When? I think it happened that night. I prayed that the little fellow inside me would come up on my shoulder and give me some inspiration. As I walked out to center stage, I didn't have the vaguest idea of what I was going to say, or how it would proceed from there.

I looked out at the dead-silent audience for a few seconds, then up at that incredible proscenium arch. "It's more beautiful then I've been told," I mused. "Oh, did I say good evening. I meant to. Good evening. Okay, he's said 'Good evening.' Now, where's the funny stuff, right?"

And the words came pouring out:

> "Ever since it was announced I was to play here, all of the great American artists who have performed for you phoned to tell me I have not lived theatrically and shall not live until I play before a British audience, particularly an audience here at the London Palladium. For here, they said, was the absolute end in appreciation." (I paused and looked ruefully at them.) "Believe me, ladies and gentlemen, I wouldn't be in your shoes tonight for all the money in the world."

My unexpected self-depreciation brought on a huge laugh. I had no idea I was going to say that, but it worked. I had hooked them, just as I had learned from watching Bob Hope many years before. And having hooked them, I decided on the spot to ignore all the warnings Val Parnell had given me.

Don't talk about radio commercials, he had said?

> "On the way to the theater, I saw a billboard advertising Schweppes sodas. The Schweppies are coming, it said. Beware the Schweppies. They're coming, all right. Soon they shall invade the BBC with these adverts, these commercials, just like we have in the States. Don't let it happen. I'll tell you what it's like."

I slid easily into all my crazy stories about commercials in the U.S. for Post Toasties, Sanka coffee, and a lot of other products. After my Schweppes billboard introduction, they knew exactly what I was talking about. Well, not exactly. But they kept laughing—and that's what counts.

Having defied Val Parnell in the matter of the commercials, I ventured into all the other no-no's he had proscribed. Contrary to what he had said about the British audience not understanding the story of the little Jewish man "and the motorcar jack," it got the biggest laugh. The reviews in the London newspapers the next day all talked about "Mr. Thomas's hilarious tale of the man with the flat tyre."

Val Parnell apparently swallowed his pride, because, without admitting he'd been wrong, he invited me back to the Palladium for its show during the coronation of Queen Elizabeth II. The Queen came backstage afterwards to shake my hand. I said to myself, "I wonder what they must be thinking about all this in Becheri in Lebanon."

But the most satisfying reaction came from the common people of London. Jack Benny was right. Men would tip their hats to me on the street and say, "Hello, Mr. Thomas, how are you?" or "Hello, Danny Boy." Cab drivers would honk and say, "Hi, Danny Boy, how's the flat tyre?"

They never forgot that story. They never forgot it.

chapter
19

It was about this time that Uncle Abe Lastfogel said to me rather sternly, "Isn't it about time you did something about that vow you made to St. Jude about building him a shrine?" I'm one of the world's great procrastinators, but Uncle Abe made it perfectly clear that *this* procrastination had gone on far too long. Funny that it took a Jew to get a Catholic off his duff to fulfill a religious commitment.

Chastened, I went to see Samuel Cardinal Stritch in Chicago, uncle of the fine actress Elaine Stritch. I knew the cardinal personally, and the two of us went back together many years. As a very young thirty-four-year-old bishop of Toledo, he had confirmed me as a Catholic when I was a boy. Later, when I began to appear twice a year at the Chez Paree in Chicago, I realized that the new cardinal in Chicago was the same man. So I went to see him.

That first visit was a very funny experience. His aide, a monsignor, and a very Irish Catholic nun who acted as his secretary kept me cooling my heels in the outer office, telling me what a busy man the cardinal was. I finally got in, for what was to be a two- or three-minute session, but it lasted for more than an hour. The cardinal recognized me immediately as the young communicant Amos Jacobs, and he couldn't stop discussing the old days in Toledo. He talked about my father and mother; he talked about what good, devout people the Lebanese immigrants were, "never causing any trouble in this country"; he talked about my career in show business. The nun-secretary kept nervously poking her head into His Eminence's office. Outside, the people with appointments were stacked up like airplanes over a fog-bound Midway Airport.

After my scolding from Uncle Abe about neglecting my vow, I was in Chicago, staying at the Ambassador East Hotel and waiting for an appointment to see Cardinal Stritch. It was a Saturday and I went for a walk down the street. As was my habit in those days, I was chewing tobacco and spitting in the breeze. Suddenly, about two blocks from the hotel, I came upon a handsome mansion with a lot of chimneys on its roof. I realized it was the cardinal's residence. Should I just barge in on him, or should I wait for an appointment at the chancery? I said, "What the hell," threw away the chewing tobacco, cleaned my mouth, and rang the doorbell.

The same nun-secretary opened the door. She looked at me with dismay and said in her beautiful Irish brogue, "Glory be to God. There goes the day." But she announced my presence to the cardinal.

He was glad to see me, but once again, I did take up the good part of his day. Instead of the usual chitchat, I brought up the whole subject of my vow, and what I was going to do about it. I told him I had thought of getting off the hook with a statue, around which candles could be lit, but that wasn't enough for what I thought St. Jude had done for me. The cardinal agreed.

Finally I said, "How about a hospital?"

His Eminence looked interested. "And where would this hospital be?" he asked.

I said, "I dunno. In the South somewhere, where there are a lot of poor children, both black and white, who need it the most. Maybe in the bayous of Louisiana, or maybe in Mississippi or Arkansas. A kind of clinic with four beds, if you had to put them to bed, and nobody asking for a Blue Cross card."

By now I had really caught the cardinal's attention. He said, "Wait a minute. How are those kids going to get out there in the boondocks? And suppose they need a specialist? You've got to be near a medical center, where a lot of facilities are available to you. Take a look at the growing city of Memphis."

He then launched into a pitch, which I swear took twenty minutes. I learned about Memphis's University of Tennessee Medical School. I learned about Memphis's airport, railroad station, and bus depot. I learned about Memphis's home-ownership rate of eighty percent. At the end of his long discourse, the cardinal said, "Besides, it's my hometown."

I said, "Your Eminence, why didn't you say that in the first place?"

He said, "It really isn't my hometown. It was my first

parish. I was born in Nashville. But I'll tell you what I'm going to do. I'm going to send you to a couple of fellows in Memphis, John Canale and Ed Barry. Ed's a big man in town, a lawyer, he's on the board of a lot of hospitals, he owns the Memphis Chicks baseball team, he owns the ballpark. If Edward takes you on, you stay there and build your hospital. If he says he has no time for it, you go wherever you want to go."

I went back to California and told Uncle Abe what had transpired between me and the cardinal. Uncle Abe said, "Wait a minute. Let's do this right. Before we go to see this fellow Barry in Memphis, let's set up a foundation—the St. Jude Foundation of California—so we can collect money and prove to those guys in Memphis that we mean business." So we set up the foundation. Uncle Abe became the President, Morris Stoller, the controller of William Morris, became the treasurer, and Paul Ziffren, who was on the Democratic National Committee, became the attorney and got us our tax exemption. Everyone worked for free.

Then we went to Memphis to see Ed Barry. He was very cordial. I suspect that he had had a prior word with the cardinal, whose parishioner he had been when he was just plain Father Stritch, the parish priest in St. Patrick's in Memphis. Barry didn't turn us down out of hand. He brought in people like the mayor, Frank Tobey, and Fred Gattis, a wealthy catalogue publisher of Lebanese descent. He also brought in some of the top medical people in Memphis.

Some were skeptical.

But Ed Barry continued to be fascinated with the idea.

He brought his entire group to Los Angeles to discuss it with us some more. Dr. Lemuel Diggs, Professor of Medicine at the University of Tennessee, eventually came up with the idea that won us an okay from Memphis. Dr. Diggs said, "What we really need here is a research hospital for catastrophic children's diseases—especially leukemia and, in black children, sickle-cell anemia." My little four-bed clinic idea went out the window, but who could complain.

All I had to do now was to come up with ways to raise a few million dollars.

Our first sizable amount of money came in at Christmas of that year. My picture *I'll See You in My Dreams* was opening, and Warner Brothers set the Midwest premiere at the Chicago Theater—a sensible move because songwriter Gus Kahn, the subject of the film biography, was a Chicagoan. Uncle Abe said, "Why don't we make this premiere the first benefit for St. Jude's Hospital?" Warner Brothers went along with the idea. You didn't often say no to Abe Lastfogel in those days.

Cardinal Stritch served as Honorary Chairman of the affair. The Catholics came. My old buddies from the 5100 Club came. Lovers of Gus Kahn's music came. Fans of Doris Day came. I was amazed at what St. Jude's had taken in that night—an incredible fifty-one thousand dollars.

Strange, but I later realized how important the number 51 has been in my life. The 5100 Club, $51,000 in my first attempt to raise money for St. Jude, the fact that the hospital itself was later built on Highway 51 in Memphis.

But it was to be a long time—more than ten years—before I would see St. Jude's materialize in stone and mortar.

chapter

⇒⇒⇒20⇐⇐⇐

In the meantime, many things were happening in my family.

I made many sad trips back to Toledo. In 1947, my Dad was diagnosed as having lung cancer. This didn't surprise me because of the strong Turkish cigarettes he had hand-rolled and chainsmoked all his life. This was one of the tragedies of first-generation Lebanese immigrants. They brought bad health habits from the Old Country, and neither doctors nor family could persuade them to stop. My father's Turkish cigarettes must have contained about one hundred milligrams of tar, compared to as little as one milligram in some filtered brands available today. Uncle Tonoose's liver had been destroyed, not only by the vast quantity of booze he consumed, but also by the fiery Middle Eastern chili peppers he ate. "Because the stomach is on fire, you fight fire with fire," he would say. He ate those hot peppers like they were popcorn. They refused to give up the old ways.

When Dad was dying, I was at his hospital bedside every

day. This man, who had once been the epitome of physical strength, was just a shadow of his former self. He kept fading in and out of consciousness. In one of his lucid moments, he grabbed hold of my hand and some of his old strength reappeared. He said, "I ask only two things of you, my son. You have eight brothers but only one sister. I leave it to you to take care of your sister. The second thing I ask is this: Don't forget your heritage."

And shortly after that, Dad was gone.

My second sad trip to Toledo was in 1952, two days after my first opening at The Sands in Las Vegas on December 15th. That's when my mother—weakened by years of hard work, and missing Dad terribly—passed away. I returned to California with a heavy heart, and I knew I had to concentrate on the new generation I had created—with Rosie's participation, of course. The kids were wonderful in helping me through these periods of grief. Marlo, in particular, reminded me of funny things involving Dad. There was the time, for example, when Dad had been visiting us in California. It was when I was making the movie *The Unfinished Dance.* Marlo was about seven at the time and I used to take her to the studio with me to play with Margaret O'Brien. Marlo became fascinated at how, when I finished a scene, the director, Henry Koster, would yell, "Okay, cut. Print it. Very good."

Well, during dinner at home one night, Marlo was piddling with her food, and Dad became angry with me because I didn't jump on her to eat properly, as he had done with me when I was a boy eating at his table. So I jumped on her. She knew it was an acting performance to please my father. I said, "Now you listen to me, young lady. I want you to eat all of that food right now, this minute, or you will go to your room without supper, and without breakfast in the morning. Do you understand?"

Marlo yelled, "Cut. Print it. Very good."

I broke up laughing, and almost fell off my chair. My father was totally puzzled. "Why you laughing?" he kept asking.

Actually, I was a very strict parent. I set rules for the kids and expected them to be obeyed. Tony was still too young, but the two girls went to church regularly and attended Catholic schools. There was no staying out late. One of my rules was that if they said "Honor bright," it meant that they were telling the absolute truth—no little white lies permitted.

Well, by now Marlo was going to Marymount High School and the dating began. I was like an old Lebanese mountain man, being fiercely protective of his daughter. "You will be home by eleven o'clock, right after the movie?" "Yes I will, honor bright," she'd answer.

Then came Marlo's first prom. A boy in a blue suit was waiting for her downstairs, his Thunderbird at the ready out in front. I was calling Marlo "Mugsy" at the time. I said, "Mugsy, what time you getting home? Midnight, right?" She said, "Okay, Daddy," and like a damn fool I said, "Honor bright?" She gave me the little shoulder take, like you do in vaudeville and said, "Aah, Daddy," as if I should believe her even if she didn't say "honor bright," which she skillfully avoided saying.

I decided to give a little, "What about one o'clock?" Still

no "honor bright." Just, "Goodbye Mom, goodbye Dad. I love you."

One o'clock came, and no Mugsy. I got my shotgun out of its case and went out into the garden to wait for her—and especially her escort. I was sitting in a lawn chair, dozing off, when suddenly the automatic sprinklers came on, soaking me from head to foot. While I was inside changing my clothes, Marlo/Mugsy came home. Seeing the shotgun, which I had left on the lawn, she dispatched her innocent young man immediately.

She came inside and ran up the stairs as quickly as she could, seeking Rose Marie's protection. I was right behind her on the stairs, beating a tattoo on her rear end. The bedroom door closed behind her and I was left standing there, still wet, and feeling like a jerk. Those were the days when girls wore seventeen petticoats, making any attempt to spank them meaningless. Marlo confirmed that in the morning, when I had calmed down, kissed her, and apologized. "I didn't feel a thing," said Marlo, adding, "Honor bright."

The kids all were very smart and precocious. Marlo was an honor student, heading for the University of Southern California. Terre was a whiz at music and sang in all of her school's stage productions. Little Tony displayed an adult wit that was far beyond his years, which is exemplified by something that happened when he was only four years old.

I had been on the road for a long time, going from one nightclub booking to another, and raising money for the new St. Jude Foundation on the side. I was at a great club, Copa City in Miami Beach, Florida, when I found I was missing Rosie terribly. We had a great sex life together, but I was afraid that if I didn't see her soon our sex life would be dead. So I phoned her and asked her to join me in Florida for a few days. She got very excited and said she would come immediately—but with the kids, all three of them, and also Tony's nurse.

I put in a lot of preparations for their arrival. Rosie would stay with me in my suite at the hotel, and the kids and the nurse would be in two connecting rooms. I bought Rosie some Arpege perfume, her favorite, a dressing gown, and high-heeled mule slippers with the little feathers on them. I ordered champagne and finger sandwiches to be ready when Rosie got there. Then I went to do my show, all the time visualizing my lovely lady awaiting me in the suite, clad in the provocative garments which I had purchased for her.

When I finished that night's show, I couldn't wait to get up to the suite. I tried my key. The door was bolted from the inside. I began to pound on the door. At the sound of this racket, my beautiful lady stuck her head out the connecting bedroom I had set aside for little Tony. "Shhh," she said and came out into the hall to greet me. No sexy lingerie, no mules with the little feathers on them, no Arpege. She was wearing my old beat-up flannel bathrobe and bedroom slippers, and she absolutely reeked of Vicks Vapo-Rub. "I'm sorry, darling," she said, "but Tony's ill. I think it's the flu. I'll have to sleep with him. Good night. I'll see you in the morning." The door closed behind her.

This went on for four nights. I never got to be with Rosie at all. On the fifth day, Tony was fine. You know how kids are; one minute they're sick and the next minute they're recovered. It was two o'clock in the afternoon, and I had him with me in the living room of my suite while I was having breakfast. Rosie was still pulling herself together in the bedroom.

As I ate, Tony was playing with a little sand-pail and shovel. He still hadn't been able to be out in the sand, but he was preparing for it, I guess.

Rosie came out and it was the first time I actually was able to talk with her. I was pretty hot. I said, "What did you come here for? Every night you sleep with the kid. When are you gonna sleep with me? I mean, this is ridiculous. I mean, you're my wife. You're supposed to . . ." She broke in and said, "Honey, all right. He's much better now and . . ."

Just then, Tony took it into his head to throw his pail toward the balcony. I rushed to get it before it went over the railing, with visions of it hitting someone in the head eight stories down. I got there too late. I could only watch it sail harmlessly through the air. Fortunately, it fell in an unoccupied patch of sand.

But I grabbed my four-year-old son, shook him, and said, "Don't you ever do that again. You know, you could knock somebody's eye out. What are you, crazy? Now you go to your room and you stay there until I tell you to come out." Little Tony started for the door. Then he turned around and said to me, "Just for that, tonight she sleeps with me."

I added that story to my act, which made Rosie pretty angry—until she saw what big laughs it got. Much later, I

even used it when I was a guest on *The Johnny Carson Show.*
More big laughs.

As a matter of fact, Rosie was providing more and more
material for my act. Unknowingly, of course. I always was
fascinated by how her mind raced ahead of mine, and how
she expected, by some sort of E.S.P., that I would know
what she was thinking before she spoke. She thought I was
slow-witted for not being able to keep up with her.

For example, we were driving to Las Vegas one day,
listening to Guy Lombardo's orchestra playing "Apple
Blossom Time" on the car radio. Rosie was deep in
thought. Out of the blue, she said, "It's a shame they split
up." I said, "They didn't split up. Guy Lombardo and his
brother, Carmen, are still very much together."

"No," Rosie said, "I'm talking about the three Greek
girls." How was I supposed to get into her mind and know
she was thinking about the Andrews Sisters, one of whose
hit tunes was "Apple Blossom Time." She thought I was a
dummy for not keeping up with her.

So quick is Rosie's mind that she does not pause to grope
for names. She uses the word "What's-his-name" a lot.
Even on the memo pad she keeps near the phone to write
down messages. Often, I'll find a message "What's-his-
name called." I'll say, "Who's what's-his-name?" She'll say,
"Don't you know, dummy? Jan Murray."

Once, I thought I had gotten back at Rosie. We had
brought home a package she had purchased on a trip we
had taken. I left it on a table near the entrance to our house.
She came to the top of the stairs to our bedrooms and yelled
down at me, "What did you do with my what-do-you-call

it?" I said, "I gave it to the whozits." She said, "Why?" It made sense to her.

Shades of Abbott and Costello and their "Who's on first" routine.

I also derived a lot of material from Rosie's parents, to whom I became very close after the deaths of my own father and mother. Example: My father-in-law and mother-in-law came over to have dinner with us just before we were to make our first trip to Rome. Rosie came down the stairs, wearing a silk jersey skirt and a lovely blouse. The skirt hung on her hips very beautifully and I let out with a wolf-whistle. Pa said, "God bless you kids. You just like lovers, like when you first married."

I said, "Well, Pa, your daughter's a very well-built lady, and I hear that when the ladies walk on the Via Veneto in Rome, the Italian men come from behind, they give a little pinch on the derriere, and they say 'Bella, bella, bellissima.' Now what do I do? What's my reaction to that? Do I let it go by as a compliment, or do I, y'know . . ."

He broke in and roared, "They do *what?*"

I said, "They pinch, y'know, on the derriere."

My mother-in-law said, "The culo."

Pa said, "Nah, they do that in my country, they cut the throat."

I said, "Pa, they do it. And what I want to know from you is what would I say to the man in Italian. Like 'Forgive me, that belongs to me,' or something like that."

Pa said, "I don't-a believe they do it."

Rosie's Mom said, "Yeah, they do it, they do it." She was

screaming now. "*They do it,* and Danny, I'll tell you what to say." She blurted out something which apparently was in the Sicilian dialect of her parents.

Now it was Pa's turn to become enraged. He was from Sicily but a firm believer that Italians should speak pure Italian, not the regional dialects. He and his wife got into a yelling match about what was the proper phrase for me to say when someone accosted Rosie on the Via Veneto.

The shouting lasted about ten minutes and now was exclusively about proper Italian syntax. The original subject was long forgotten. Finally I said, "Settle down, Pa. I mean you're here for dinner. All right, Pa. Now just tell me what I would say."

Pa, who by then was conjugating Italian verbs in his argument, screeched to a dead stop. "Scuze me," he said, "whose ass are we talking about?"

This story, too, went into my repertoire, though I had to clean it up a bit to fit my image. This was all well and good. I was enriching my material, and my act was making a lot of money for me and my family. But, as I said before, I wasn't spending enough *time* with my family. Those weeks and months on the road with my nightclub act were taking their toll. The kids did a lot of kidding around about it, like their famous Father's Day telegram to me, "Daddy, dear old Daddy, you're more than an uncle to us." But they were kidding on the square. They felt a void, and I felt a void.

Marlo wrote something as an eighth grader that summed up this void as well as anyone can. It was an essay, which she called "Viva Today":

What's the matter with today? Everybody's rushing to secure tomorrow. Aren't the twenty-four hours in today as important as the twenty-four hours in tomorrow? My father travels all over the country, and sometimes all over the world, trying to secure tomorrow for his loved ones and himself. But unfortunately, when his tomorrow comes, his loved ones will be grown and gone. So I say, "Viva Today."

When I read this, it broke my heart.

I had procrastinated in my dealings with a lot of things. But this was a matter in which I knew I could *not* procrastinate.

I went to Uncle Abe and asked him to try to come up with work that would keep me at home a reasonable amount of the time.

chapter

»21«

Television had quickly blossomed as a major entertainment medium. People were staying home to watch Milton Berle's *Texaco Star Theater* and Sid Caesar's *Your Show of Shows.* Most TV production was being done in New York, but some programs, including the fabulously successful *I Love Lucy,* were coming from Hollywood.

Uncle Abe Lastfogel got word, through his ear which was always to the ground, that NBC was planning a Hollywood-based variety series. There would be four hosts, each head-lining a show every fourth week. It sounded like a good vehicle to keep me at home at least a quarter of the time, and I was signed for what came to be called *The Four Star Revue.* The other hosts were Ed Wynn, Jack Carson, and Jimmy Durante. Quite a cast. It's a shame we couldn't work together. We hardly ever saw one another.

Alas, *Four Star Revue* was just not right for me. It was a mishmash of singers, dancers, jugglers, and sketches. I introduced the acts and worked with the fine comedian, Julie

Oshins, in the sketches, which I enjoyed. But as far as using my own material was concerned, it just wasn't good. In *their* segments of *Four Star Revue*, Ed Wynn and Jimmy Durante could use quick little bits of comedy—which was their style. My style was slow-development storytelling, for which there just wasn't time. I had to get on and off and introduce the jugglers.

For instance, the producer, Pete Barnum, loved my "Ode to a Wailing Syrian" routine. He allotted me seven minutes to do it in one of my early shows. In rehearsal, though, it took me seven minutes just to get into the nub of the routine—basically the absolutely necessary introduction, so the audience would know what I was talking about. Pete threw up his hands. "In a one-hour show with commercials," he said, "we just don't have the time to do it." So the Wailing Syrian was thrown out. So was my Jack Story and most of my other good stuff.

Another disappointment was that the show didn't give me the time at home with my family that I thought it would. Part of that was my fault. With three weeks off every month, I felt underutilized and rushed off to do nightclub dates and fund-raising for St. Jude between shows. In the one week I was home, my time was pretty much taken up with rehearsals and script alterations.

Remember, this was an extremely experimental time in television. In the fall of 1951, the format of the show was drastically changed. Instead of four rotating hosts, there would now be a profusion of headliners, a different one topping the show each week. Among them were Martha Raye, Victor Borge, Spike Jones, Olson and Johnson, and the Ritz Brothers. The name of the show was changed to *The All Star Revue;* it later evolved into *The Colgate Comedy Hour.* The original four hosts were invited to stay on, but only Jimmy Durante did. When I realized I'd only be on the show two or three times a year, I opted out and went back full-time to the saloons, as I called the nightclubs—something which I did many times in troubled periods of my career. The saloons were my safe haven.

But my constant *kvetching* about wanting to be home with my wife and kids certainly caught the attention of Uncle Abe Lastfogel. He had that on his mind as he watched the inauguration of a totally new television network, ABC. Before that, there had only been NBC, CBS, and the now long-forgotten DuMont network. Since they were starting from scratch, ABC was hungry for shows. As I mentioned before, one of the people they desperately wanted was Ray Bolger, a proven talent both on Broadway and as a TV guest star.

But to get to Bolger, they had to deal with his agent, the wily old horse trader Abe Lastfogel. That's when Uncle Abe said to ABC, "Okay, you can have Bolger for a half hour show, but only if you also take Danny Thomas for a half hour as well." They reluctantly agreed.

And that's how the greatest career break of my life came about.

But as I previously indicated, it wasn't easy. Nobody had any idea about what I was going to do, least of all ABC. My feeling was that they were hoping I wouldn't be able to come up with *anything,* and then they'd only have to fall back on the escape clause Uncle Able had negotiated with them: for me to do a fifteen-week *radio* show, the type Bing Crosby and Rosemary Clooney had at the time.

As far as the television project was concerned, all I heard was what I *couldn't* do. No variety show ("There are enough of them already"), no Danny Thomas Comedy Hour ("Your material takes too long to develop in a short TV show"), *maybe* a situation comedy ("but it's a shame you're not handsome, like Desi Arnaz").

I needed help. The William Morris people told me that Lou Edelman was available. Lou had been the producer on my film, *I'll See You in My Dreams.* He was close to Mel Shavelson, who had been one of the movie's writers—as well as having been a writer for Bob Hope for some years. I prevailed on Lou to come over to my house to kick around some ideas, and he brought Mel along.

It started out as a pretty desultory meeting. They quickly decided that a sitcom was the only way to go, and I agreed. But then we discarded every idea that came up, even my own favorite concept—a theatrical boarding house with kooky show-business characters. It just didn't work.

That's when Mel Shavelson got up to leave, and I began my long pleading to come up with *something* that would allow me to stay in Los Angeles, at home with my kids. That I was away on the road so much that they hardly knew me, that they called me "Uncle Daddy," that I didn't know my girls' dress sizes, that I wanted my son to know me as something more than a telephone pal.

And that's when Mel leaped to his feet and yelled. *"That's* the concept. I can write it overnight."

I said, "*What* overnight? That wasn't a concept I was telling you. I was just wailing about my problems."

Mel said, "That's the essence of comedy, going back to Charlie Chaplin and even before. Show me a man in trouble, and I'll show you a funny man. I was still bewildered. Rosie had been listening at the door, and she wasn't bewildered. She thought the idea was great, and she offered her title for the series: *Make Room for Daddy.* I can explain that: while I was away, the two girls slept in our bedroom with their mother. The dresser drawers, which usually held my shirts, were filled with my daughters' little panties, stockings, sweaters, whatever. Making room for Daddy (when I was coming home) meant that they had to clean out their little panties, stockings, sweaters and whatever, and move them to their own dressers in their own rooms.

Lou and Mel loved Rosie's title and it went on Mel's script, which he finished, not quite overnight, but in two days. It was essentially the story of Danny Thomas's dilemma—how an entertainer struggles to maintain a normal family life while pursuing his offbeat itinerant life in show business. My character on the series was to be named Danny Williams. Once again, I used one of my brother's names, the "Williams" coming from the name of my brother Bill.

What can I say? The network liked the script, we shot the pilot, and the series went on the air in September 1953. It remained on the air, in one form or another, until 1964. I had finally found a way to stay home with my family—by doing a show about me and my family.

Show business is full of ironies. We shot *Make Room for Daddy* on Soundstage Five at the Desilu Studios. Next door, on Stage Six, was Ray Bolger's show, originally titled *Where's Raymond?* Remember that I had been tacked on as an unwanted appendage to the deal that brought Ray to ABC? Unfortunately, it seemed that that hugely talented man didn't have the kind of help I had.

The Ray Bolger Show only lasted two years.

chapter

22

We assembled quite a cast on Soundstage Five. To play my wife, Margaret, we signed an accomplished stage and screen actress, Jean Hagen. She had been in *Another Part of the Forest* and *Born Yesterday* on Broadway and had earned an Oscar nomination for *Singing in the Rain.* We found two darling kids to play my six-year-old son, Rusty, and my eleven-year-old daughter, Terry. They were Rusty Hamer and Sherry Jackson. I loved them because they reminded me so much of my own children.

And then there was Hans Conried. There are no words to describe this literate, witty, urbane man. At first he played guest roles—my ne'er-do-well Cousin Carl, my Uncle Oscar, a nudnik named Derik Campbell—and he finally settled in as my Uncle Tonoose, patterned after my own Uncle Tony. Hans took great delight in insulting me, and I loved every minute of it. Once, watching my habit of chewing tobacco and using spittoons which I had set up all over the soundstage, he said, "I once did a scene with an un-housebroken bear who was neater than you are." He said terrible things like that with such delightful haughtiness that I could never get mad at him.

A lot of very good actors and actresses passed through our show—in the beginning and later on. Horace McMahon began in the role of my agent, and was replaced by Jesse White—both to become big-name character actors. The elevator operator in the Williams home was played by a young man named Bill Dana. His character's name was José Jimenez—and you may remember how Bill went on to parlay José Jimenez into a major TV attraction. We had Pat Carroll, Pat Harrington, Jr., Sid Melton (very funny as the boss of the nightclub where I worked), Annette Funicello, and Stanley Myron Handleman in continuing roles—all future stars.

After just twelve weeks on the air in 1953, we won the Sylvania Award, tying the prestigious *U.S. Steel Hour* for the distinction of being named the best new show of the year. It would be nice to say that everything was going smoothly, but it wasn't.

On one level, it was fine. I loved the two kids in the show, Rusty Hamer and Sherry Jackson. In a way, I had two families at one time—my own kids at home at night, my show-kids for several hours in the daytime. When I bought presents for Marlo, Terre, and Tony, I also bought them for Rusty and Sherry. Between shots, Rusty and I would go outside and toss a baseball, a football, or a basketball— according to the season. Poor Rusty suffered a tragedy in his young life not long after the series began when his real father died. So I redoubled my efforts to show him love and to keep his mind occupied. One day, he came up, threw his arms around me, and said weepingly, "You're the only Daddy I have now."

On a second level, things were not so fine. Jean Hagen, in the all-important role of my wife, was aloof in her dealings with the rest of us, sometimes even snobbish. I guess it had to do with her stage training, and the fact that she had played fairly significant roles both in the theater and in films. Her professional and personal habits tended to annoy me as well. Onstage, she began by being just as cool in her part as she was in real life. I finally had to say to Jean, "Look, we're supposed to be married. The audience thinks we sleep together at night. Yet, you never come close enough to me to even touch. Married people are supposed to touch and hug. I'm supposed to be able to inhale the smell of you, your perfume." I guess I was like a peasant berating a queen, but she responded.

Another thing that bugged me about Jean was that she was a *schlump.* On rehearsal days, we all wore jeans and sloppy clothes, but she carried it too far. You know, I love the lady beautiful. I raised a couple of them and I married one—not in that order, of course. So when I heard that Robert Kintner, the top network executive was coming to the set, I said to Jean, "For God's sake, put on high heels, put on a little lipstick."

One of the complications was that Kintner liked Jean a lot. I'm not saying he was enamored of her or anything like that, but he certainly was pushing her career. He was the one who insisted on her for *Make Room for Daddy,* and he always made it clear that he considered her the pivotal character in the series. That put the entire show into a mess later on.

All of which goes to prove that the public—even with a zealous press digging away—rarely knows what is going on behind the scenes in a show-business operation.

For example, a behind-the-scenes flap involving Jean nearly derailed us early on in the series. Our first director was Bill Asher (who married Elizabeth Montgomery), very kindly loaned to us from the *I Love Lucy* staff by my good friend Desi Arnaz, who wanted us to get off to a good start. Asher directed our first nine episodes. At about the same time, the William Morris Agency had sent over Sheldon Leonard, then an actor renowned for his tough gangster roles. Norman Brokaw of William Morris told me that Sheldon wanted to become a director, and asked if he could look over Bill Asher's shoulder to learn TV directing techniques. We said fine.

Well, Sheldon was such a quick learner that by the time Bill Asher was finishing his nine weeks, he was letting Sheldon handle a lot of sequences. He obviously was good at it, so when Asher left, we hired Sheldon as the full-time director. That caused an immediate hassle with Jean Hagen's husband, who told me, "I don't want my wife to be directed by that gangster actor." We stood firm, and Sheldon Leonard remained as the director of our series. A good thing, too. Because that was my first association with a man who eventually became my partner in television production—and my lifelong friend.

But more of that later. At that time in the infancy of *Make Room for Daddy,* Sheldon and I and everyone else were

The cast of *Make Room for Daddy* was my second family and provided me with some of the happiest days of my life. Clockwise, my second family consisted of Rusty Hamer, Sherry Jackson, me, Angela Cartwright, and Marjorie Lord.

(Left)
With Jean Hagen, my first
wife in the series. We won
two Emmys in 1954.
(Photo courtesy Jack Albin)

(Right)
Marjorie Lord succeeded Jean
as my spouse, and this is the
only time in my entire career
when I got hit in the face
with a pie.

(Right)
Jack Benny was one of
my greatest friends of
all time.

(Left)
But no one was greater
than my "Uncle Abe"
Lastfogel, the head of
the William Morris
Agency, who was my
tutor, the architect of
my career, and loved by
me like a member of
my family.

(Above) An interesting collection of talent surrounding Richard Nixon, then the vice president. Listening to a Jack Benny joke are Milton Berle, George Burns, Eddie Fisher, and me. How young we all looked!

(Top right) Here I am clowning with Jerry Lewis.

(Right) Rosie looks on as I put my handprints in concrete at Grauman's Chinese Theater in Hollywood.

Kidding around at the Friars Club.
I'm pretending to be a priest taking
Buddy Hackett's confession.

(Below)
Phyllis Diller appeared in one
of my NBC specials. Her nose
may have been fixed: mine
definitely wasn't.

(Left)
Here I am with three show-
business greats—Bob Hope,
George Jessel, and Eddie
Cantor, who was rarely
photographed in his
later years.

President Ford came to visit the young patients at the
St. Jude Children's Research Hospital in Memphis.

(Above)
Sammy Davis, Jr., Senator George Murphy, and George Burns enhanced one of my St. Jude benefits.

(Right)
Helping celebrate dear Mr. Burns's eighty-fourth birthday.

With my beloved Abe Lastfogel, not long before he died.

(Photo courtesy Carl Y. Iri)

(Above)
My current act is "The
Legends of Comedy," and
features my good friends
Milton Berle and Sid Caesar.

(Left)
The late Sammy Davis, Jr.,
the greatest of the great,
never failed to appear at my
St. Jude benefits.

(Photo courtesy Lee Salem)

(Above left) This is my absolute favorite photo of Frank Sinatra and me.
(Photo courtesy Jim Laurie)

(Below left) How proud can a father be? Two of my kids, Tony and
Marlo, won Emmys in 1988.

(Above) And how proud can a father be, Part II—there's no one like my
son-in-law Phil Donahue.

(Above left) It was truly an historic moment for me when
President Ronald Reagan awarded me the Congressional Medal at
the White House.
(Photo courtesy The White House)

(Below left) And the whole family was there to see it,
right down to my grandchildren.
(Photo courtesy The White House)

(Above) We're a family that believes in frequent get-togethers. This is a
recent photo of my family, with Phil very much a part of it.

Here we are today, Rosie and me. We've come a long way together since that little radio station in Detroit—and she's still the love of my life.

involved in a lot of tension on the set. Nevertheless, all of us—including Jean—worked hard and turned out a good show every week, presenting a happy face to the public. In the first year we won the Emmy for the best new show. We were renewed for the next year, and then the next. In our second season, I won the Best Actor Emmy. The series got the Emmy for Best Comedy Show.

When it didn't interfere with Tony's school, I brought him to the set as often as possible, to play with Rusty Hamer. The two kids scared me to death by climbing up into the scaffolding and rigging over the soundstage, but they were sure-footed and having such a good time that I didn't yell too much.

At home, things couldn't have been more pleasant after my years of being away. All three kids were a delight to be with every night and on weekends, and for Rosie and me it was like a prolonged second-honeymoon period—especially considering that we never had a first one. Also I had plenty of time to devote to improving and expanding the house. I commissioned a statue of St. Jude for the backyard, and I had a sculptor carve a bas-relief of *The Last Supper* for a wall in the dining room—using a thirteen-foot single piece of Honduras mahogony. I was very proud of this work of religious art. I had it carefully lighted, with a single spot picking up Jesus's face. Then I invited several of my friends over to see it. Among them were Mel Shavelson and Harry Crane, one of the best comedy writers in the business. Harry also happens to be Melissa Gilbert's grandfather.

When we assembled in the dining room, my friends all

stared at the sculpture with awe. I said, "Look at that light on Jesus's face. It's so realistic you can just about see him talking. I wonder what he's saying."

To which Harry Crane, the iconoclast, said, "Separate checks."

That's a joke that's been told about me in Hollywood for years. It ranks with Bob Hope's gag about my having stained-glass windows in my car.

But back to the show. In the third year, Jean Hagen announced that she was leaving. She said she wanted to get back to more serious work in the theater and the cinema. We couldn't dissuade her, and she was gone. That's when network boss Robert Kintner's concern for her became apparent. He had said she was the mainstay of the show, and with Jean no longer in it, he seemed to lose interest. We were scheduled opposite powerhouses like Burns and Allen, and Bob Hope. In many cities, we were scheduled at odd-ball times like Sunday afternoon, when practically nobody was watching.

But we didn't give up. And, in fact, we pulled together a pretty good premise for our fourth year—*without* Jean. The story line was that she had died and I was now a widower trying to rear the kids by myself. I was to date a lot of beautiful ladies (one of them turned out to be Marilyn Maxwell), who would try to convince the kids that each was the best candidate to become their stepmother. Unfortunately, I had to play most of the year in a wheelchair. During the summer, the real-life Danny Thomas had broken his leg playing basketball with some college kids in his backyard.

This led to a classically funny interview between San Francisco columnist Dwight Newton and Artie Stander (of the old Fanny Brice radio show) who had come to work with me as a writer:

NEWTON: Is this year's show going to be funny?
STANDER: Oh, very funny. I got a widower with two kids and a broken leg.

So I tooled around the soundstage in an electrically driven wheelchair, with my leg in a cast. It was an interesting experience. The old character-actor instincts came out in me. I could be grumpy, yet loveable, like Lionel Barrymore. It was fun working with a new beautiful woman every week or two. The only problem was that none of them really fit the bill as a permanent replacement for Jean Hagen.

Then one night, with nothing better to do, Rose Marie and I went to see a play, *Anniversary Waltz,* at a small theater on Wilshire Boulevard. We both were taken with the young woman who played the female lead. She was a perky little thing, and very, very lovely. What I liked about her performance in the play was how she stood up to her husband, fought him tooth and nail, and was realistically funny about it.

Her name was Marjorie Lord. I went to see her backstage and invited her to come down to our studio to discuss her playing one of my weekly dates in the series. The writers and Sheldon Leonard were quite intrigued when they met her. So they sat down and wrote a sequence in which Rusty had the measles and Marjorie was a nurse I had to hire to tend to the boy. She was so snap-crackling good in that episode that the writers dreamed up continuing sequences, in which *she* contracted the measles from Rusty and had to be quarantined in the house with Rusty and wheelchair-bound me. We reacted so naturally together that our close proximity led to a romance and—in the season's last episode—a proposal of marriage. The way it was written, *she* proposed to *me*—after I had botched up my own proposal, in song, patterned after the Gus Kahn role I had played with Doris Day in *I'll See You in My Dreams.* It was the how-can-a-face-like-this-say-I-love-you-to-a-face-like-that sort of thing.

Today, that scene might be considered overly cute, but it worked. The entire stage relationship between me and Marjorie worked. Her cast name was Kathy. She was to be my wife in the series for the next seven years. We loved each other; no hanky panky, just close friends.

But first we had the problem of just getting into the *next* year.

The whole situation was typical of the crazy ways of television. With Jean Hagen gone from the show, it was fairly obvious that ABC's Robert Kintner was reluctant to continue with the series—even with the surprise emergence of Marjorie Lord. Yet, with all this uncertainty, ABC invited me to be their master of ceremonies at their big bash in Washington, D.C., for the nation's top television and radio writers.

While I was preparing to extol the virtues of the shows on ABC's next-season schedule, Uncle Abe Lastfogel was doing some fancy footwork behind the scenes. If anything was needed to prove what a genius Uncle Abe was, this is it. He was a good friend of Tom McDermott of the Benton and Bowles advertising agency. In those days, unlike today, television network time was controlled by the advertising agencies. They bought a block of time, 8:00 to 8:30 on Saturday night, say, and they filled it with a show of their own choosing, wholly sponsored by the product of one of the companies they represented. The networks had little more than veto power over the programs that filled their schedules.

I didn't quite know what Uncle Abe was up to, but I had some idea. The night before I left for Washington, I couldn't sleep. I had a switch in my bedroom that flicked on the light on the St. Jude statue in the backyard. I put it on and went outside, pacing up and down in front of the statue. I didn't pray. I was just talking. A prayer would mean urgent need, which this wasn't. I had had four good years with my family, and I could always go back to the saloons to make money. I just kept saying as I paced in front of St. Jude, "This is a good family show. It deserves to be on the air." I said, "I know what you're thinking. It's *not* my pride." I'm glad it was two in the morning so no one could see this hook-nosed idiot babbling to a white marble statue.

I flew to Washington in the morning, and at about the same time, Uncle Abe flew to New York. It was a Friday. The next afternoon, I was in my room at the Sheraton Carlton Hotel preparing for that night's ABC dinner, when the phone rang. It was Uncle Abe. He said, "You're one-twelfth away." I said, "One-twelfth away from what?" He said, "I'm with Tom McDermott of Benton and Bowles, and he's dickering with his client, General Foods, to buy your show. He's convinced eleven of the twelve brands. Now he just has to convince Tex Cook, head of the Maxwell House Coffee division. We'll know on Monday."

An hour later, I was helping to set up the stage for that night's dinner performance, when Uncle Abe called back. He simply said, "Sweetheart, *mazel tov.* Book a room at the hotel for me and Aunt Frances. We're coming down to celebrate." I got so excited that I touched two microphones together and nearly electrocuted myself.

I learned the details when Uncle Abe and Aunt Frances got there. Maxwell House was going to sponsor the show. We were going into General Foods' 9:00 to 9:30 spot on Monday night on CBS, one of the most prestigious times on the air. It had just been vacated by *I Love Lucy,* when Lucille Ball decided she wanted a rest after six years.

Although I now was going to be on CBS, I still had to do that dinner for ABC that night. I couldn't say a word about the switch. Talk about being nervous. President Dwight Eisenhower was on the dais. In his honor, I wanted to read a moving tribute to Abraham Lincoln, which I had found in Carl Sandberg's biography. But I was so lit up that I couldn't memorize the words.

So I wrote them on a shirt cardboard and read them from the lectern. If Abe Lincoln could do the Gettysburg Address from notes on the back of an envelope, why couldn't I emulate him by using a shirt cardboard?

It worked fine.

chapter

❋❋❋ 23 ❋❋❋

In the last show on ABC, I had proposed to Marjorie Lord's character, Kathy. In the first show on CBS, we were married, and Kathy's daughter, Linda (Angela Cartwright), had come to live with us, adding a third kid to my TV family.

The ways of television were strange indeed, and with our move we were given a new name: *The Danny Thomas Show.* This came by edict of the head honcho of CBS, William Paley. He didn't like the title *Make Room for Daddy.* In fact, Paley didn't like our show altogether. He was in Florida when Uncle Abe closed the deal with General Foods, and Paley tried to move the show out of the schedule. But sponsors were mightier than network presidents in those days, and with General Foods/Maxwell House Coffee literally owning that 9:00 to 9:30 P.M. Monday time slot on CBS, there was little Paley could do about it. I guess he changed his mind, however, when, with our very first CBS show in October 1957, we shot up to the Top Ten in the ratings and stayed there.

With all these good things happening, I felt more than ever that I had to continue to fulfill my obligation to St. Jude.

The money for the hospital was coming in briskly—both from Abe Lastfogel's group in California and from Ed Barry's in Memphis. But we had to do something dramatic to stimulate more contributions. So on May 27, 1955, we scheduled a huge show outdoors at Crump Stadium in Memphis. A capacity crowd of more than fifteen thousand people showed up, each making a donation to our St. Jude project. Dinah Shore was one of the many guest stars who helped draw them in.

The weather in Memphis in May is "totally unpredictable," which means lots of rain. The day of the show, I wondered if I hadn't made a mistake in not moving the event indoors. There were black churning clouds all over the area. The Weather Bureau predicted four inches of rain, and it grew so dark that the streetlights were turned on in Memphis at 3 P.M. I was sure we were going to have a disastrous washout.

But the crowds kept pouring into the stadium. Like me, they were looking nervously up at the black clouds overhead. When the show was about to begin, I took one last look at the sky. I couldn't believe what I saw. The clouds had pulled apart, leaving a clear crescent-shaped space directly over the stadium. I had never seen anything like it in my life. We were onstage for two hours and fifteen minutes, and that clearing in the clouds never moved. It was only when we were finished that the downpour began, soaking the people as they rushed for their cars.

The newspapers played up that weather phenomenon nationally, and contributions—large and small—flowed in from all over the United States. When I returned to Memphis in 1957 for another fund-raising show for St. Jude, the weather forecast again was for huge downpours of rain. The page-one headline in the *Memphis Commercial Appeal* read: "Rain Predicted, But Never Fear, Danny's Here."

The miracle happened again. The clouds swirled all around the stadium, with angry lightning flashes, but not a drop of rain fell on another overflow crowd, which had come to see—among others—Elvis Presley, the King, at the height of his popularity. At the end of the show, as the crowd was filing out and the lightning still flashed, I walked to the front of the stage and addressed the medical people, who were seated in the first few rows. I said, "Please come forward and tell me what to do. I'm just a mere minstrel passing this way." That started a spirited discussion among the doctors about how the yet-to-be-born hospital should concentrate on the specialized research into sickle-cell anemia, leukemia, and other blood diseases in children.

This mere minstrel stayed out of the discussion, though their enthusiasm cheered me considerably. After all, my role was to think up gimmicks to raise money—such as telling Maxwell House Coffee to donate all the money I made for the TV commercials I did for the product.

One of the most unusual money-raising ideas came out of my part ownership of the Miami Dolphins football team. That resulted from my long-standing friendship with a fellow Lebanese-American, Joe Robbie. We Lebanese take great pride in each other's accomplishments in the United

States, and I followed Joe's career from the time he graduated from law school and was elected to the South Dakota legislature, to his move to Miami, where he became a supersuccessful entrepreneur.

Anyway, when the old American Football League was forming, Joe wanted a franchise for Miami. This was at about the same time the New York Jets, the New England Patriots, and other teams were being organized to compete with the National Football League. It was a risky gamble then; no one even dreamed that the two leagues eventually would merge into today's powerhouse N.F.L. So Joe needed money, and knowing what a football fan I was, he came out to see me with Lamar Hunt of the league organizing committee. I was appearing at Harrah's in Lake Tahoe.

I remember that Rosie cooked a bang-up dinner for them, and then Mr. Hunt put the question to me: Would I own fifty-one percent of a new team, the Miami Dolphins? I said I couldn't do that, but Joe and I could get enough people with money to put together the fifty-one percent in a syndicate, with me in control of it as president. Hunt agreed, and that's what we did. I was a pro-football owner, though Joe Robbie was the real managing partner. For me, it was like being a kid turned loose in a candy store.

As such, I went crazy in my very first game as an owner. A Miami player named Joe Auer took the opening kickoff and ran it back for a touchdown. I got so excited that I ran the length of the field alongside him, though I was careful not to step over the sideline. When Auer reached the end zone, I was all over him—jumping on his back, pounding on his helmet, wringing his hand. The next thing I knew, the referee was standing there, looking at me with a very stern expression. I said, "Uh-oh." The referee said, "You know, Mr. Thomas, I could disallow this touchdown. Owners are not supposed to walk beyond the thirty-five-yard line, and you not only walked, you *galloped.*" My face must have betrayed my feelings when I heard this, because the nice ref allowed the touchdown to stand. He said, "Oh, Danny, this is your first game, so forget about it."

What does this have to do with raising money for St. Jude? Well, I sold out all my shares in the Dolphins—all except three percent, which I returned to Joe Robbie, with the proviso that the earnings be donated to the St. Jude Hospital in perpetuity. In addition, Joe donated a lot of money on his own and became a member of our board of directors. I remained a minority owner of the Dolphins and received a diamond-studded championship ring—as did the coaches and the players—the two times the Dolphins won the Super Bowl.

The sun also shone on my efforts to find a top architect to design the hospital. Who could believe that I would come up with the great Paul R. Williams, one of the most famous architects in the world, who also happened to be black.

Paul and I got to talking about my hospital project, and he became interested when I mentioned our goal to help conquer sickle-cell anemia among black children in the South. He said, "Let me take a crack at drawing up the plans." Well aware of the astronomical fees Williams commanded, I asked nervously, "How much will you charge us?" He said, "Nothing. You'll just have to pay my draftsman."

We still needed an organization that would guarantee the

three hundred thousand dollars it would take to run the hospital's administration every year. This old Phoenician's mind started working. I remembered what my father had told me on his deathbed: "Never forget your heritage." I thought of the hundreds of thousands of people of my heritage who had come to America. They had prospered, they had educated their children, and they had passed on. They had made individual contributions to society, but they had never united in a common cause all their own. Maybe St. Jude Children's Research Hospital could become their common cause.

I met with the scattered leaders of the Lebanese-American and Syrian-American communities and showed them the dramatic pictures of the proposed hospital. From the start, one of the biggest supporters was a remarkable man named Michael F. Tamer. A forceful, dynamic executive with a booming voice, Tamer also was the president of a federation of Lebanese-Syrian clubs in the Midwest. He became the driving force in assembling leaders of Arabic ancestry from all over the country.

It was the beginning of the American Lebanese Syrian Associated Charities (commonly called ALSAC today). I wrote the preamble to the organization's constitution on a sheet of brown wrapping paper and delivered it verbally. I held the audience better than I ever had in my show-business career—but it was my sincerity that held them, not any performer's tricks. I was followed by Dr. Diggs of the medical staff-to-be in Memphis, who gave them a straight-forward picture of how the much-needed research would be done to conquer catastrophic childhood diseases. As a result of that first ALSAC meeting, twenty-two thousand members were enrolled.

It didn't happen right away. I did benefits; I made personal appeals. In the summer hiatus periods from my TV show, Rose Marie and I would go to the Midwest, meet Mike Tamer, and travel by station wagon from one town to another where there would be Lebanese-Syrian communities in Indiana, Ohio, Michigan, Missouri, you name it. It was tough on Rosie. We'd do a luncheon in one town and then head off in the station wagon for a dinner in another town. We'd stop along the way so Rosie could change her clothes in a gas station rest room. The luxuries of Beverly Hills were forgotten on these long treks.

But it all paid off as membership in ALSAC grew. With the long-term maintenance of the St. Jude Hospital in their hands, the construction of the hospital could proceed.

When the building finally was completed and dedicated on February 4, 1962, I made the principal address to the nine thousand ordinary people and dignitaries who showed up. In thanking everyone, I said, "It took a rabble-rousing, hook-nosed comedian to get your attention, but it took your hearts, loving minds, and generous souls to make it come true. If I were to die this moment, I'd know why I was born."

There wasn't a dry eye in the house, especially mine.

chapter

24

While all this was going on, *The Danny Thomas Show* on CBS was just humming along. Frequently we were Number One in the ratings, almost always in the Top Ten. Remember, we were only the second big situation comedy to emerge in television (*I Love Lucy* being the first) and we could get away with a lot of experimental things—which are now done so often they don't seem so fresh anymore.

For example, Sheldon Leonard, now the producer of the show, worked constantly with me until we developed what we called "the treacle cutter" as one of our trademarks. The "treacle cutter" was the technique of giving me lines to build up a scene to almost unbearable sentimentality—only to zap the audience with an unexpected, totally unsentimental comedy line. Case in point: My son, Rusty, feeling rejected, has run away and enrolled himself in an orphan asylum under the name Elvis Earp. I go to fetch him home. I tell him all the wonderful things we are now going to do together—fishing, baseball, swimming—"and we'll have dinner together, with you standing up, because your bottom will be so sore from the tattoo I'm going to beat on it.'' Cutting the treacle. We did it at least once in every show. In a comedic way, it neutralized my reputation for becoming *over*sentimental at times.

Also, I think we were the first to introduce the ''warm-up'' for the studio audience, to put them in the mood to laugh during the filming of the show. I did the warm-up myself, using my nightclub material, testing out new stories, re-rehearsing old ones. Mel Shavelson says that sometimes the warm-ups were funnier than the shows. In fact, they became much more than warm-ups. I also had to entertain the three hundred-or-so people in the studio *during* the filming, just to keep them from walking out. You see, in those primitive days of television, there was no taping, no instantaneous editing the way it's done today. We used three 35-millimeter cameras, and every time there was a fluff or a gaffe, we had to stop the cameras and do the scene all over again. There was no laugh-track, so we even had to make sure the laughs from the live audience were in the right place. Sometimes they got tired and didn't laugh. For a half-hour show, they might be sitting there for six hours.

So when their interest flagged while film was being reloaded, and so on, I'd run out on the stage and do my *shtick* to keep their interest up. Sometimes, I'd banter back and forth with Sheldon Leonard, who was out of sight of the audience in the control booth, but they could hear him on the P.A. system. Sheldon and I insulted each other pretty good in these exchanges, and the people loved it.

The exchanges led to a lot of new material for me, which

I used in my nightclub act (I kept doing the act when I had a few weeks off from production on the TV series) and in my pre-show warm-ups. For example, when things got hopelessly fouled up, Sheldon used the Yiddish word *fartumult,* which, loosely translated, means "hopelessly fouled up."

One day, Marjorie Lord, my lovely, definitely non-ethnic leading lady, asked me for a more precise explanation of the meaning of *fartumult.* I thought back to my days with Mrs. Feldman and came up with the following:

"An old Jewish grandmother is asked by her son and daughter-in-law to sit with their young child while they go out for the evening. Her daughter-in-law tells her, 'Under no circumstances let the child wake up because he won't go to sleep again.' So the old lady settles in for the evening but eventually gets bored and decides to bake a cake for her grandson. The cake is in the oven when the doorbell rings. The old lady is totally confused: If she answers the doorbell, the cake will fall and be ruined. If she stays with the cake, the doorbell will keep ringing and wake up the child. *Fartumult.*"

I used that story in my warm-ups from then on.

Thinking back on the incredible eleven-year run which the show enjoyed, I can only attribute its success to two things. First was its ingenious format—an entertainer whose show-business career put him in conflict with wanting to enjoy a normal family life—continued to work. The combination was effective, and not just a story of parents with kids, as in *Ozzie and Harriet* and *Father Knows Best.* The nightclub stuff played beautifully against the family stuff and was perfect for me. I could use fragments from my nightclub routines; I could even bring in people I knew in that other world, to play characters in the show—such as the very funny husband and wife vaudeville team, Patty Moore and Benny Lessing, known as Aunt Patty and Uncle Benny to my kids in the show.

The second reason for the show's continuing success was the remarkable harmony we developed. It would be more interesting, I'm sure, to report conflict between me and Marjorie Lord, but I can't remember one cross word that passed between us. We're *still* good friends. I had the same wonderful rapport with the children in the show—Rusty Hamer, Angela Cartwright (who played Marjorie's daughter), and Sherry Jackson (later replaced with Penney Parker when Sherry grew too old-looking for the part). The only problems I had were with my own children, who sometimes grew jealous of my attentions to the show-kids. I remember that Marlo once was furious because I sang *her* song, "Daddy's Little Girl," to Sherry.

It was the same with the crew. I had the same technicians for years, and I don't think I ever fired anybody. Behind my back, the grips, electricians, cameramen, etc., called me "The Toothless Tiger." I'd scream and yell a lot, but they knew I'd soon get over my ire. The closest I came to drastic action was when one guy, through an act of gross negligence, cost my production company thousands of dollars.

I called this man in for the express purpose of hearing from me that he was fired. He arrived with his ten-year-old son. With the kid there, I didn't know what to do. All my life I have said that if anyone dishonored me in the presence of my own children, I'd kill him, because every man is a hero in the eyes of his own kids. This is the Lebanese mountain tradition, of course. So what did I do? I spent about fifteen minutes telling the kid how important the man was to my organization. Then, instead of firing the father, I sent him back to work in his usual job—which he held until the show went off the air maybe five years later.

My greatest joy in those days was sitting around a table every Wednesday to discuss the beginnings of the next week's show. That's the kind of tight schedule we worked on in those days—not planning four weeks ahead, as in most cases today. My writers were all brilliant young guys who went on to become famous writer-producers in the industry—men like Shavelson, Jack Ellison, Chuck Stewart, Bob O'Brien, Danny Simon, Bob Schiller, and Bob Weiskopf. One of them was a boy, Larry Gelbart, the son of my barber, Harry Gelbart, who pleaded with me to give his 16-year-old son his first comedy writer's job in show business. Larry Gelbart, of course, went on to become the creator of *M*A*S*H* and the writer of great movies like *Tootsie* and Broadway hits such as *A Funny Thing Happened on the Way to the Forum* and the current smash musical *City of Angels.*

These men would constantly talk about stories from their personal family lives, which we would weave into the show. Mel Shavelson, for example, was president of the Little League baseball organization in the San Fernando Valley and came up with a very funny script about how my character, Danny Williams, becomes coach of a Little League team and has to cut his own son, Rusty, not knowing that he is about to be replaced himself. In their mutual agony, they can only take solace in the song from *Damn Yankees*—"You Gotta Have Heart." Who replaces Danny? Joe DiMaggio.

But aside from coming up with story ideas, these guys were very funny people, just in their casual conversation. Bob Weiskopf nearly floored me with one story about his personal life. He was married to a lovely Japanese woman. He was also a friend of Herman Wouk, the great novelist. In World War II, Wouk was in the navy and was exasperated with how the navy censors sliced up his letters home. Finally Wouk figured out a solution. He'd write things like "Last week, we were visited by Mrs. Weiskopf's relatives." According to Bob Weiskopf, no censor ever caught this canny reference to a brush with the Japanese enemy.

Two of our best writers were Frank Tarloff and Mac Benoff. Unfortunately, those were the days of McCarthyism, "Red Channels," and the Hollywood blacklist. Frank and Mac were on the list—God knows why because I never heard them say anything more subversive than "Richard Nixon is a jerk." But they couldn't work anywhere else in the industry.

Sheldon and I kept them on. We had to use pseudonyms for them, or we might have been blacklisted, too. Frank became David Adler; for Mac, we used my real name, Amos Jacobs, and Sheldon's real name, Leonard Bershad.

Later, when the industry honored Sheldon and me for all the shows we made on the old Cahuenga lot, everybody got up and thanked us. But Frank Tarloff got to his feet and yelled, "Wait a minute. We've all got some reason to thank these two guys. But I have got the *real* reason. Without them, there would have been no food on the table."

When the nonsense died down, Frank went on to win the Academy Award for *Father Goose,* the delightful Cary Grant movie.

Mel Shavelson never ceased to tease me about the deal we had had to make with him at the beginning of the show. When he wrote the pilot in 1953, there was very little optimism about the future of *Make Room for Daddy,* and very little money. So Mel was induced to take one-half of his regular fee, with the balance paid out over the first thirteen weeks the show was on the air. No one expected it to go longer that. But the series kept going on, and on, and on—and Mel kept getting paid, even though he left us after our third year. He got paid for every episode we made for years thereafter. He's *still* getting paid—for the reruns. Talk about a long-shot gamble paying off with a bonanza. As a businessman, I never resented the financial consequences of Mel's gamble with that pilot script. Without it, there would have been no show.

As a businessman, I soon had to take my own financial gambles, which fortunately turned out to be a bonanza for *me.* Remember when I said that success came to me when I wasn't looking. That's how I became a tycoon on a forty-thousand-dollar investment—all the while continuing to produce and act in my own series.

In 1957, Uncle Abe Lastfogel came to me and said, "We have a show here at William Morris which we're sure is going to be a big success. We want your Danny Thomas Productions to own it. All you'll have to put up is forty thousand dollars." I protested that I only had seven hundred dollars in the bank, which Uncle Abe knew was a lie, and I eventually provided the money. Sheldon Leonard, by now my partner, directed the pilot. The show was *The Real McCoys*, starring much-respected actor Walter Brennan, with Richard Crenna and Kathy Nolan. It was on ABC and then CBS for six years—nearly always high in the ratings. When I sold out my interest in the show in 1962, I got my original investment back nearly fifty-fold.

Through Uncle Abe, other TV-show investments kept dropping into my lap. The next one was *The Andy Griffith Show*. Both the William Morris people and Sheldon Leonard correctly guessed that the next big thing on television was to be rural comedy. But we used an innovative gimmick this time. Instead of financing an expensive pilot, we invented the technique of the "spin-off." We did an entire episode on *The Danny Thomas Show,* in which I travel through a small town called Mayberry and am arrested by the local sheriff, played by Andy Griffith. In the bullheaded tug-of-war that ensues between me and Andy, the entire background of Griffith, as sheriff, comes to light. *The Andy Griffith Show* was sold on the basis of that one episode of *The Danny Thomas Show.* It ran on CBS for nine years—another super hit.

Another superhit was what came to be called Danny's Famous Deli. We conceived the idea to provide constant refreshment for the people on our shows, and my prop man, Stewart Stevenson, actually set up a delicatessen in his prop room, which had two refrigerators. He would go to nearby delis like the popular Nate-'n-Al's in Beverly Hills, and stock up every day with corned beef, pastrami, lox, cream cheese, whatever. There were soft drinks in abundance, and Stewart even kept frosted glasses in his freezer. My set became known as an oasis on the lot. Writers from other shows flocked there. So did stars like Desi Arnaz, Lucille Ball, and Red Skelton.

One day, a hot and frazzled Jack Benny came staggering into my dressing room. He was working in an episode of *December Bride* across the street and apparently wasn't needed in the scene they were shooting. It was a terribly hot day, and my humming air-conditioning unit had attracted him.

When he saw me, Jack said, "Excuse me, Danny, I didn't think anyone was here."

I said, "That's all right, Jack. How would you like a nice cold drink?" His eyes shined with gratitude, and I sent Stew Stevenson to come back with an orange drink in a frosted glass. Jack gulped it down. He was amazed when I also sent Stew for a pastrami sandwich for him. He said, "What have you got here, a branch of Nate-'n-Al's?"

I then had to go back to my own set. I said to Jack, "Eat, rest up, lie down on my couch here where it's cool, until you have to go back to work." Jack, still munching on his sandwich, nodded—radiating more gratitude.

When I got back to my dressing room an hour later, Jack was gone. He left behind him the remains of three more sandwiches, also a note, which read:

> Dear Danny:
> Go frig yourself.
> Love,
> Jack

So typical of those guys. Such were the inscrutable ways of my comic colleagues of that period.

Speaking of Nate-'n-Al's, there's a great story involving my friend, writer Harry Crane. Harry suffers from hypoglycemia and occasionally requires a quick infusion of sugar into his system. He was walking down Beverly Drive one day when he realized he needed such a fix. He walked into Nate-'n-Al's, stepped up to the counter and said, "Quick, give me an orange."

The counterman, busy with his slicing and chopping, said to Harry, "Sir, we can't sell oranges here. You'll have to sit at a table, and the waitress will take care of you."

Harry said, "No time. Give me an orange. Quick."

The counterman said, "Sorry, sir," whereupon Harry keeled over in a dead faint. They had to call an ambulance and Harry was rushed to West Side Hospital.

Joey Bishop heard about the occurrence and phoned Harry at his room in the hospital. "How are you, Harry?" Joey asked.

Harry said, "I'm fine now. Thanks for calling."

Joey said, "Where are you?"

Harry said, "You know where I am. You're the one who phoned me."

Joey said, "No, what I mean is how do I get there?"

Harry said, "Just go to Nate-'n-Al's and order an orange."

We did an episode of *The Danny Thomas Show* with Joey Bishop playing my press agent. Uncle Abe parlayed that into another spin-off—and *The Joey Bishop Show* was born. Another acquisition for our rapidly growing Supermarket of Sitcoms. It was the same when *Gomer Pyle* spun off from our *Andy Griffith Show*.

The most interesting and prestigious of the new wares in our Supermarket was *The Dick Van Dyke Show,* which Sheldon Leonard (God knows how he found the time) helped Carl Reiner develop. If you remember, the show, now considered a TV classic, had a show-business background, like mine. The principal characters were a trio of comedy writers, Dick Van Dyke, Rose Marie, and Morey Amsterdam, in constant, hilarious conflict with the neurotic star of their mythical show, Alan Brady, and his pompous brother-in-law, Melvis Cooley, the show's producer. Intertwined, as in my series, was the family life of Van Dyke's character, Rob Petrie, and his wife, Laura.

The casting of Laura is one of those legendary stories of that hurly-burly era of television—a legend which I think has never been fully told before. It goes back to when we had to replace Sherry Jackson, the daughter in my own show, because she was getting too mature-looking. We eventually replaced her with Penney Parker, but in the meantime we interviewed dozens of lovely young girls. One of them impressed us all, but I turned her down because she was a bit too mature for a kid about to go to college; in fact, she had just had a baby. That same season, 1959, this young woman was hired to play an answering service operator in *Richard Diamond, Private Detective,* but the audience never saw her face, only her lovely legs.

So now, we're about to do *The Dick Van Dyke Show* pilot, and we're having a devil of a time finding the lady to play Dick's wife, Laura, in the series. Sheldon Leonard and Carl Reiner finally came up with someone they thought was perfect—a young stage actress from New York. We interviewed her and tested her, and Sheldon and Carl asked me what I thought. I suppose I was less than enthusiastic. I said, "She's all right, I guess. I wouldn't stand in your way if you want to hire her."

An hour later, totally dejected, Sheldon and Carl stuck their heads into the doorway to my office and said, simultaneously, "Screw you." I said, "Why screw me? If you like this girl so much, sign her up." Reiner said, "That's not enough. What we want from you is *enthusiasm.*"

I said, "Enthusiasm you want? Let me think." I thought for a few minutes. They believed I was reconsidering my assessment of their choice for Laura, but I had something else on my mind. I said, "Sheldon, do you remember that girl we brought in to test for Sherry Jackson's part, and I turned her down because she was too mature?"

Beginning to catch the drift, Sheldon said, "Yes."

I said, "Well, she's been working in *Richard Diamond.* At least her legs have been working. That's all you see."

Sheldon said, "Go on. I remember her."

I said, "All I remember is she's got three names."

Carl Reiner said, "John Charles Thomas."

I said, "Very funny. Get the actor's directory."

Sure enough, there she was.

And that's how the girl with three names, Mary Tyler Moore, had her fabulous career launched by our Supermarket of Sitcoms.

Lest this gives you the impression that I was the hands-on Emperor of our TV Empire, I was not. I had too much to do to keep the *Danny Thomas Show* on track every week.

The man who deserves most of the credit for running the Empire (we frequently had three shows in the Top Ten) was the indefatigable Sheldon Leonard. How he did it, I'll never know. He'd sit in on the first reading of my show and then scamper through a lot of little doors, which led to our other productions. All of our shows were concentrated on various soundstages at the Desilu-Cahuenga studios, and Sheldon got a lot of exercise running between them. It kept him thin and lanky.

I turned the *Andy Griffith Show* over to Sheldon completely. On the other shows, I read scripts and helped with the casting. It was more business than show business. Working on my own show all day, I missed fooling around with Andy Griffith, Joey Bishop, and the others.

The one exception was the *Dick Van Dyke Show,* where I'd sneak over once in a while to hobnob with the guys, especially the funny ones, Morey Amsterdam and Rose Marie Guy—because the subject matter of comedy-show writers was so close to me, I expect. I loved the way they'd sit around and tell funny stories—only to say, "We can't use that one. It's too old." I got in some old stories of my own, which they couldn't use. Once in a while there were stories they couldn't use—for other reasons aside from age.

The principal perpetrator of these tales was Morey Amsterdam, whom I'd known for years. Morey is like Milton Berle, with an encyclopedic mind that can toss out a joke on any subject. Many of them were off-color, but we constantly faced the challenge of trying to sanitize them for use on the rather straitlaced television of that period.

One of the Morey Amsterdam stories on which we

wasted a lot of time is his favorite. He still tells it to me when I run into him (he lives in my neighborhood in Beverly Hills). The story goes as follows:

A woman in a rural town looks up one day and she sees an elephant eating cabbages in her backyard. The animal probably has escaped from a touring circus, but the lady has never before seen an elephant in her entire life. She calls the police and reports, "There's a real big horse in my cabbage patch. He's pulling up my cabbages with his tail. And if I told you what he's doing with the cabbages, you'd never believe it."

Try to clean *that* one up for family television. No matter how Morey tried, he could never convince the CBS censors, who would say, "No matter how you cut it, you're still implying the woman thinks the elephant is shoving the cabbages up his ass." There was no one to censor the censors' comments.

But to get back to Sheldon Leonard, the genius who held all this together (including the fights with the censors), not only was he my partner but my closest buddy. I loved the man. When my son, Tony, went into production much later, I told him he had to find a partner like Sheldon—and he did.

In our eleven years together, Sheldon and I had only two fights. Only one of them was significant. He was directing an episode of *The Danny Thomas Show* and he had too many people on the stage to fit into his three cameras. He asked me to step aside because I was the only one who didn't have a speaking line coming up. I guess I sulked a bit. I said, "What are the people in the studio audience going to think, seeing me standing over here by myself. Maybe I should smoke a cigar. Maybe I should get a cloth and dust my cigar ashes off the tables. Why do I have to be out of the shot?"

Sheldon said, "From everything I know, the director is in charge of the set, and that's what I want." I left the soundstage in a huff.

In a few minutes, Sheldon came to my dressing room. He said, "Seeing you sitting there behind your desk, I know you're the boss. But on the stage, the director's the boss, or the show never gets done." I had long since realized he was absolutely right, and I jumped up and hugged him. Our only crisis was over.

There was one other time when I acted like a schmuck, and it involved not only Sheldon but other people on our staff. I always had been sensitive about my lack of formal education, my having been a high school dropout in my freshman year. I must confess for the first time that with all the power suddenly in my hands, I became a reverse educational snob. Sheldon was a Syracuse University graduate, most of my writers had gone to the finest colleges in the country.

I actually used to tease them about their education—an education which I lacked. Once I screamed at Sheldon, "The trouble with you is you're iliopedantic." For days, Sheldon and the others went crazy trying to find the word in their dictionaries. There is no such word. I made it up.

Then, to taunt them, I used to tell them one of my favorite stories: There was this janitor who couldn't read or write. Totally uneducated. He worked in a building for several years and then he was fired. He made his living for a while, picking up junk in the street. Then he started his own junk business. From that he opened a surplus store and made a lot of money. He invested in Wall Street, eventually became a millionaire, and bought the building where he once worked. Everyone said, "Amazing about Joe. I wonder where he'd be today if he could read and write?" Someone answered, "He'd still be the janitor."

In a way, I guess I was saying to my people, "If you guys are so smart, how come *you*'re working for *me?*"

It was a shameful thing, but it soon passed. Before long, life and experience taught me that there is nothing more valuable than education. Today, this high school dropout is one of the biggest boosters of the world's colleges and universities.

chapter

25

My kids were growing up, and Marlo, of course, was the first to attend U.S.C. She had done very well scholastically at Marymount High School and easily was admitted to this hard-to-get-into university. She still lived at home. In my Lebanese heritage and also in Rosie's Sicilian tradition, a daughter doesn't leave unless she's wearing a white veil and a ring on her finger. Rosie, in particular, played hardball in this matter.

So Marlo commuted to college every day, driving about fifteen miles each way in Los Angeles's crazy freeway traffic. She was a brilliant student, ending up with a 3.8 average. She was seriously planning to be a teacher, and, in fact, spent many months—as part of a U.S.C. educational project—working as a teaching assistant in the barrio schools of East Los Angeles. Very few people know that about Marlo.

From Day One, I had tried to talk her out of an acting career. I told her I didn't want her to have to suffer the heartbreak and rejection I had seen so many times with young women trying to make a go of it in my profession. And when Marlo seemed so enthusiastic about teaching, I thought I was succeeding. Little did I know. After all, she was carrying my genes.

Marlo tried out for dramatic productions at U.S.C. and was cast in some of them. Rosie and I went to see her and she was quite good. But I kept up my drumbeat of what I call "hairy stories" about the perils of show business, and she seemed to be listening. She was listening all right, but she had inherited another genetic characteristic from me— stubborness.

On the day we came home from her commencement, Marlo steered me into my office at home. She threw her diplomas down on my desk and said, "This is for *you.* Now, how do I become an actress?" What's a father to do? I told her that if it's what she really wanted, I'd do all I could to give her the proper advice.

But that was only the first of a double-barreled shot. Marlo said, "Dad, I want to leave home and go out on my own. I don't even know how to open a can of sardines. I've been too sheltered and protected. I've got to become more independent. What if, Heaven forbid, something should happen to you and Mommy, where would I be? You've got to talk to Mom about letting me go."

That's when I first began to call Marlo "Miss Independence." And it didn't surprise me at all when she later turned out to be one of the foremost advocates of women's rights.

Anyway, back then after her graduation, I took the case

of Miss Independence to Rose Marie. As I expected, there was a lot of screaming and yelling from my wife, but I said, "C'mon, Rosie. The kid's right," and after more screaming and yelling, she gave in. We went out with Marlo to help her find an apartment. Nothing seemed safe enough to Rosie until we came across one which Marlo liked—in Hollywood, just behind the Methodist Church on Highland Avenue. Even though we knew it was safe, Rosie called my friends in the Los Angeles County Sheriff's office to implore them to get extra locks installed on Marlo's door. Three locks—top, middle, and bottom. With all this protection, Marlo finally moved in.

About a week later, I got a phone call from my firstborn. She asked for her Mom. I knew something was wrong. I said, "What's the matter, honey?"

She said, "Oh, Daddy, it's awful. It's awful. This place is overrun with ants."

Rosie was upstairs and I yelled, "Rose Marie, Miss Independence has ants." In a matter of minutes, Rosie had rocketed out of the house, her car laden with every insecticide she could lay her hands on.

So true independence came slowly to Miss Independence, but when it did, it took hold with a vengeance. She took acting lessons; she pounded the streets looking for acting jobs. She had made up her mind that if she hadn't gotten anywhere in a year, she'd quit and go back to teaching. Gradually she began to get somewhere, on a small scale. Uncle Abe Lastfogel's people at William Morris helped her (on my urging, of course) but she did most of it herself. In small regional playhouses, she starred in stage productions of *Sunday in New York, Under the Yum Yum Tree,* and *Gigi.* She was like any kid trying to get started in the business. The William Morris guys kept tracking her, but apparently she wasn't sending out any sparks for them.

Finally, Miss Independence *really* declared her independence. She told me, "I don't want William Morris to handle me. I don't want *you* to keep pushing me, either." Marlo then wrote a beautiful letter to Uncle Abe, which he told me about later. She wrote: "I don't want to come between you and my father. I love you as my Uncle Abe, so please just continue being that. If I'm going to get anywhere in this business, I have to do it myself—without any undue influence from you or Dad."

And do it herself, she did. Director Mike Nichols came out to Los Angeles to cast a girl for the road company of Neil Simon's Broadway hit *Barefoot in the Park,* which had starred Elizabeth Ashley and Robert Redford in New York. Nichols must have interviewed a hundred girls for the Ashley role (Corie) and my daughter was among the hundred. I don't think Mike had any idea she was related to me, but he ended up giving her the part. He didn't realize he was dealing with Miss Independence. She shocked everyone by *turning down* the role.

No one was more shocked than I was. I asked her, "Why?" She said, "Daddy, I'd be doing this play all over the country for the great privilege of ending up here in the Huntington Hartford Theater in Los Angeles. And what good would that do me? I've been playing in Los Angeles already, and I can't get arrested here. It would be different if Mr. Nichols were casting for the role of Corie in the movie." Miss Independence was getting ahead of herself. That part went to Jane Fonda.

Uncle Abe told me, "That kid of yours is a beautiful person, judging by the letter she sent me, but she's crazy." Another William Morris bigwig, Sam Weisbord, said, "She's crazy, period." Crazy or not, she was my daughter and I had to stick by her.

It turned out that we *all* were crazy and that she was right in turning down the touring national-company role.

A few months later, Marlo was in New York. She saw some agents and casting people, and one afternoon she dropped in to a Schrafft's restaurant to refresh herself with a milk shake. She was sipping her shake at the counter, when a man slipped onto the stool beside her. It was Mike Nichols. Pure happenstance.

Nichols said, "I know you, don't I? You are . . ."

"Marlo Thomas," said Miss Independence.

"Oh, yes," said Nichols. "You know, you never should have turned down that part in the *Barefoot in the Park* tour."

Marlo carefully explained to him why she had done so.

According to Marlo, Nichols looked at her reflectively. Then he said, "By the way, Saint-Subber has a deal to do the play in London. He's got Mildred Natwick and Kurt Kasznar from the original cast, and Raymond Massey's son, Dan, is going to play the lead, the Redford part. They're still looking for the female lead, Corie. I don't have anything to do with this production, but I could set up a reading for you."

I wasn't there, of course, but I could visualize my little Mugsy whooping with joy, like she did when she was a little

kid. She went to the reading, with the obvious recommen-
dation of Nichols as his previous choice, and she got the
part. She was almost inarticulate with excitement when she
phoned us with the news. This would not just be a second-
string road company production that would come and go.
In England she would be the star of a play the British had
never seen. It could run for months, years maybe. I said,
"Honey, I have to admit you were right in being so stubborn about what you really wanted."

So Marlo came home, packed, and rushed off to London
to start rehearsals. Rosie, ever overprotective, wanted to
send a bodyguard with her, but I said that would be going
too far. I promised that we'd join Marlo in England as soon
as my TV show went into hiatus for the summer.

By the time we got there, the play had already had its
out-of-town tryout in Brighton, the rough edges had been
rubbed smooth, and the big opening in London was only
a couple of days away. But when Marlo met us, we were
overcome with worry. She was limping badly. She also was
crying.

I said, "What is it, honey?"

She said, "I tripped over something when I was running
on stage down in Brighton, and they say I ruptured my
Achilles tendon. The doctors want to put my leg in a cast."
Sobbing, she threw her arms around me. She said, "Oh,
Daddy, I didn't come all the way to London to have my
understudy open for me." The way she was clutching me,
I thought back to when she was four years old and had to
have an ear infection lanced. Back then, the doctor had her
wrapped up tight in a blanket like a straitjacket and she was

screaming, "Daddy, Daddy." I said to the doctor, "But she's only four years old." He said, "But she'll move and I might puncture her eardrum." I said, "Let me hold her. She won't move. I promise you."

So I held her and said to little Mugsy, "Now you just look at Daddy's nose. Keep looking at Daddy's big nose, and don't take your eyes off Daddy's nose, and don't move, and it's not going to hurt, and I'm gonna hold you." Before we knew it, the lancing had been done and the infection was draining.

So here we were, eighteen years later in London, England, and I was holding Marlo in the same way, and she was saying, "Daddy, Daddy, don't let them keep me off the stage because of that Achilles tendon."

We had a long conference with the doctors, a physician and a surgeon. Finally, I said to the surgeon, "Can't you kill the pain with Xylocaine or something, just to get her through these first few performances?" The surgeon said, "Well, it's your responsibility." I kept thinking of the possible risks, but Marlo kept saying, "Please, Daddy," and finally I said, "Use the Xylocaine."

The play opened that night, and Marlo was a smash. She got nine curtain calls when it ended, and Rosie and I had tears streaming down our cheeks. At the champagne party afterwards, the playwright, Neil Simon, made a toast to Marlo and her two doctors, saying that Marlo was exactly what he had in mind when he first wrote the part of Corie— and he thanked the doctors for helping her pull it off. The critics, unaware of the gimpy leg, were ecstatic the next day. One wrote, "A young lady from America hit the stage last night. Hit it? She demolished it. Marlo Thomas is a fantastic performer."

The fantastic performer insisted on doing a couple of more performances that week—abetted with the Xylocaine. But then came Saturday—*two* shows scheduled. The surgeon, Mr. Goodsmith, said, "This is insane. She'll be crippled. She'll only do one show tonight, whether the management likes it or not, and immediately after that, she goes into a cast."

And that's what happened. Goodsmith got no arguments from me or from Rosie. Nor from Marlo. She had proved the point that, while "she couldn't get arrested" in Los Angeles, she had made it in the big time. Now they would wait for her injury to heal. When it did, she returned to the play and it ran, with full houses, for nearly a year.

She returned home in triumph, and we gave her a good old-fashioned Lebanese-Sicilian welcoming party. I was never more proud than when big shots from all over the industry kept calling to say, "We have a project that might interest your kid. Where can we find her?"

But, of course, Marlo had her own ideas. The year before, she had made a pilot for ABC called *Two's Company*. Edgar Scherick, the head of programming at ABC, had liked Marlo but not the pilot. "We think you have a real chance of being a television star," Scherick told her, "and I'm going to look for something for you."

Now with all these new offers that didn't appeal to her, Marlo came up with her own idea, taken straight from the dilemmas she herself was facing—a show about a single young woman on her own, a college graduate who wanted to be an actress, and about her overprotective father who wanted her to marry and have a family, fearing all the time that men grew on trees in his daughter's living room.

Marlo took the idea to Scherick. He loved it, and they got Bill Persky and Sam Denoff to create the sitcom about a young woman from Brewster, New York, who leaves her parents' home to find a career for herself in the Big City. The series was a huge hit on the network for five years. It also was a forerunner to other series about struggling young women—such as *The Mary Tyler Moore Show* and *Rhoda*, which came later.

When I first heard about the show, I suggested they call it, "Miss Independence."

They ignored me. They called it *That Girl*.

chapter

I had previously met Franklin D. Roosevelt and Harry Truman, but in 1955, I had my first one-on-one visit with a sitting U.S. president. The president was Dwight D. Eisenhower, and our meeting came about in a strange way.

I was touring with Mike Tamer to raise money for St. Jude during my summer vacation. We did a benefit in Paterson, New Jersey. Our next stop was to be Washington, D.C. I was asleep in my motel room in Paterson when one of the guys came in and said, "Hey, Danny, you just got a phone call from the White House."

I said, "Cut the joking and lemme get some sleep."

The man said, "No, it's true. It was the chief of protocol in the president's office. He said the president knows you're going to be in Washington and he wonders if you can come in a little earlier and get to the White House at about eleven-thirty or so."

I still thought it was a joke. I said, "Okay, wiseguy, what's this chief of protocol's name? I'll call him back." He gave me the name, I called him back—and it was true. I couldn't believe it. The president wanted to see *me?* About what? I didn't have a clue, and neither did the chief of protocol.

I left the others to make their way to Washington in the station wagon, and I took a plane. I got to Washington's National Airport, where I had a shave and a shoe shine before I went by cab to the White House. The guards let me in at the gate, and I was taken up to the president's residence. On the way, we passed through the White House press corps. The reporters asked, "What's cookin,' Danny?" I said, "I don't know. Ike and I have to solve some big problem, I guess."

Ike was waiting for me in a sitting room upstairs. He was on a couch and he put me in an easy chair just opposite him. He asked me if I wanted something to eat, and I said, "Just a tuna fish sandwich and a Coke, please." A servant brought the food, and the president and I indulged in a lot of small talk. He said, "You see that painting just behind your head? That slides back and there's a television set behind it. This is where we watch your show every Monday night." He seemed to be stalling for time, and I couldn't figure out what was going on.

The president started talking about how he liked TV shows with a message—like teachers and policemen should get more money. Then he said, "I understand your parents were immigrants," and we had a discussion about how immigrants are the lifeblood of America. He said, "Other countries all have the same heritage, the same thinking. Here, it's the *mix* of cultures that make us great." I agreed and decided that since he seemed to be wasting time, I'd tell him a few of my immigrant jokes. There was one that made him howl. I never saw a president laugh so hard.

The story was this:

There was this fellow named Istvan, who had just come over from Hungary and was working on the iron-ore docks on the East Side of my hometown, Toledo. He couldn't speak English at all. When the noon whistle blew, those who lived alone and didn't have a lunch bucket, went to the nearest diner. Istvan just sat there and didn't eat. He didn't know what to say.

Finally, he went to a friend and said to him in Hungarian, "Got to have something to eat. Something sweet to make me strong from breakfast to supper." The friend taught him to say, "Apple pie and coffee." Istvan learned how to say that, and when he told it to the cute waitress in the diner, she brought him the apple pie and coffee. That's what he had for lunch every day for about six weeks.

Then he said to his friend, in Hungarian, "Up to here already with apple pie and coffee. Got to have something different." The friend taught Istvan to say, "Cheese sandwich."

Then he went into the diner. The same cute waitress came over to take his order. Istvan said, "Cheese sandavich."

The waitress said, "Certainly, sir. On whole wheat or rye?"

He stared at her for a minute and said, "Apple pie and coffee."

Ike was still laughing at that story when Mamie Eisenhower came in. She offered me another soft drink. I said,

"No thank you," and she left. Ike kept talking. I kept getting up, saying, "Am I keeping you, sir?" Ike said, "No, no. Sit down."

Finally, Mamie came back into the room. She said, "Danny, I've got to tell you the truth. Our granddaughter wanted so much to meet you. We thought she could get out of school early, at eleven-thirty, but they wouldn't let her go. I hope you don't mind waiting."

So that was the mystery of why the President of the United States was so doggedly keeping me there. The little girl came in at about one o'clock, we had a fine time together, and then I left—with Ike and Mamie's thanks.

On the way out, the press corps swarmed around me, saying, "What was it about, Danny?"

I said, "Classified, fellows."

Between Eisenhower and Bush, I knew and entertained every president—with the exception of Richard Nixon. Jack Kennedy, Lyndon Johnson, Gerald Ford, Jimmy Carter, Ronald Reagan. Each had his own special sense of humor and seemed to enjoy some of my routines more than others.

Possibly because of his own medical problems with his back, President Kennedy relished my stories in which I teased my orthopedist. Some examples of lines that made Kennedy laugh: "When my arthritis in my elbow was bothering me, I said, 'Doctor, it hurts when I do that.' The doctor said, 'Don't *do* that.' " . . . "When I told the doctor I had pain in my left leg, he said, 'It's age.' I said, 'Doctor, I respect your medical degrees and your standing in the profession, but my right leg is the same age as my left leg, and the right leg doesn't hurt.' "

President Ford loved it when I teased my mother-in-law and father-in-law about being such big eaters: "When they came to the dinner table, it was like the Indianapolis 500—with spoons." . . . "One day, my father-in-law rushed into the dining room so fast, he got his false teeth in upside down. He like to chew off half of his head before he realized it."

Both President Truman and President Reagan seemed to laugh a lot at my routines in which I kidded Rose Marie for her dress-buying habits: "When Rosie buys a dress for an affair we have to go to, she always gets the dress two sizes too small. That means we all have to go on a diet so she can fit into the dress. We eat a lot of sprouts with vinegar and lemon juice, and we walk around all puckered up. My boy's belts don't fit him anymore and his pants fall down. . . . When I started out in show business, I worked for one dollar a night, just to eat. Now I make a thousand times more, and I *don't* eat."

President Johnson always loved my remarks about how women are infinitely stronger than men: "Did you ever see a busload of widowers going through Europe?" He also liked my exaggerated stories about trying to keep up with my neighbors in Beverly Hills, like his friend, oil-millionaire Ed Pauley: "Mr. Pauley had Persian rugs on his floors. I had live Persians, lined up side-by-side, wall to wall. Cost me a dollar-forty an hour for every Persian."

So with all due respect to my good friend Bob Hope, he's not the only one who was able to make presidents laugh.

chapter

⋙27⋘

I enjoyed my work and I had wonderful times with my comedian friends. As George Burns has explained it, we used to meet regularly for lunch at the Hillcrest Country Club, where there was a special "comics' table" set aside for us to amuse one another and to tell show-business lies. It was probably as famous as the Algonquin Round Table for writers in New York.

Hillcrest was originally formed as a country club for Jewish people in the Beverly Hills–Los Angeles area, at a time when Jews were not admitted to Gentile clubs. After a while, the Hillcrest people decided that it was wrong for them, too, to practice discrimination, so they started admitting non-Jewish members. Uncle Abe proposed me, and I came in waving my check. They said, "Danny, wait a minute. We decided that if we're going to take Gentiles, we should take Gentiles who look like Gentiles." That story was printed in Harry Golden's newspaper, *The Carolina Israelite*. But I *was* taken in, and I was delighted. Most of my colleagues in show business were already there.

The conversations at the Hillcrest comics' table were hilarious—sometimes funnier than the shows we put on in public. For example, the impish George Burns would tell endless private stories about how he would harry his best friend, the sweet, affable Jack Benny. Typical was a tale about the time George and Gracie were in London for an appearance at the Palladium, and Jack phoned him from Beverly Hills to wish him well. In those days, making a transcontinental call would require the same time and patience as phoning Tibet or Zambia today. Not only that, but George was staying at the ultraswank Savoy Hotel, where they screen all calls and announce the caller to the guest before putting him through.

"Well," said George, puffing on his cigar, "the phone rang in my room and the operator said, 'Mr. Benny calling you from California.' I said, 'Put him on.' Jack came on the phone and before he could say more than 'Hello,' I said, 'Send up a corned beef on rye,' and I hung up the phone."

Continued George, as he related the story with another puff on his cigar, "I waited for Jack to call back, as I was certain he would. Sure enough, in about a half hour, the hotel operator was on the phone: 'Mr. Benny is on from California again, sir.' I said, 'Put him on,' and this time, before Jack could even speak, I said, 'And don't forget the mustard.' Then I hung up again."

By this time, Jack Benny, who was listening to the story, was laughing so hard that he almost fell to the floor. So was everyone else. But Jack was carrying on as if the victim of George's gag was someone else—not him.

I have my own personal true story about George. For his eighty-fifth birthday, my wife, Rosie, bought George a handsome black Japanese kimono with a dragon embroidered on it. She sent the kimono to George, and he wrote her a thank-you note as follows:

Dear Rosie:
    The kimono is beautiful. My girlfriend came over the other night and I ran upstairs and put it on. I came down the stairs and she looked up and said, 'Wow!' Then I opened the kimono, and she put on her hat and coat and went home.

Love,
George.

Steve Lawrence can be hilarious. He once broke us up by telling us about an experience he had with a cop outside the CBS Television studio in Los Angeles. Steve was a guest on the Carol Burnett Show that night, and he was late. He made an illegal left turn in his car from Fairfax Avenue and immediately was stopped by this big burly Los Angeles policeman.

Said Steve, "The cop asked me for my driver's license, and I frantically looked in all my pockets, but I didn't have it with me. I said, 'Officer, I forgot my license. But I'm Steve Lawrence and I'm appearing on the Carol Burnett show tonight—in about a half hour, in fact.'

"The cop said, 'Oh, yeah. You *look* like Steve Lawrence, but how do I know you *are* Steve Lawrence?' I was beginning to panic. I didn't know what to do. I knew they were waiting for me inside, but all my identification was in my wallet along with my license, which I'd left at home. In desperation, I picked up my script for that night's show and I said, 'Look, officer, here's my script.' The cop sniffed. *'Anyone* can have a script,' he said.

"I said, 'Okay, I guess the only way to prove to you that I'm Steve Lawrence, is to read to you my lines in this script, which I've memorized, and you read the lines of the person who's talking to me.' The person who was talking to me in the script was Carol Burnett.

"The cop picked up the script and said okay. So here, right in the middle of Fairfax Avenue was this big guy with the deep bass voice reading lines like 'Darling, you're so late for dinner,' and 'Sweetheart, you better go in and have a look at the children.' A crowd began to gather and I said to the cop, 'Those are Carol Burnett's lines. Could you read them a little louder?' He raised his voice to a bellow, saying, 'Darling, things don't seem to be the same between us anymore.' By now, the crowd was going to pieces, laughing. The embarrassed cop finally realized I was who I said I was, and that he had been had—and he let me go."

Those pals of mine really are quick-witted—and one of the quickest-witted is Joey Bishop. As I said, he always reminded me of dear Mrs. Feldman of my childhood, who was also very sharp with the unexpected ad-lib. There's a classic story about Joey and his very good friend the late Sammy Davis, Jr., whom we all loved very much.

It seems that Sammy bought himself a new car, a Rolls-Royce, and he said to Joey, "Let's drive it up to Las Vegas, break it in, and have a little fun when we get there." Joey said, "Sure," and he and Sammy took off up Interstate 15 from Los Angeles to Las Vegas.

Sammy, of course, had only one eye because of a horrible car accident several years ago, but he was a good driver and was humming along the highway with his new toy. Apparently, he was humming along too fast, because a California

Highway Patrolman stopped the Rolls before they got to the Nevada border, where the cops are less strict.

The California trooper recognized Sammy immediately and he said, "I'm sorry, Mr. Davis, but you were really exceeding the speed limit. Can I see your driver's license, please?" He took the license from Sammy and pulled out his pen to write a citation. That's when Joey got into the act. His hand shot out and grapped the policeman's arm. "What are you writing?" he said. "The man's got only one eye. What do you want him to watch—the road or the speedometer?" The cop broke up and Sammy never got the ticket.

I myself was the object of Joey's sharp wit on several occasions. Once, we were both entered in Bob Hope's golf tournament in Palm Springs. We got out to the country club early, and we each got a bucket of balls to practice our swings. I began with a seven-iron. I swung so hard that the club slipped out of my grip and sailed about fifty feet down the fairway. Joey said, "What are you worrying about with all your money. Just get yourself another bucket of clubs."

One of Joey's sharpest ad libs came when I was M.C.'ing a show at The Sands Hotel in Las Vegas. Joey was on the bill and I gave him a super-flattering introduction. Then I gave him a little love-tap on the cheek and said, "Go get 'em, kid." Joey looked up at the audience and said, "You all saw it folks. An Arab hit a Jew."

The crowd was howling with laughter, but I couldn't let Joey get away with it. I said, "You're trying to make an anti-Semite out of me? Look what I have here." In my pocket was a cigarette lighter with the blue-and-white Star of David on it. A novelty salesman from Philadelphia had given it to me that afternoon. When I flicked the lighter on, it played "Hatikvah," the national anthem of Israel.

Joey didn't let the music finish. He said, "When El Rancho Vegas burned down and the firemen investigated the fire at the hotel, they couldn't find gasoline or rags or anything else that looked like arson. But they kept hearing a funny sound." And Joey gave a perfect piping rendition of "Hatikvah," exactly as it was played by my cigarette lighter.

I'm a collector of show-business ad-libs, and this rat-a-tat exchange by Joey ranks as one of the best. Another one also took place at The Sands. I M.C.'ed the annual anniversary show there and that particular year, there was quite a collection of talent on the stage and the performance went on forever. There was Frank Sinatra (who I introduced as "the master of all he surveys"), Sammy Davis, Jr. ("Pound for pound, the best entertainer in the country"), Dean Martin, Joey Bishop, Desi Arnaz, Red Skelton, and many, many more. It got to be a wild, hilarious night, with all of us ending up on the stage at once. There were so many people in the audience that there was absolutely no aisle space. I began to wonder if the Las Vegas Fire Department was on vacation. If anybody in the audience wanted to go to the bathroom, they'd have to walk over the tables.

I realized it really *was* getting late. So I said to Mr. Sinatra, our peerless leader, calling him by his nickname, "Cheech, we've been on for over two hours. Let's get off."

Sinatra said, "You're right, Jake. C'mon guys, let's go." They obeyed him then as they do now. But it was as they began to move offstage, that the greatest ad-lib in my memory occurred.

Dean Martin picked up Sammy Davis bodily, held him up to the audience, and said, "I want to thank the NAACP for this trophy."

I've never heard such a loud prolonged laugh from an audience.

The second best ad-lib in my experience came in the latter days of my *Danny Thomas Show* series when Marjorie Lord and I went to Europe to do several segments. The premise of these scripts was that Danny and Kathy Williams were on vacation and were keeping in touch with their kids back home by telephone. We did shows from Ireland, England, France, and Italy, with distinguished local guest talent.

One of the best of these was Noel Purcell, the great Abbey Players actor in Ireland. In that week's script, Kathy is visiting her relatives in the village of Lusk, near Dublin. Her uncle is played by the big, bluff, white bearded Purcell. He and the others take it for granted that I am Irish, too, calling me Danny Boy.

In a pub scene, Purcell announces, "My darling niece's Danny Boy is a fine singer in the pubs in America. Sing us a song, Danny Boy. I think for a moment and I say, "OK. This is the favorite song of my wife's father." I sing, "Are You Beautiful Because You're Irish, or Are You Irish Because You're Beautiful." Everyone cheers wildly. Then Purcell says, "It's only fittin' now that you sing the favorite song of your *own* dear father."

I am nonplussed, but I go over to the piano, strike a

chord in a minor key, and sing an Arabic song. It is authentic, from my own personal memory, but it sounds like a lot of wailing. That's supposed to be the end of the scene, designed to provoke a big laugh.

But then came the great ad-lib, from the mouth of Noel Purcell. He came over, tapped me on the shoulder, and said, "That's a fine tune, Danny Boy. Are there any words to that?"

That's the *real* show business.

chapter

The reason I did those episodes in Europe with Marjorie was because *The Danny Thomas Show* was in its eleventh year and the level of our premise-barrel was getting low. You can't keep using the same premises over and over again. Besides, we were all getting tired and wanted to go on to other things. So, although the ratings were still good, we decided to bring our series to an end in 1964.

How many other sitcoms in the history of television have lasted eleven years? Today, a five-year run is considered a great success, and they only do twenty-one or twenty-two shows a season. We did as many as thirty-nine a season.

So we reached the end of the road. But CBS ran a full season of reruns in prime time, from April to September 1965—the year after we went off the air. The show has been on the air, including its time in reruns, for thirty-five consecutive years—and it's still on.

The other Danny Thomas productions were still prospering, too. *The Dick Van Dyke Show, The Andy Griffith Show,*

Gomer Pyle, The Joey Bishop Show, and *The Real McCoys,* among others, were all on national TV. Nobody felt they had to run a charity benefit for me and my partner, Sheldon Leonard.

The year 1965 was also when Sheldon and I finally split up. It was a wholly amicable parting, and we have remained good friends to this day. We decided to split because Sheldon had developed a new television property to which he had to devote all his time. When you hear what it was, you'll understand why. It was a new series called *I Spy,* starring Bill Cosby and Robert Culp. Taking over for Sheldon in my company was my brilliant nephew, Ronnie Jacobs, my brother Ray's son. He had been handling business affairs for Danny Thomas Productions for some years—and still does.

We signed to do one-hour specials for NBC. Fun and profit for three years. Then Uncle Abe Lastfogel arranged for me to team up with Aaron Spelling in Thomas-Spelling Productions. This led to my becoming part owner of other fabulously successful shows such as *The Mod Squad.* As I said, things kept dropping in my lap.

One of the things Aaron and I did was *The Danny Thomas Hour,* which ran on NBC in 1967 and 1968. I produced and hosted. Every week, we did an hour of variety or serious drama, concentrating on drama. The writing was excellent, and our guests included terrific stars such as Richard Kiley, Anne Baxter, and Olivia De Havilland. I still harbored ambitions of becoming a character actor, but I limited myself to introducing each drama and serving as a kind of narrator. One of the ironies of television is that we were positioned in the TV schedule opposite my own Andy Griffith Show on CBS, at least for the first half hour. We got beaten by Andy in the ratings every week—except twice.

Those two ratings wins came about because I developed the idea of bringing back the *Make Room for Daddy* crowd for a couple of one-hour specials. The first one was *Make More Room for Daddy,* in which little red-headed Rusty has grown up (by this time, Rusty Hamer is about eighteen) and gets married. All the old cast was there—me, Marjorie Lord, Penney Parker, Angela Cartwright, Hans Conried—plus Joanna Taylor as my new daughter-in-law. We had a marvelous old-fashioned Lebanese wedding, with singing and dancing. Hans, as Uncle Tonoose, went crazy at the wedding, much as my real Uncle Tony would have, and he was simply wonderful. There must have been a lot of nostalgia in people to find out what happened to the old *Make Room for Daddy* bunch, because the ratings went through the roof. Almost half of the TV sets in America were tuned in to us.

The second ratings-buster came later in the season, when the segment of *The Danny Thomas Hour* was called *Make Room for Granddaddy.* It was the same cast, except Rusty and his TV-wife have presented me with a new grandson. Once again, we creamed Andy Griffith and the ABC opposition in the ratings. I guess everyone wanted to see how gruff-but-sentimental Danny Williams would deal with an infant showing up in the family.

The response was such that the network people and the ad agencies began to wonder if this old Phoenician and his troupe should be brought back as a regular series. In 1970,

Make Room for Granddaddy went into ABC's schedule as a weekly half-hour sitcom.

It wasn't easy this time. My grandson, now six, was played by one of the cutest kids in all creation, Michael Hughes, and I brought in a lot of friends to play themselves—Frank Sinatra, Milton Berle, Sammy Davis, Jr., Diana Ross. But ABC moved us around in the schedule from Wednesday night to Thursday night and we died. So did the shows of Henry Fonda and Shirley MacLaine, which took over Wednesday night. The ways of network programmers are weird indeed.

But we had other problems as well. People in the audience complained that Marjorie Lord and I both looked younger than we did when we were newlyweds, and that we were unbelievable as grandparents. (I must confess that I now was tinting my hair black and had grown long youthful sideburns.) And then there was poor Rusty Hamer. I had always said Rusty was the best boy actor I'd ever worked with, but in *Make Room for Granddaddy,* he was an adult and much of the youthful ebullience was gone.

That happens to many child actors when they grow up, but Rusty took it harder than most. I had kept using Rusty as an actor, but other producers didn't. According to his brother, the boy was bitter and depressed after *Make Room for Granddaddy* folded, and he dropped out of sight in Southwestern Louisiana, where he had a series of odd jobs working in the oil fields and delivering newspapers. On January 18, 1990, he committed suicide by shooting himself in the head. He was only forty-two. It was one of the saddest days of my life when I read that in the newspapers.

247

He *had* been my surrogate son, and I had loved him the way I loved my own Tony.

But to go back to happier times, *Make Room for Grand-daddy* was profitable, even though it was on the air for only one season. It helped me develop an entire new line of grandfather jokes for my nightclub act—which I kept doing, maybe as an insurance policy, all through my years of success in television.

Another reason for my new grandfather routines was that I actually *became* one, thanks to my second daughter, Terre—she of the beautifully sweet singing voice, like her mother's. Terre sang in grade school, she sang in high school, and she sang in college. Now she wanted to sing in the clubs.

I had learned my lesson with Marlo. No hairy stories for Terre about the perils facing a young woman wanting to make a go of it in show business. If she wanted a career as a singer, so be it. And she was good. Her voice always reminded me of Peggy Lee.

And we, as a family, gave Terre all the help we could. Marlo used her in an episode of her show, *That Girl,* playing the important role of a singing nun. The director, John Rich, thought up a gag for that show that's still talked about in the TV world. Without any announcement, he sneaked me into the show as a priest who, in one scene, is accidentally jostled by Marlo. She says, "Oh, excuse me, Father," and I say, "That's all right, my child." My ugly face, of course, was instantly recognized by the audience, working with my *own* child—in fact, two of them. I'm told that that episode has been replayed on the air more than any other segment of *That Girl.*

With Terre's singing voice constantly improving, I made her my opening act at The Sands in Las Vegas and at Harrah's in Lake Tahoe. I treated her like any other singer I ever worked with—Lena Horne, Diana Trask—coming onstage and saying, "Welcome to the Danny Thomas Show—and here's Terre Thomas." After that, she was on her own, singing three or four songs with the full orchestra. Terre got good reviews, she kept gaining confidence, and agents were talking about booking her into clubs as just plain Terre Thomas.

But then romance reared its lovely head—just as it had with Terre's mother, who met me when *her* singing career was taking off. In Terre's case, it was a young man named Larry Gordon, who was in the music publishing business. He came up to see her when Terre was appearing with me at Harrah's. I must say she looked irresistible in that glamorous setting, wearing her beautiful gowns. They had been going together, and Larry finally popped the question. Rosie and I gave them our blessing, and they were married a short time later.

It's amazing how history repeats itself. Terre gave up all thoughts of continuing with her singing career, just as Rosie had done, and she settled into the roles of housewife and mother. A few years later, she presented us with our first grandchild, Dionne, named after Dionne Warwick. Then came our first grandson, Jason. Unhappily, Terre's marriage ended in divorce (there was also an annulment from the Church), but Terre has remained a super mom to this day—an accomplishment which I consider as important as the successes of my other children. It is only lately—with Dionne and Jason grown up—that

Terre is resuming her singing career, and I have no doubt that she'll go far.

But it was the birth of little Dionne twenty years ago which caused me my greatest excitement. I was *playing* at being a grandfather in *Make Room for Granddaddy,* but this was the real thing. It led to one of my most successful nightclub routines—like so many other things that came out of my own personal life and experience.

All of what I said in that grandfather routine is true. I started with a quotation I had read in an old magazine: "A father is a man who gives his daughter to another man who isn't half good enough, so they can give him grandchildren who are twice as good as anybody's." Then I went into a long recitation of how boring grandfathers always had been to me.

Once there was a guy who sat next to me on a plane, while I was trying to read *Playboy*—which I read for the same reason that I read *National Geographic:* I like to look at places I'm never gonna visit. Anyway, while I'm concentrating on the photography in *Playboy,* this guy next to me pulls out sixteen snapshots of his new grandson, the ugliest wrinkled mutt you've ever seen. "Isn't he handsome," he kept saying. "Don't you think he looks like me?" All I did was to try to keep reading my *Playboy.* Every boring experience with a grandfather seemed to be just like that.

"Not me," I said to myself when Terre became pregnant. "Not old Sophisticated Sam here."

Oh yeah?

There I was in the waiting room while Terre was in labor, just as nervous as the young expectant fathers, pacing up and down. I said to one boy, "Don't worry, son, the Lord's on your side. What do you want, a boy or a girl?" I got the stock answer, "I don't care."

Then the nurse showed him his baby through the glass and yelled, "It's a boy." He said, "I know it's a boy, but a boy *what?*" I never saw a kid go into shock the way he did.

Finally it was my turn, and Sophisticated Sam was just like all the other grandfathers I hadn't been able to stand. The baby was red and wrinkled, with long black hair, but to me, she was the most beautiful thing in the world, gorgeous as a model in baby-food commercials.

Then they let me hold my grandchild in the first hour of her life. You think you're a man of the world, you think you're sophisticated. But wait, Buddy, wait until this happens to you. I held her ever so gently. I was trembling. I was afraid I'd break her. Then, as I held her, I could feel that little heart beating against my chest, my child's child. A feeling which I'll take to my grave.

Then the doctor broke the silence: "She resembles you quite a bit, Mr. Thomas." I wanted to hit him in the mouth. Then I realized I was holding the baby upside down.

So was I as bad as all those other guys I used to make fun of?

Nah! Worse!

The birth of a baby is a wonderful thing. But some people feel differently—namely my blessed mother-in-law, who at the age of eighty-two insisted that her doctor give her birth control pills. She had so many of them around the house that she could have sterilized her entire bridge club.

Her doctor said to her, "Mrs. Cassaniti, you don't need those pills at your age."

She said, "They make-a me sleep good."

The doctor said, "But Mrs. Cassaniti, they're not sleeping pills. You don't need them."

She said, "Don't you tell me. I tell you. I gotta granddaughter, eighteen-years-old, she looks like Gina Lollobrigida. Every morning, when she gotta date, I slip one of these in her orange juice. And every night, I sleep like a baby."

My Rosie had the greatest birth-control method ever. She pretended she was asleep. Now *I* pretend I'm asleep. Unfortunately, most of the time I'm not pretending. I guess *my* biological clock's telling me I need sleep!

But I digress. I was talking about my first granddaughter. I even wrote a song for the new baby—"Dionne"—which I sang on the Merv Griffin Show, then on the Lennon Sisters Show with Jimmy Durante.

And I was just as insufferable when the next four grandchildren came along—Terre's Jason, and Tony's Tracy, Kristina, and Kathryn.

chapter

In addition to deriving new material from my experiences with my family, I was still using my tried-and-true method of picking up short jokes and expanding them into one of my long drawn-out stories. Just as when I was first getting started at the 5100 Club in Chicago, the ideas would come from anywhere—a chance encounter on the street, an old friend or a total stranger telling me about something he had heard at a party the night before.

One of Marlo's favorite Danny Thomas routines, for example, originated with my barber, Harry Gelbart. If you remember, I had given Harry's brilliant son, Larry Gelbart, his first writing job—and Harry seems to have been repaying me ever since by telling me every joke he has heard—while I am a captive in his barber chair. One day, Harry told me a joke about a parrot, which took him all of two minutes to relate.

I said to myself, "Hey, wait a minute. In those few sentences, there's the germ of an idea that I could build up to eight or nine minutes on the stage." It was not for nothing that Jackie Miles used to kid me for my propensity to drag things out in an amusing fashion.

So I thought about my barber's parrot joke for a long time, and this is what came out (the short version):

This old Jewish man is walking down a street in his Midwestern hometown, and he happens to pass a small pet store. It's a very warm night, and the door of the pet store is wide open. And through the open door, out into the night air, there comes to this man's ears a familiar strain of music. He slackens his pace, and he hears chanting. *(I do the voice of a cantor chanting the liturgy of a Sabbath evening prayer in the synagogue.)* The man stands still in his tracks. This is the chant of his favorite prayer. And the chanting continues. *(I do more chanting.)*

The man walks, as though hypnotized, toward that pet store. He stands in the doorway, amazed, in awe of what he sees and hears. The chanting *(I chant)* is coming from a parrot. And I say, incredible though it might be, there was this parrot chanting those sacred and semi-sacred Hebraic hymns. The man decided then and there that he had to have that parrot. It was costly, but whatever its price, please the Lord, the man could afford it. And buy it he did.

He took it home and every night the parrot would chant to him. Sometimes simple little Sabbath hymns like *(I chant),* sometimes more complicated ancient Hebrew chants. The man was so happy he could hardly wait for the High Holidays to come.

Finally it was the week of Rosh Hashanah, the holy Hebrew New Year. Off the man goes to the tailor shop, and he has a little *tallis*—a prayer shawl—made for the parrot. He also orders a little black *yarmulke*—a skull cap—made for the parrot. The Pope wears a white *yarmulke (in the long version I go into an aside about the Pope's skull caps).* With the parrot outfitted, the man has an identical *tallis* and *yarmulke* made for himself. Like mother and daughter lookalikes, they come out father and bird.

The big day, Rosh Hashanah, arrives, and off they go to the synagogue. The spritely old man is running up the steps, with the bird following closely behind. They get to the front door and are stopped by the *shamus.* A *shamus* is like a sexton. He takes care of the temple, also takes the tickets on high holidays. The *shamus* sees this incredible sight and says, "Wait. Where are you going with the green chicken?"

The man says, "Dummkopf, that's not a chicken. That's a parrot, a talking bird. That bird don't just talk. That bird could *daven.*" This is the Hebrew word for chanting prayers. The man goes on, "That bird could chant the prayers better than you, the cantor, and the whole congregation put together." Naturally from the *shamus* comes the most inevitable of all clichés: "put the money where the mouth is." They make a small bet. While they're wagering, other members of the congregation come up and want to get in on the action. Before you know it, there's four hundred dollars bet against the parrot's capacity to *daven.* The old man says, "You crazy? You lost already the bet. Wait, you'll hear."

Now he says to the parrot, "Sweetheart, make a chant." *(I bend down on the stage and people tell me they actually can visualize the parrot.)* The old man says, "Go ahead. Make a chant. Don't be nervous. Say anything. I'll start you off." *(I chant.)* But not a peep comes out of the parrot. Not even "Polly wants a matzo." Nothing. The old man is disconsolate. He loses the bet. He can't wait for the services to be over.

He goes home, throws the bird on the floor, goes into the kitchen, gets the biggest butcher knife he can find, and starts to sharpen it. In comes the parrot. It looks up at the old man and says, "What you doing?" The old man says, "You got back the voice, huh, chicken? What I'm doing? For the four hundred dollars you lost me—you wouldn't even make one chant—I'm gonna take that knife and cut off your head." The parrot says, "No, wait. Wait. Wait for Yom Kippur, the next holiday. We'll get bigger odds."

Forgive me for telling this story at such length, but I wanted you to have at least one verbatim account of the kind of thing that kept me going in show business for so many years. It's not Milton Berle, it's not Bob Hope, it's not anybody else who tells fast one-liner jokes for a living. What it is is typical Danny Thomas storytelling.

All this was for my nightclub act, of course. In television, the shows I did were mostly scripted by other people. I didn't want to use my own material on TV because that might result in my giving my entire act away in a single night. It's different in nightclubs, where you tell the same stories over and over again, and people can't wait to hear them—often mouthing the familiar punch lines before you can say them. Red Skelton actually used to place cards on the tables in nightclubs, listing his stories, with boxes for people to check to indicate which they wanted to hear.

But I certainly kept active in television—along with my endless rounds of benefits for the now-rapidly-growing St.

Jude Hospital. In TV, during this period, I hosted specials for NBC—about two or three of them a year. One of them, *Danny Goes Country* (with the great country singer Eddie Arnold as my co-star), garnered the highest rating in television to that date. Another did almost as well and was, to my way of thinking, the best variety show ever done on the air. It was *The Wonderful World of Burlesque.* Among the people walking on and off the stage were Frank Sinatra, Dean Martin, and Jack Benny. I told some of the stories I remembered from watching Abe Reynolds at the old Empire Burlesque when I was a boy in Toledo.

A third memorable special of that time was a show celebrating the fortieth anniversary of the Coconut Grove, the famous old Los Angeles nightclub. Jimmy Durante was in it, along with Eddie Fisher and Joey Bishop. I loved Jimmy and it was wonderful working with him—comparing nose sizes and all. I heard one of the great stories about Durante while we were working together on that show—and I still tell it.

It seems that Jimmy and his beloved wife Marge had gone to a party and Jimmy became enthralled with a gadget in the front door of the house. It wasn't just a peephole to look out and see who was there; it was a little hinged door, with a barred grill—like the old-time speakeasies had.

Jimmy said to his wife, "Marge, I want one of them at home."

Marge said, "For God's sake, why?"

Jimmy said, "Because when I'm home alone and somebody rings da bell, I could open da little door, and if I don't want to talk to 'em, I could say 'Durante ain't home.' "

Durante actually thought that his unique gravelly voice was undistinguishable from anyone else's. He was a great man, never turning me down for a St. Jude benefit, and now that he's gone, he remains memorable in my mind.

So does Lucille Ball. She was a lovely lady and the greatest comic actress of all time. No one could improvise slapstick like she did. I think the funniest one-hour TV comedy I ever did was a Westinghouse special called *Lucy Makes Room for Daddy.* You may remember it. It was one of her classics.

The premise of the show was that Desi was going to Hollywood to make a movie, and he and Lucy leased their house to me and my wife, Kathy. But the movie was postponed, and with us in their house, Desi and Lucy had to move in with the Mertzes, next door. But Lucy couldn't stand being away from her own house, so she kept coming in to water the plants, pick up her mail, and so on. The whole thing turned out to be a hilarious comedy of errors, with Lucy wandering into my bedroom while I was asleep to steal a check to force me into default; me thinking she was Kathy and slapping her on the rump and nuzzling her; Kathy walking in and seeing us—the whole thing ending up in a huge brouhaha, with an ensuing court action. Never did I have more fun in my life than I did in that hour. Lucy's improvisations were brilliant.

So that was Danny Thomas, the TV performer. Danny Thomas, the producer and TV executive, was still going strong. In addition to *Mod Squad,* Aaron Spelling and I picked up two Walter Brennan shows, *Tycoon* and *The Guns of Will Sonnett* (a fair-sized hit). We also did a show starring Tim Conway.

The Conway series didn't work, but Tim provided me with some great laughs offstage, usually in the corridors of our production company. I'd run into him in the hall, and I'd say to him—the same as I would to anyone—"How are ya, Tim?" The problem was that he would always *tell* me, in great detail: "Well, I've got a boil on my neck, and yesterday I had a stomachache, and this morning I woke with a hacking cough." And so on and so on. I'd continue down the hall, with Tim following close behind. It got to be a running gag with us. Finally I shortened my greeting to just "Hi!" It didn't help. He looked at me cunningly and said, "Do you really want to know?" and, without waiting for an answer, he started all over again.

Ah, the idiosyncracies of the performer! I'm as bad as the rest. I was actually hurt when Don Rickles never insulted me the way he did everyone else while he was doing his act. I said to a mutual friend, "Doesn't Rickles like me? How come he never picks on me?" Apparently the message got through. The next time I walked into the Las Vegas lounge where Rickles was appearing, he boomed out at me, "Well, look who's here. It's Moses with a cigar." And he never failed to insult me since.

So in a minor way, I had tacked on another item to my list of accomplishments in life.

Like any insecure performer, I wondered what would be next.

The answer, surprisingly, was in my own home.

chapter

⟫⟫⟫ 30 ⟪⟪⟪

Who would have thought that my youngest child, Tony, would have turned out to be as spectacularly successful as he did? He grew up like any normal boy, mostly interested in sports and rock music. When he was a little guy, I used to bring him to the set to play with Rusty Hamer. Later, he came to the set on his own, keenly interested in what I was doing, both as an actor and a producer. When I performed at The Sands in Las Vegas, he almost always came along. He'd watch my show, then sit with me as I cooled out afterwards having a 4 A.M. snack of Chinese food. Tony always listened avidly to my analysis of what had worked in my act and what hadn't, though he had trouble just keeping himself awake. I wanted all my children to find their own ways in life—as I had done—so I no longer pressed them to tell me what their ambitions were. But one night at The Sands, Tony blurted it out: "I want to go into show business, but I can't sing, I can't dance, I can't act, I can't tell jokes." I said, "That's quite a handicap, son—but you'll find *something."* As was my habit, I then put it out of my mind.

The next thing I knew, Tony had formed a rock band. He was the drummer. I remember two of his buddies who were also in the group: David Goldsmith and Bobby Wallerstein. The kids hung quilts and blankets all over the inside of our garage to block out the sound, and that's where they rehearsed. It was then that a former favor for a friend came back to haunt me. A couple of years before, Ed Sullivan's daughter, Betty, had been attending U.C.L.A. and one of the faculty members asked, "If any of you knows an entertainer who can make an appearance here, put up your hand." All show-business kids can't resist putting up their hands in cases like this. Once, Marlo offered me as a way of getting Red Skelton for an appearance at her high school, and Red, a nice man, got me off the hook and did about ten minutes of his act at the school.

When Betty Sullivan put up her hand at U.C.L.A., she said, "My dad knows Danny Thomas. I can get *him.*" The next thing I knew, I got a phone call from Ed in New York. He said, and these are his exact words, "How would you like a father to stand ten feet tall in the eyes of his daughter?" He explained about Betty raising her hand, and I said, "Okay, Ed, I'll do it."

Now it's two years later, and my son, Tony, thinks his rock group is ready for the big time. He comes to me and says, "You gotta help me get on the *Ed Sullivan Show.*" Ed's show was still a big-time television showcase. I said, "Well, your sister never lets me interfere with her career." Tony said, "I don't care about that nepotism crap. I want to get on that show." He must have been all of sixteen then.

So I called Ed Sullivan and I said, in Ed's exact words, "How would you like to make a father stand ten feet tall in the eyes of his son?" Ed immediately remembered his debt to me and said, "Okay, but will you come on the show and introduce Tony?" I said I couldn't get away to New York, but Ed put Tony and his group on the show, anyway.

Despite this enormous boost, Tony's combo made one record, which never got anywhere. It was a teenage dream that didn't work. The next thing I knew, Tony was studying theater arts, cinema, and television at U.S.C. He was the third of my three kids to attend that fine university. My granddaughter, Dionne, goes to U.C.L.A., U.S.C.'s archrival, which forces me to question my loyalties when I go to U.S.C.-U.C.L.A. football and basketball games.

When Tony got out of college, he asked if he could come to work for me in my production company. I said, "Sure, but in this business, everybody's got to start in the same place—the mail room." That didn't faze him. I was partnered with Aaron Spelling at the time, and we were doing *Mod Squad* as well as *Make Room for Granddaddy.* I also had acquired the TV rights to *Captain Newman, M.D.,* from the author, my friend Leo Rosten. We were making the pilot for a series, but in the crazy ways of television, my long-ago writer, Larry Gelbart, was simultaneously making a pilot for a show called *M*A*S*H.* We both wanted Alan Alda for the lead role. Needless to say, *M*A*S*H* won out over *Captain Newman, M.D.* They not only caught Alda but also caught the brass ring of television. It was a smash hit on the tube for years.

In any event, with all this going on in our company at

Paramount Pictures, Tony received a rapid TV education. Eventually, he came to me and said, "I want to be promoted from the mail room, maybe to assistant to the producer of one of our shows." I said, "There's no opening here for such a job. Son or no son, you just don't throw somebody out."

To his credit, Tony applauded me for this antinepotism statement, and in almost the same words his sister, Marlo, had used years before, he said, "Actually, Dad, if I'm going to make it in this business, I want to do it on my own."

I said, "You're right, Tony, but if you end up with a partner, just make sure its a relationship like the one I had with Sheldon Leonard."

That's exactly what happened. Tony went to work at Columbia Pictures, where he became the assistant to Paul Junger Witt, who was, to Tony, exactly what Sheldon Leonard had been to me. Paul is an extremely bright young man, who, at the time Tony joined him, was doing a Civil War series called *The Young Rebels.* Their next project after that was one of the finest TV movies ever made—*Brian's Song.* It was a true story about two football players with the Chicago Bears—one black, one white—named Gale Sayers and Brian Piccolo. Piccolo develops cancer, which eventually takes his life. The entire film is about the unique relationship between these two men, and how the dying Piccolo's illness affects the entire team. Critic Leonard Maltin calls it, "A milestone of excellence in made-for-TV movies."

What happened to Tony after that is nothing short of miraculous. He *did* become Paul Witt's formal partner in Witt-Thomas Productions—later to be joined by a fine writer, Susan Harris, in Witt-Thomas-Harris Productions. They did *Soap* and *Benson.* Among their more recent TV series are *The Golden Girls, Empty Nest,* and *Beauty and the Beast.* In the last Emmys, they got no less than thirty-nine nominations. Their one movie last year was *Dead Poets Society,* starring Robin Williams, which won the Oscar for best writing.

I'm proud of all my children, but I have a special respect for Tony, who made it the hard way. There's no tougher, more dog-eat-dog field than TV and movie production. I know.

Throughout all this, Tony remains my loving, respectful son, which is par for the course in Lebanese immigrant families—even to the third and fourth generations. He has given me three more darling grandchildren, Tracy, Kristina, and Katie; and his wife, Glenn, is an integral part of the family. Many of the holiday dinners are at Tony and Glenn's house. She's a great cook. She makes the greatest pumpkin soup in the entire world.

Tony gets very sentimental about expressing our family ties. About five or six years ago, he and Paul Witt moved their operation to the same old Desilu Cahuenga lot, where I had done *Make Room for Daddy* and most of the other Thomas-Leonard shows.

Tony said, "I looked around that studio courtyard, where I spent so much time with you when I was a boy, and I looked at Paul Witt, realizing that we have the same brotherly relationship that you had with Sheldon Leonard."

Then Tony started talking about the route he followed going to the studio every day. He lives on the same street that we did when he was a child—Elm Drive in Beverly Hills. Tony said, "I go exactly the same way you did when I was a little boy sitting next to you in the car. I never vary it. It's funny, but as I drive, I can see *your* hands on the steering wheel, going down Melrose Avenue to the studio. Today, I think of you a lot as I follow that same route on Melrose. I'm under the same pressures now that you were then, and I can understand now why sometimes you were a little grumpy, and what must have been going through your mind when there were problems on your show. Knowing how it all came out for you, it reassures me. There's a lot of comforting nostalgia for me as I drive every day along Melrose."

I'm afraid I loused up Tony's feelings of nostalgia and sentimentality.

I said, "I didn't drive on Melrose, I went on Willoughby."

To this day, it's Tony's favorite story. Another treacle-cutter.

chapter

The sense of family was so strongly instilled in my three
children that I was deeply touched—though not surprised—when they teamed up to do something for me that
I won't forget as long as I live.

They grew up knowing all about that old Lebanese tradition. My eight brothers and their wives were constantly in
our lives—either as visitors or as workers in my operations.
My sister, Emily, lived with us for years. My son, Tony,
thought of his Aunt Emily much as I had thought of my
Aunt Julia. He remembers Emily as the matriarch of our
household, a master cook who kept surprising us with ex-
quisite Arabic dishes. He kept saying, "Someone should
write down Aunt Emily's recipes, so we can keep them in
the family after she dies." Unfortunately, no one ever did.

Later, Emily and her husband, Ed, lived on the 116-acre
farm which I had bought as a weekend retreat for the family
in Beaumont, California. I called it the "Big Muz Ranch,"
after my Arabic name, Muzyad. When I no longer had time

for weekend retreats, I turned the Big Muz over to Emily and Ed to inhabit as they pleased. They both spent their last years there.

But back to what my three kids did for me. It was 1976. My Danny Thomas Productions was kind of dormant, mostly because I was so heavily involved in nightclubs and St. Jude activities, so Tony and Paul Witt operated it for a while. They did some successful TV movies (like *Blood Sport* with Gary Busey; *Griffin and Phoenix* with Peter Falk and Jill Clayburgh; *Satan's Triangle* with Kim Novak) which came out under my banner.

Then Tony and Peter were approached by a very good writer, Steve Gordon, who later did Dudley Moore's smash movie, *Arthur.* Gordon, who was from my hometown Toledo, wanted to do a television series about an old Toledo doctor, now practicing in New York's Puerto Rican neighborhood. His Dr. Jules Bedford character definitely was of the old school. He made house calls; he treated people whether they could afford to pay him or not. As counterpoint, he had a son, Dr. David Bedford, who had a lucrative Park Avenue practice, and couldn't understand what he thought were his father's rather outmoded ideas about administering health care.

Tony came to me, told me about Steve Gordon's premise, and said, "Dad, we want to do this."

I said, "Fine. And I would like to play the part of the old doctor."

Tony said, "Come on, Dad. You're sixty-three years old. Do you really want to go back to working five tough days a week?"

I said, "That would be great. You know I always wanted to be a character actor. This part might be it."

Tony shook his head in disbelief. "You're *sure* you want to do it?"

"Yeah," I said, putting on my last angry man act, which I was before Alan King came along.

Still shaking his head, Tony went away, saying, "I'll talk to NBC about it."

The next day, he came back and said, "They don't want you."

I said, "NBC doesn't *want* me. That's impossible."

He said, "Dad, you haven't done a series in six years. The NBC people see you in a tuxedo, with the red handkerchief in your breast pocket, and 'Good evening, ladies and gentlemen,' and you do a stint on the nightclub floor. They don't see you as an old fuddy-duddy."

I said, "Fine. Then I'll stop tinting the hair black, and let the gray grow back, maybe use a little bleach to make the hair more white. Great. I'll play the part."

Tony said, "But they don't want you, Dad. They don't see you in this character. They want our company to produce the series—but with some other actor."

He must have seen the hurt in my face, "Let me give it another shot. We'll talk again tomorrow."

The next day he came back and said, "You know, Dad, Robert Young tested two or three times before they gave him the Dr. Welby part. Even Marlon Brando has to do screen tests occasionally."

I said, "What are you getting at?"

He said, "Are you willing to go to New York and do a test for this part?"

He was positive that after all my years in the business, I would consider it demeaning to be tested on film or tape, like a newcomer. He nearly fell over when I said, "I'll be happy to test for the part." Tony still couldn't believe it, but he went out and got me some airline tickets.

When he handed me the tickets, he said, "Marlo will be waiting for you at the airport in New York." At this point I became aware that my children had something in the works. Marlo was living in New York, where she had been making movies ever since *That Girl* had gone off the air. She had just finished a film called *Thieves* with Charles Grodin.

When she met me in New York, Marlo kissed me and said, "Let's not waste any time. We've got three days to prepare you for this test."

I said, "Prepare? What prepare? I was acting in movies while you were still wetting your pants."

She said, "But Daddy, this is different. You never had a part like this before. So Chuck Grodin is going to coach you, and then he'll direct the test."

Charles Grodin was already a big-name actor/director on the stage. In fact, he was doing a play on Broadway at that time.

I said, "Hey, wait a minute. Who's paying for this test? Is it NBC?"

She said, "No, Daddy. Tony, Terre, and I are paying for it. It's our present to you for all you've done for us."

From my experience as a producer, I knew the cost of these things. "But that's forty or fifty thousand dollars out of your own pockets."

"Don't worry about it," said Marlo. I hugged her and I cried.

So I went to work with Grodin. Tony had given me a ten-minute scene from Steve Gordon's script, and we slaved over it in my hotel room—even on Chuck's matinee day. He's a skilled director, and I learned a lot about serious acting from him. When he thought I was ready, we went to a studio and taped it. Grodin seemed pleased. I learned later that he didn't charge my kids a nickel for his intensive work.

When we finished the taping, Marlo hugged me and kissed me and said "Okay, Daddy, go home. Chuck and I are going to do the editing." They were up all night until the tape was ready for presentation to the network. I flew back home.

I didn't learn until later what happened next. In the morning, Marlo called her contact at NBC's New York headquarters and said, "I want to come over. I have a tape I want you to see." The NBC people got all excited. They thought Marlo wanted to show them a project for *herself*— and ever since *That Girl,* all three networks would give anything to get her back in a series.

She showed them the tape, and they were totally confused. They said, "My God, is that your father?" Marlo said, "That's my daddy." They didn't recognize me with my white hair and bushy moustache.

Marlo then asked, "Is there anyone else who should see this?" Dave Tebbett, a top NBC executive and friend for years, was brought in. Marlo said, "My dad wants to play this part, and no one thinks he can. But this tape proves he can, and it proves what a fine actor he really is." They reran the tape for Tebbett, and he agreed. So did Antonowsky.

Happily, Marlo went on, "Is there anybody else who needs to vote on this?"

"No," everyone said. "If Danny wants it, it's his."

Marlo ran down into the street, found a pay phone, and made what she still calls the most thrilling call of her life. When I picked up the ringing phone, my daughter said, "Daddy, you got the part!".

Back in Los Angeles, Tony came running into my office with a telegram from NBC, which he had had framed. The telegram stated that NBC was buying the show, "with the understanding that Danny Thomas has to be in every episode." The NBC people in Los Angeles—who had turned me down—were dumbfounded. But they had to put the series, called *The Practice,* into production.

The Practice was a good show—one that I'm proud of. The critics liked it. Old Dr. Bedford was a fascinating character, absentminded, gruff, angry at society. If a man came in with a slight cold, he'd say, "Get outta here. I got sick people to take care of. Go home. Go to bed." My snooty doctor-son was played by David Spielberg; his wife was Shelley Fabares; my nurse was Dena Dietrich; Didi Conn was my dingbat receptionist. All in all, a good cast, with good scripts. But those were the days of the Big Slump at NBC, and it was hard for them to counter the fluff shows on the other networks, such as ABC's *Charlie's Angels.*

It doesn't matter that *The Practice* lasted only one year on the network.

What matters is what my blessed children did to help me.

chapter

⟫≫32≪⟪

I didn't fret too much about the short life span of *The Practice*—I'd be lying if I didn't say I fretted a *little*. But it did set my mind back to thinking about the great Al Jolson.

In my opinion, Jolson was one of the finest entertainers of all time. The instant he stepped out on a stage, there was electricity in the air. You knew something terribly exciting was going to happen, and it usually did. No one could raise an audience to a fever pitch the way Jolson did, just by singing a song or chatting up the crowd. Frank Sinatra has the same effect on audiences today.

The first time I met Jolson was back in World War II, when Uncle Abe Lastfogel had brought me out to California for the first time, for my stint on the Fanny Brice radio show. Uncle Abe got me a four-week guest card at the Hillcrest Country Club so I could play golf, and he personally took me to the club so I could meet the other show people who hung out there. We sat at a table with George Jessel, George Burns, Jack Benny, Lou Holtz, Groucho

Marx—and Mr. Jolson. Sadly, only two of us are left from that group—George Burns and I. I don't get to the club very often anymore.

That day I met Jolson, we all chatted over lunch for a while. Then, Uncle Abe and several of the others went off to get dressed to play golf. George Burns went off to play bridge. I was left at the table with the great Al Jolson. My knees were knocking. I was too shy to even try to start a conversation.

He did. He said, "What are you doing, son?"

I told him about the Fanny Brice show, and how I was about to go overseas to entertain the troops, and that when I got back, "there's a little contract waiting for me at the Chez Paree in Chicago." I was being Humble Dan in the presence of this show-business idol. I didn't realize at the time that Jolson hadn't worked in fifteen years. His bravura personality and singing style had gone out of fashion, but in the public's mind, he was still a superstar.

Jolson said, "I envy you, boy."

I said, "You envy *me,* Mr. Jolson?"

He said, "They want you. I'd give a million dollars if somebody wanted me."

I said, "Gee, Mr. Jolson, why don't you put on another Broadway show, or do a movie, or . . ."

He said, "No, son. That would be *me* wanting *me.* Like I said, let me tell you, boy, when they want you, bathe in it. Because the day could come when they don't want you anymore."

I never forgot that. Later I told the story to my audience at The Sands and brought tears to their eyes. They were applauding and applauding. I could only get off the stage by using one of my treacle-cutters. I said, "And believe me, ladies and gentlemen, as much as you want me, and as much as I *want* you to want me, the management wants you gambling in the casino right now."

But Jolson's words came back to me in a more serious vein after my series *The Practice* folded—and again, when two other series of mine didn't work. As a matter of fact, I actually derived inspiration from what Jolson had said about being wanted.

Because I *was* wanted.

My old series were doing very well in TV syndication.

Nightclubs around the country wanted me, and I always played to capacity audiences.

I was constantly wanted by other TV stars to appear as a guest on their shows.

And, most important of all, I was wanted by my fellow members of ALSAC to carry on the task to which we had dedicated our lives.

chapter

»»33«««

Dealing with my fellow Lebanese Americans in ALSAC at the hospital and around the country led me to think more and more about my heritage. My father had spoken about it constantly, but I wanted to learn firsthand.

I read about our forebears, the ancient Phoenicians, whose small boats had opened up most of the trading routes in the Mediterranean. We produced great scholars, poets, and philosophers, including Kahlil Gibran, whose book *The Prophet* once outsold the Bible in a single year. What interested me most was that Gibran had lived in my parents' village, Becheri.

Becheri. I decided I had to see my true homeland. So Rosie and I made two trips to the land of my ancestors, the first in 1962, then again in 1974. It amazed me that my name was known even in that remote region.

We flew into Beirut, which at the time before the war was the most beautiful city in the Middle East. There were hundreds of people waiting to greet us at the airport. They knew we were coming. That was no accident. The Minister of Tourism is Habib Kyrouz, a cousin of mine. When you come from Lebanon, you have cousins all over the place.

We drove about fifty miles up into the breathtaking mountains. I choked up when we finally got to Becheri. There were ten thousand people—probably the entire population of the village—crowded into the square in front of St. Saba's Church. There were signs everywhere, in both Arabic and English: "Becheri Welcomes Her Son."

I was taken on a tour of the village, which was made up of stone houses hundreds of years old. I saw the houses where my mother and father had been born. Looking at the rocky slopes, I could see how tough life must have been for them. Wherever we went, cousins came up to me, identifying themselves as either Kyrouz (my father's family) or Touck (my mother's). Their warmth was overwhelming. But I guess it's the same when any immigrant's child returns to the Old Country.

Finally, I went back to address the crowd in front of St. Saba's Church. I was very nervous. Was my Arabic still good enough to make a coherent speech? After the first few sentences, I knew I was all right. I harked back to my father's Kyrouz family and my mother's Touck, to one or the other of which everyone in the village belonged. I said, "My father's blood in me is Kyrouz, my mother's milk was Touck, but I am all Lebanese."

Never in my life—on the stages of America, England, or elsewhere—did I ever hear such an uproar of applause. They fired off salutes. Fireworks, guns, cannon—it was incredible. Rosie said, "Duck, they're shooting at you."

That was before we realized it was all going up in the air.

In 1974, I was invited back to take part in a show to benefit the Lebanese Red Cross in Beirut. The hostess was Madame Franjieh, wife of the President of Lebanon. That was a quieter time, a year before the start of the devastating civil war between Christians and Muslims.

My first show in Lebanon caused me a lot of worry. I knew they would understand my jokes in English, but I knew I'd have to sing some Lebanese songs. I decided to take a chance with some of the Lebanese songs I had heard from my father. I didn't remember all the words, but that was all right because those mountain-folk songs in Arabic are mostly improvisations, anyway. God knows what I improvised, but it seemed to work.

To give myself some time to figure out what I was going to do next, I introduced a young man who improvised some intricate melodies on a Lebanese instrument called the Ood, which looks something like a mandolin. When he finished, I asked him, "What's your name, son?"

He said, "Marcel."

I said, "Marcel, Pierre, Emile, Edmond . . . doesn't anyone have a good honest Arabic name anymore?" The people cheered. That got me into one of my sermonizing dissertations about people denying their heritage. And then, believe it or not, I came up with a long story on the subject, which I had been telling for years—a Yiddish story. I just transposed it from Yiddish to Arabic.

The Yiddish story was this:

Irving Lefkowitz started out with a little store in downtown Chicago. He prospered, moving up to larger shops, and he ended up owning a good-sized department store. He now lived in one of the wealthy suburbs north of Chicago.

As his wealth grew, Irving's wife, Zelda, became more and more snobbish, which to her meant becoming more and more French. She changed her name to Claudette, she hired French maids for the house, and a French chef, too. Her conversation was sprinkled with French expressions. Irving didn't pay much attention. As long as she was happy, that was all that mattered. The only thing he resented was that he lived so far out of town that he couldn't play cards— casino—with the boys anymore.

The Lefkowitzes had two children. Then Claudette became pregnant again. She wanted to go to Paris to have the baby delivered, but this time, Irving put his foot down. "You'll have the baby here in the house," he said, "just like you did with the other kids. And Dr. Weinstein will come here to do the delivery."

Came the night that Claudette went into labor. She was upstairs with the nurse. Irving and Dr. Weinstein were downstairs playing gin rummy. As the evening went on, Irving heard a scream from upstairs. "Mon Dieu!" Irving said, "Go upstairs, already. The baby must be coming." The doctor just kept playing out his cards. "It's not time," he said.

Another fifteen minutes, and another scream from Claudette, "Mon Dieu!"

"It's time!" Irving said. "Go on up, already. What are you, some kind of quack?"

The doctor calmly said, "It's not time."

So he and Irving kept playing cards. And then there was another scream from upstairs. This time, Claudette yelled out that most explicit expression of Yiddish agony: *"Oy, vey iz mir."*

The doctor put down his cards. *"Now* it's time," he said.

Well, in Beirut, speaking Arabic, I transported the entire story to Lebanon. The husband was a wealthy merchant, as many Lebanese men are. The wife had totally Frenchified herself, as Claudette had done, and as many Lebanese women had done. She, too, kept screaming "Mon Dieu!"

The only thing I changed was the punch line of the story. It was *"Yah boutell"*—the Arabic version of the Yiddish *"Oy, vey iz mir."*

The audience went crazy with laughter. They hadn't heard that mountain-man expression in years. The president's wife asked me, "Where did you hear that mountain word?" And I said, "From my father and mother."

All of which proves a point—that people are basically the same all over the world, no matter what their culture or background happens to be. They have the same gripes and they laugh at the same things.

I was on the cover of a Middle Eastern magazine a few days later, with a headline which read: "He Came, He Cried, He Conquered."

Of course I cried, but then you can't go by me. I cry at basketball games.

chapter

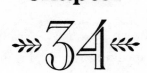

In the 1980s, I began to slow down. Rosie talked me into
it. It was funny, because she was the one who had wanted
me to become a grocery clerk in the old days because I
wasn't making enough money in show business. Now she
was saying, "Enough, already. You've got plenty of money
coming in. Why don't you retire?"

I pulled myself up to my full five feet eleven inches and
I said, "Retire? *Me* retire? Never. A retired man with nothing constructive to do is a dead man." But I did cut back
a little. The funny thing is that even when I have nothing
to do, I still live on the same schedule as when I was doing
nightclubs for weeks at a time. I can't go to sleep until three
or four in the morning; I sleep until noon, breakfast at 1
P.M. It makes for a topsy-turvy world, but that's the only
way I can live. I see a lot of late-night television shows,
including my own from years back.

All the shows from the old Danny Thomas Productions
days are still in TV syndication. The company remains in

production and is being run by my nephew, Ronnie Jacobs. In actuality, though, I have not been an active producer for some time. I hate desk work, which is why I split up amicably with Aaron Spelling in the 1970s. When we meet these days, Aaron and I still call each other "pardner."

My son, Tony, came to me and said, "I have to ask you something, but you don't have to answer me now. Paul and I have a series concept to do with Diana Canova. If you agree to play her father, I know we have a cinch sale. Think about it, Dad, and let me know."

I said, "I don't have to think about it. If it's a cinch sale for you, I'll do it." So I became Diana Canova's father, a dentist, who moved in with her and her young daughter after she was divorced. The series was dropped after one season.

A year or so later, Tony and Paul came to me with another series idea which they had in the works. This one was called *One Big Family,* and it was for first-run syndication—you know, the kind of series you see on your local TV station before they come on with the network news.

One Big Family had an interesting premise. I was Uncle Jake, a second-rate performer who played conventions, weddings, bar mitzvahs, and such, who inherited a large family of kids when their parents were killed in an accident. One of the kids was Dom DeLuise's son, Michael, and it was a lot of fun working with him. He's just a skinnier version of his father.

All in all, the show was a grind for me, however. Pushing seventy, I didn't have the vitality I had when I was working on *Make Room for Daddy* and my other projects. Tony had said to me again when he sold the series, "Dad, you shouldn't be working five tough days a week, so we've set this up so that you'll only have to be on the set for, say, three days." It didn't work out that way. I felt I should be there at all times to help the kids in the show. One of the directors was that talented young comedian, David Steinberg, who was beginning to work behind the camera. David insisted that I take off early—whenever he could spare me. To tell you the truth, I appreciated it.

One Big Family was on the air for one season. In a way, I was glad it wasn't renewed, though I felt sorry for the kids, whose careers were just getting under way. The year was very confining for me. I had a lot of St. Jude benefits to do, which meant I had to make a mad rush on weekends to fly across the country for things like the annual Miracle Ball in Miami. "Slowing down" meant that I had cut my St. Jude appearances to six or eight a year. And I was still doing my nightclub engagements in Las Vegas and Atlantic City. Rosie said, "Some slowing down."

And then there were the guest appearances I made on friends' TV shows. One of the wonderful things about being in show business is how friends always come to one another's aid. Typical was a series of incidents involving Bob Hope. One day, someone in Bob's office called, sounding frantic, and said, "Bob needs you. Can you get over here right away?" I knew Bob was in rehearsal for one of his specials, which was scheduled to tape that night. I said, "I'll be right there. But I'm not at home. I don't have my tuxedo." The man said, "No tux. Bob says to please get your ass over here right away." I said, "Tell him I'm out the door."

When I got to the studio, I could see that things were in a shambles. Redd Foxx was supposed to be on with Bob that night, but for some reason he'd dropped out. Bob said, "Thank God you're here." I took my coat off and began rehearsing a series of sketches Redd was going to do with Bob. The writers already had changed the lines slightly, because my style is not the same as Redd's and the lines were written in large letters on the cue cards.

As you probably know, Bob Hope is obsessive about everything having to be read from cue cards. This, too, is not my style. I learned the lines quickly, and at one point, Bob said to me, "What are you looking at me for?" I said, "Because I'm talking to you." He said, "Just look at the cards. Don't give me any of that New Haven crap." This comment was a throwback to Bob's days in the theater, when everyone was still trying to memorize his lines in pre-Broadway performances in places like New Haven, Connecticut. I dutifully kept looking at the cue cards, and the sketches went well.

A short time later, I was filling in for Frank Sinatra at a party in Palm Springs for former Vice President Spiro Agnew. It was a big party, and I didn't notice that Bob and Dolores Hope were there until they were ready to leave. I had been stewing about what entertainer I could get for my St. Jude Shower of Stars event in Memphis that year. By the time I saw Bob, he was already outside and about to drive away in his car. I leaned in and said, "I need you in Memphis on May twenty-ninth." Bob said, "You've got some case. That's my birthday." Dolores said, "Since when are you home on your birthday?"

Bob fiddled with his pocket diary and said, "Hell, it's not

only my birthday, but I promised to do a benefit for Les Brown that night in Columbia, South Carolina." (Les Brown and his Band of Renown have been with Hope for years.) Bob thought for a minute and said, "Your affair is for St. Jude, right? Tell you what I'm gonna do. I'll have Les switch his date to the next night, and I'll come and do your gig in Memphis first." And that's exactly what happened. Friends.

By the same token, I came to Bob's rescue when his brother, George, died. No one knows why Bob takes on some of his engagements, but for some reason, he was scheduled to do a show at the Pike's Peak Race Track in Colorado. It was the day of George's funeral.

I was attending the bar mitzvah of Buddy Hackett's son—very Orthodox, and I was trying not to mix meat with milk—when I got a call from Norman Brokaw of the William Morris office. Norman said, "Bob Hope would like you to fill in for him, at the matinee and evening shows, at Pike's Peak."

"When?" I said.

"You've got to leave now. Your accompanist, Wally Popp, has been told, and he's on his way to the airport. We've picked up your wardrobe, and that's on the way to the airport, too."

"Oh," I said, and I told Sherry Hackett to stop looking for non-dairy creamer for me.

I flew to Denver, then to Colorado Springs. A sheriff's car met me and we drove for miles and miles, until, as I like to say, we ran out of telephone poles. When we got to the racetrack, the grandstand was jammed. I did the two shows, and the audience didn't seem to mind the substitution. Company H of the Air Force Academy was there, and they gave me a hat that had been designed for Bob.

Then I collapsed. But what are friends for?

I often marvel at the number of friends I have in show business, and how they've always helped me when I needed them.

I also marvel at how few *enemies* I have developed. I can tell you about one—Walter Winchell—and that enmity came and went. Actually we weren't permanent enemies at all. Most of the time we were buddies, and I remember doing soft-shoe dances with him in the lobbies of Miami hotels. But twice, I got so furious with him that we weren't speaking.

The first time was when he wrote in his column, "Friends are disturbed that the Danny Thomases are acting like children." The implication was that I was fooling around and Rosie was upset about it. Nothing was further from the truth.

I got hold of one of Winchell's flunkies, and using some of the terminology I had picked up from the *shtarkas* in the nightclubs, I said, "You tell your boss that if he doesn't retract that statement, I'm gonna bust both his kneecaps."

The flunky said, "He's in Florida."

I said, "I don't care where he is. You tell him to retract."

The man said, "You know he doesn't retract."

I said, "I repeat. You tell him he'll walk stiff for the rest of his life." I made myself sound pretty tough for a guy who's devoted his whole life to saving children's lives. But I'd never been more angry.

A couple of days later came the retraction. Winchell wrote: "Friends assure us that all is well with the Danny Thomases."

But Winchell and I didn't make up for some time. The reconciliation came about in an unusual way. I was appearing at the Copacabana in New York when a note arrived in my dressing room at the Hotel Fourteen next door. The note read: "I am here with seven holders of the Congressional Medal of Honor. Please acknowledge their presence. W.W."

Winchell was pretty shrewd. He knew I was as patriotic as he was, and that I couldn't turn my back on some of America's greatest war heroes. So when I got onstage, I cut my show short by twenty minutes, and went into a spiel about the Medal of Honor winners—the guests of Walter Winchell. The crowd got to its feet and Winchell came onstage and hugged me. That was the end of our feud—until the next time.

The next time came after I had done a show on my *Danny Thomas Hour* with Sid Caesar and Don Adams. It was a harmless playlet about three con men in a hotel, who want to get their hands on a diamond so they can hock it, bet the money on a sure-thing horse, and then return the diamond. In the course of this foolery, Sid Caesar, playing an out-of-work Shakespearian actor, ends up impersonating a distinguished guest in the hotel, Prince Abdullah. With Sid's foreign-language double-talk, it was hilarious.

The next day, Winchell wrote in his column, "Hollywood is agog. Danny Thomas is doing a show about Arabs and other America-haters."

By this time, Winchell's mind was slipping—sort of a sad dotage—and I didn't bother to threaten his kneecaps again. But we stopped speaking, for the second time.

I next saw him at a Dodgers-Chicago Cubs baseball game in Los Angeles. I was in the press box along with a photographer, and when Winchell came in, the photographer said, "May I have a picture of you two gentlemen?"

Winchell said, "Maybe this gentleman doesn't want a picture with me."

I said, "You're right. This gentleman *doesn't.*" Then I lit into Winchell: "Walter, you're a schmuck. You really are a schmuck. You were an absolute legend. You *were,* but now you've lost it completely. You know, Walter, you're going to die alone."

And he did, too. His daughter had a private burial for him.

But remembering his former greatness as a journalist, I pray for him. I swear I do.

chapter
35

But enough of long-ago feuds. I'd rather reflect on the happiness I was enjoying with my family. There is a delightful word for it in Yiddish—*nachas*—which loosely means total pride and satisfaction with one's offspring. I had plenty of *nachas* from my growing array of grandchildren, from Tony's success, from Terre's healthy adjustment to life as a single parent, from Marlo's varied and fascinating activities. But especially when Marlo called us one day and said, "Mom and Dad, I'm going to marry Phil Donahue."

Ever since *That Girl,* Marlo had cut quite a swath across the entertainment and political scenes. After she did *Thieves* with Richard Mulligan on the stage, she made *Thieves,* the motion picture, with Charles Grodin and Mercedes McCambridge. She had become one of the most vocal advocates of such public interest issues as women's rights and the environment.

She had made other films (*Jenny,* for one) and then had plunged heavily into TV movies, one of the best known of which is *The Lost Honor of Kathryn Beck,* a remake of a famous German film. She received the Best Actress Emmy for *Nobody's Child,* in which she played a patient at a mental institution who was released, went to college, and went back to become head of the institution. But with her father's blood in her, Marlo wasn't satisfied with being just an actress, so she became a producer of films for both TV and the big screen.

Anyway, Marlo was winging along on her career when she was invited to be a guest on Phil Donahue's talk show. Apparently it was a case of love at first sight. There were sparks. Phil kept asking her back, and soon he was asking her *out.* They were dating regularly. They were of the same mind on politics and everything else. As for me, except for my one fling with Hubert Humphrey, I keep my politics to myself.

A few months later, *I* was asked to be a guest on Phil's show. We chatted about this and that, and then came the time for questions from the audience. A woman asked me, "How about Marlo and Phil. Are they serious?" Something like that. I said, "Well . . ." Phil said, "Well . . ." And then there came the distinctive voice of my daughter, over the loudspeaker from the control room: "Don't you two make any decisions without me."

So I wasn't exactly surprised when Rosie and I got that call from Marlo a few months later, telling us that she and Donahue were going to be married. I jumped with joy, and so did Rosie. Not only did I like Phil a lot, but I'm an old-fashioned father, I guess, and I had been nagging Marlo about her single state for a long time.

The wedding was held in the new house I had had built after we had sold our home on Elm Drive in Beverly Hills. This new house is also in Beverly Hills, but on a hilltop in the mountains overlooking the city. It is completely fenced, with heavy iron gates—perfect for the total secrecy Marlo and Phil insisted on for the ceremony. They wanted to avoid the press—especially the tabloid press, which has been known to put photographers in helicopters to hover over such affairs.

But everything went without a hitch. Applying for a marriage license—which you must do in person—is the usual giveaway to the press. But I arranged with Mayor Tom Bradley for Marlo and Phil to be driven into the police garage at City Hall, from where they would ride up a back elevator to the clerk's office. They were not spotted.

No one was invited to the wedding on May 21, 1980, except for members of the immediate families. There was only one other person I wanted there, and that was Uncle Abe Lastfogel. But I even had to keep it secret from *him.* On the day of the wedding, I called and said, "Uncle Abe, I want you to come up to the house."

He said, "Fine, I'll have Sam Weisbord drive me."

I said, "No, I'll come and get you myself."

So I drove to downtown Beverly Hills, and only when Uncle Abe and I were halfway up the hill to my house, did he say, "What's going on?" I told him he was about to become the only outsider to attend the wedding of Marlo to Phil Donahue, and tough old Uncle Abe managed to shed a tear or two before we got to the gate.

Because Phil was a divorcé, he and Marlo couldn't be

married in the Church, so a judge friend of mine performed the ceremony. But then our family priest, Father Pat McPoland, blessed the marriage. After that, the celebrating began. It was a wild time. There were Irish songs and jigs, Lebanese songs and dances. Even with all this noise, there were no complaints from the neighbors. So the world didn't know about the wedding until a couple of days later.

Phil has been a wonderful addition to the family. Being Irish, he has a great repertoire of Irish stories. So do I—from my Crotchy Callahan days. So whenever he comes over to the house, we break out a six-pack of beer and try to outdo each other with classics of Hibernian humor. This can go on for hours. When we go East, Rosie and I frequently stay with Marlo and Phil, either in their apartment in New York or their house in Connecticut. We always have a happy time together. After a couple of beers together, "When Irish Eyes Are Smiling" and "Danny Boy" are almost certain to be vocalized. My children and grandchildren love it—from this man, who is literate and erudite on his television show. On my seventieth birthday celebration at the Hillcrest Country Club, Phil got up and sang a parody of "Danny Boy" which brought down the house.

Marlo and Phil lead an interesting life together. They have two separate careers, and one does not impinge on the other. Phil is up-to-his-ears busy with his *Phil Donahue Show* five days a week, with both his work on the air and the many hours of preparation that contribute to the making of each one-hour show. Marlo's production company has about a half dozen movie projects in the works at all times. Her days are taken up with meetings with writers, directors, technicians, and network and movie-studio executives. Her weekend times with Phil are most precious to her.

Marlo's business frequently takes her to the West Coast—alone, without Phil. On those occasions, she stays with Rosie and me in our house, rather than at a hotel. Marlo is a strong, self-sufficient woman who would be perfectly safe in the Beverly Hills Hotel, but she indulges one of my idiosyncracies. I'm *still* an overprotective father. So now she stays with us, and I feel more comfortable knowing she is safe in the bosom of her family. Besides, this outspoken advocate of women's independence likes to hang around the kitchen and shmooze with Rosie about Sicilian and Lebanese cuisine.

Marlo and Phil usually come to see me when I perform in Atlantic City once or twice a year. Marlo always begs me to do my "old stuff" for Phil, because he loves my Yiddish stories from the old days, as well as my Irish ones. She insisted that I do my parrot-that-*davens* story in one of those Atlantic City performances. I had never done it in Atlantic City before. "It's too long for this audience," I told Marlo. "Test it out on Phil," she insisted.

It was a tough test. If it could make Phil Donahue laugh, it could make anyone laugh. Donahue loved it, and so did the rest of the audience. In fact, they laughed at Phil laughing at the story.

I loved it because how many people can get to use Phil Donahue as a guinea pig?

In all, I'm delighted that with the addition of Phil as my son-in-law, my family has become even more ecumenical. Now we have an Irishman, a WASP (Tony's wife, Glenn), and an Italian (Rose Marie), along with us descendants of the old Phoenicians. Also part of the family is Maury Foladare, my wonderful press agent for more than fifty years—a Jew. My steadfast, long-time secretary, Janet Roth—also very much a part of the family—is a German Presbyterian from Des Moines, Iowa.

Now that's ecumenism.

And this is a good place to say a word about Janet Roth. She has been with us for forty-two years. She is not only my secretary, but also my friend and confidante. She came to us just before Tony was born. Every time Rose Marie flew to join me where I was playing on the road, Janet took over the house and the care of the children. I wouldn't know what to do without her.

We have an arrangement, Janet and I. She can't quit, and she can't be fired.

chapter

August 25, 1984, was one of the saddest days of my life. Uncle Abe Lastfogel died.

I had had a lot of experiences with deaths over the years, but nothing like this.

Only two of my siblings are still alive. Some of them died violently. My brother, Paul, for example, was killed in an automobile accident on his way to see me perform in Las Vegas.

One of my most curious dealings with death came with the passing of Harry Cohn, the fabled head of Columbia Pictures. In spite of the fact that he had once told me, "Y'know you could be a helluva actor, so why don't you get your beak chopped off, for crying out loud," I loved the man. I was at his house many times, and he would ask me to tell stories, and he kept giving me boxes of expensive cigars. Danny Kaye delivered the eulogy at Mr. Cohn's funeral. It was written by Clifford Odets and there was a great line in it: "Harry Cohn had a fire that warmed a few, and burned many." I was one of the few that his fire warmed.

It was before that eulogy at Mr. Cohn's funeral that I got a phone call from his widow, Joan. She was in Arizona, where Harry had just died. Apparently Joan had heard all the stories by Bob Hope, Red Buttons, and others about how religious I am. I'd like to be half as religious as they say! In her distress, she apparently thought of me as something of a clergyman. She said, "Danny, I want you to read the prayers for Harry."

I said, "What do you mean?"

She said, "Well, I don't want to have a rabbi, and I don't want to insult his family and friends by having a priest. So would you . . ."

I said, "But Joan, he was born and raised in the Jewish faith."

She said, "Let me tell you something. When Harry was dying, he said, 'Jesus, help me!' I'm a Christian, as you know, and I'm sure he was turning to Jesus in his final moments."

I said, "Are you sure he wasn't just exclaiming, 'Jesus Christ,' like we all do in tense moments? I knew Harry, and . . ."

She interrupted: "I knew him a little better than you. I shared his bed and I'm telling you he said, 'My Jesus, help me.' So I went and got a glass of water, sprinkled it on him, and I said, 'I baptize you in the name of the Father, the Son, and the Holy Ghost.' Now, will you please say the prayers over him at the grave site?"

I said yes, but I didn't know what to do. I was an entertainer, not an ordained priest. I went to see Monsignor Concannon, the pastor of the Church of the Good Shepherd in Beverly Hills. Most of the big Catholic actors are parishioners there, and all of my kids went to that Catholic school. I told the Monsignor the story of Harry Cohn's last moments, as Joan Cohn had related them to me, and I said, "Is it all right for me to read the prayers, as she asked me to do?"

The Monsignor was a very wise man. "Under the circumstances," he said, "I'll give you my permission." I hadn't asked for permission, just advice, but here I was with some sort of dispensation. He gave me the funeral book and he said, "Now, wherever it says 'Jesus Christ,' you substitute the word 'Lord'—meaning the Lord God of us all. That way, you will not offend anybody."

So that's what I did, reading from the book as I headed the cortege at Harry Cohn's final resting place in the Hollywood Cemetery just behind his Columbia Studios. I stood right alongside the casket and recited the Twenty-third Psalm. And no one got offended. As I said, Monsignor Concannon was a very wise man.

More distressing to me was the death of Frank Sinatra's mother, Dolly, who was in a private plane that crashed into a mountain on its way from Palm Springs to Las Vegas, where Frank was performing. As soon as I heard the news on the radio, I got into my car and sped to Palm Springs. I knew Frank already had arrived there. I wanted to be with him.

I got to Frank's house, and his wife, Barbara, met me at the door. She said, "He's sitting alone in the dark. I don't think he wants anyone to . . ." I said, "I understand, sweetheart," and I turned to go.

But Frank's voice came weakly from the next room. "Jake," he mumbled. I went in and embraced him. I said, "I'm not going to say anything. Nobody can say anything." Then he said something that made me cry. They hadn't found the wreckage of the plane yet, nor Dolly's body. Frank said, "Oh, my God, Jake, it must be awfully lonely up there." I bawled like a baby and just walked out of the room, leaving him in solitude.

Dolly was buried in Palm Springs, but the day before, a memorial service was held for her at the Church of the Good Shepherd in Beverly Hills. Frank's daughters, Nancy and Tina, asked me to do the eulogy there, to accommodate the many who couldn't get to Palm Springs—Gregory Peck, Bing Crosby, Ray Bolger, and many others. Feeling Frank's sorrow as I did, my eulogy was mostly about his deep abiding love for his mother.

But none of this could match the sorrow I felt at the death of Abe Lastfogel. I was informed by Norman Brokaw, who had worked side by side with Uncle Abe in handling my career since the early days of the Fanny Brice radio show. Uncle Abe was eighty-six when he died. He had had a slight stroke fourteen years before—when he was seventy—but he was still going into the William Morris office every day. He and Aunt Frances lived just up the street, in an apartment on the eighth floor of the Beverly Wilshire Hotel. They had lived there since they first moved to California in the 1930s. They never bought a house or a car. They had no children. The people at William Morris were their children. So was I, and other favorite clients, like Warren Beatty, who once took a Beverly Wilshire apartment just down the hall from them, so he could be near his Uncle Abe and Aunt Frances. Warren dropped in on them all the time.

Uncle Abe often dropped in on me. He'd suddenly say to Norman Brokaw, "Let's go up to Danny's house tonight." They'd come by, and no matter what Rosie and I were watching on television, he'd immediately switch the set to something *he* wanted to see. Usually, it was some client's show, but sometimes, he just wanted to scout what was going on in the business. I remember once when he flicked on *The Dorsey Brothers' Show.* He wanted my opinion of a new young singer. "Nobody knows about that kid yet, but he's going to be a big star." I agreed. The kid's name was Elvis Presley.

Uncle Abe loved to munch on nuts and other goodies Rosie had lying around in dishes and bowls. He also took delight in *fressing* (gulping down) her Italian and Lebanese hors d'oeuvres. I'll always remember how he probably was the only person I knew who didn't object to my cigars. He actually liked them. He'd sit close to me, better to breathe in the heavy blue smoke. Nearly everyone else used to flee when I lit up—except for guys on my payroll, of course.

Those were some of my thoughts as I headed for Uncle Abe's funeral at Hillside Memorial Park. Naturally I sat with the immediate family during the services in the chapel. When I was called upon to speak after the main eulogy by Sam Weisbord of William Morris, I choked up—though, by this time, I had had a lot of practice at this sort of thing.

I can't remember my exact words, but basically I said,

"My Uncle Abe was my father, my mother, my mentor, my friend, my adviser, my companion. Without him I wouldn't be standing here today. I would have had no career at all. For the rest of my life, there won't be a day when I will not be thinking of him."

And it's true. There hasn't been a day since then when I haven't thought of my Uncle Abe.

chapter

37

I missed Uncle Abe the most when I was presented with the Congressional Medal by President Reagan in the White House, some eight months after Uncle Abe's death. How I wished he could have been there with me in the White House on that auspicious occasion. After all, he had had so much to do with what *I* had done to earn the medal. Without Uncle Abe, neither my career nor the St. Jude Children's Research Hospital would have gotten off the ground. It was his goading that pushed me into both.

I take some solace in the fact that Uncle Abe knew I had been awarded the medal, even though it hadn't been bestowed on me before his death. The bill had been introduced in Congress in 1983 and that's the date which appears on the gold medal, "By act of Congress, 1983." For my portrait on the medal, the engraver was kind. It is a head-on shot, not showing my hook nose—a fact which did not escape President Reagan in his private comments to me when he handed me the medal in the ceremony at the White House.

As I said before, my entire family had flown into Washington for the event, and so did the Board of Directors of the St. Jude Hospital. I had asked them to do so because I considered the medal to be as much for them as it was for me. Newly installed on the Board was Norman Brokaw of William Morris, who had taken Uncle Abe's place in all St. Jude activities. Norman also had taken Uncle Abe's place as the principal overseer of my entertainment activities. He later became chief executive officer of the agency and helped soften Abe Lastfogel's loss considerably. He has much of the acumen of Uncle Abe. For example, he guided Bill Cosby's career to its current exalted state—also many other stars, plus statesmen and former presidents.

My own career was in a state of semi-abeyance for a while. I only worked when I wanted to. I was over seventy now, but I kept remembering the words of Al Jolson: "Keep going as long as the people want you." And they still wanted me in the nightclubs and on TV.

Another thing that kept me going was watching the career of my old friend George Burns. After all, *he* didn't reach his zenith until he was nearly eighty—when he filled in for Jack Benny in the film, *The Sunshine Boys,* after Jack passed away. That picture brought George his first Oscar.

But I had more time now to spend with the love-of-my-life, Rosie. And I managed to get together with my fellow comics at least once a month—and still do. The old comics' table at the Hillcrest Country Club was gone, but we managed to find another Hillcrest that would let us assemble there—the Beverly Hillcrest Hotel in Beverly Hills—after we had been kicked out of a lot of other places for raucousness.

The hotel has a little restaurant on the first floor, where we can make noise. We go Dutch, and we all bring our wives. If the women talk too loudly about shopping, we glare at them. The regulars in our group are Sid Caesar, Jan Murray, Harry Crane, and me—but we always have drop-ins like Alan King or Milton Berle. Jan Murray is the wildest. He must have undivided attention when he speaks. He'll say, "What are you, interrupting? What I'm gonna say is funnier than what you're gonna say." Harry Crane will say, "You wanna bet," and then it starts with everyone trying to outdo one another's jokes.

Harry Crane is not a performer, but he's written for every top comic in the business, including me. He has a dry sense of humor that I love—like Joey Bishop's and Mrs. Feldman's—and he has a computer for a mind, with a joke on the tip of his tongue for every subject known to man. He once said to me, "If you did drunk jokes, I got material to last you twenty years." He wrote them all for Dean Martin, who used them once and forgot them. Harry assembled them all into a looseleaf book as thick as Webster's Dictionary.

Harry's drunk jokes for Dean Martin are hilarious: "Dean was driving up a one-way street on the wrong side of the road. A policeman caught up with him and said, "Didn't you see the arrow?" Dean said, "Hell, I didn't even see the Indians!" Or like the ones where Dean doesn't admit he's drunk: "If you can lie down on the sidewalk without holding on, you ain't drunk."

Jan Murray is one of my best friends, and he's one of the funniest people alive. He once did a routine with me that had me rolling on the floor. He was filling in for Sid Caesar on one of my later shows and all he did was read the instructions on how to set the clock on his VCR. Whatever he tried, the numbers kept on blinking: 12-12-12. He can find great humor in an ordinary experience like that, and everyone can identify with him. That's what makes him such a great comedian.

The interesting thing is that no matter how proficient Jan is on the stage, in everyday life, he has six thumbs. I mean, he's a total klutz. If anything goes wrong with the plumbing or wiring at home, his wife, Toni, has to take care of it. Leaving it to Jan would mean absolute disaster.

Everybody knows this. When Buddy Hackett's father died, Jan was out of town and phoned Buddy about coming to the funeral.

"Don't come," Buddy said. "You'll fall in the hole."

A lot of great material comes out of these free-for-alls at the Hillcrest Hotel. Remembering the two thousand paying guests jammed into Rosie's last St. Jude gala, Harry said to Rosie, "Here's a joke you can use next year: 'I hope the scientists at St. Jude Children's Research Hospital will one day research a way to get you all seated where you all want to sit.'" Rosie used it and got a big laugh.

Rosie and I, too, are both the butt of much of this Beverly Hillcrest Hotel humor:

"Talking about Rosie's cooking, the trouble with eating Italian food is that in four or five days you're hungry again."

"The Pope has a statue of Danny on his dashboard."

"Danny's house is so big that when he's in the bedroom

and wants to phone Rosie in the kitchen, he has to use an 800 number."

"When I played golf with Danny and we approached a water hole, he didn't walk around it, he parted it."

"When Danny was eighteen, he hurt himself playing football. He got holy water on the knee."

And so on and so on and so on. That's why I dearly love those sessions at the Hillcrest Hotel. Someone suggested taping them, but Jan Murray said, "Uh-oh, if Berle ever gets his hands on that tape . . ." Then he answered himself: "Milton doesn't steal jokes. He finds them before they get lost."

I love Milton. He was very important in my life.

And he was about to be a very important part of it again.

chapter

It happened when a writer named Rosemary Edelman, Lou Edelman's daughter, wrote a script for a TV-movie, *Side by Side,* which CBS was very interested in. The movie was about three old codgers in the garment industry—all tops in their field—who are frustrated by age discrimination in the business and decide to form their own company. They hire older workers, who are similarly discriminated against, and their company becomes a sort of cooperative of old-fashioned craftsmen who compete against the younger, more ruthless sharks in the "rag business." The three principals are a master salesman, a master cutter/designer, and a master business manager.

When the network honchos saw the script, a light bulb went off. Why not cast Milton Berle, Sid Caesar, and Danny Thomas as the three factory owners? When our agents presented us with the idea, we said, "Why not?" It was a cute concept and the money was good. And, perhaps most important, Milton, Sid, and I had never worked together before as a threesome, and it looked like fun.

So we did it, and it *was* fun—except for poor Sid, who had broken his hip and had to hobble about in terrible pain. The movie aired and, though it wasn't Shakespeare or Ibsen, it got pretty good ratings. That led other people to believe that our names still carried a lot of weight with the public, and we were approached to do a three-man show in places like Caesar's Palace in Las Vegas and Atlantic City. We would perform two nights in each location. The act was called "The Legends of Comedy."

Looking back on it, we *were* legends—in terms of longevity, anyway. Milton, who worked in vaudeville, movies, and radio for some time, began his fabulous television career in 1948 on NBC and became the universally loved "Uncle Miltie" on the *Texaco Star Theater.* Sid's *Your Show of Shows,* a television classic, goes back to 1950. I, of course, started doing *Make Room for Daddy* in 1953. All in all, we have a total of nearly two hundred years in show business, considering our pre-TV activities.

Who can forget Milton's slapstick classics on the old *Texaco* show? My favorite is one he did with Steve Allen (and which they reprised later on our "Legends of Comedy" tour). In this skit, Milton begins by singing "September Song," and Steve comes out, yelling, "What's with this singing? What happened to the Milton Berle who told all the stories about all the great slapstick comedians like Chaplin, Laurel and Hardy—feet stuck in cement, pianos rolling downhill, slipping on banana peels? Let's do some slapstick."

Milton says, "Yeah, like what?"

Steve whips out a black grease-pencil and draws glasses

and a beard all over Milton's face. He says, "You don't think that's funny?" Milton says, "No, that's not funny."

Steve comes back with a huge powder puff loaded with cornstarch. He slaps him across the face. Now Milton is all white. He says, "I don't think that's funny."

Steve goes offstage and comes back with scissors. He cuts Milton's tie off, then cuts his suspenders. Milton's pants fall to the floor. Milton says, "No, that's not funny."

Steve gets a seltzer bottle and sprays Milton, back and front. Milton is now a mess, with the cornstarch and black grease paint turning into gray mush. "Not funny," says Milton.

Now Steve cames back with the classic whipped-cream pie. He's about to throw it into Milton's face, but Milton slaps Steve's hand and pushes the pie into *Steve's* face.

Milton says, "Now *that's* funny." Guaranteed huge laugh.

With Sid Caesar, so *many* of his skits and pantomimes from *Your Show of Shows* are classics, but nothing can top his Crazy Professor in the battered top hat, who professes to know everything but cons his way through the questions of a reporter (Carl Reiner) without knowing much of anything at all.

Best of all, I liked Sid's Professor routine in which he combines his very funny evasive answer with his genius-talent for spouting authentic-sounding foreign-language gibberish. He's asked the question, "Professor, why is it that a bestseller book in one language doesn't make it when it's translated into another language?" Sid says, "Dot's easy. It's all in the telling."

He then describes a scene, in English, in which a man is making passionate verbal love to a girl. He follows with the same scene in which he spouts German gibberish, Italian gibberish, and finally Japanese gibberish. Each nation's lovemaking characteristics are included in the telling. Mass hysteria from the audience.

I wondered if the audiences for "The Legends of Comedy" would be mostly older people who remembered us from our earlier days, but I was wrong. I was amazed at how many younger folks showed up, many of whom would be classified as "yuppies." People kept coming up to me, saying, "We know you guys from clips and reruns on cable and in syndication." One of them really flattered Sid by saying, "Hey, I love *Saturday Night Live,* but what *you* were doing back then, wow!"

Anyway, beginning in 1988, we opened to packed houses wherever we went—and still do. We played the Riviera in Las Vegas, Caesars in Atlantic City, Caesars Palace in Las Vegas, and the refurbished old Palace Theater in Cleveland. We felt a lot of love coming across the footlights from the audience. It seems to me that we got a standing ovation from the audience just for showing up. It's been the same since we've gone on to Miami and other places. I have to tell you, there's nothing in the world like performing in front of an audience. And as much as the fans love it, I love it, too—in fact, I thrive on it.

Our show isn't complicated—in fact, it's very simple, but that might be why it works. I enter from stage left and Milton and Sid come on from stage right. We banter back and forth a bit. Then we each do our own act, coming together for a little more fooling around at the end. But nothing is fixed. Sometimes Milton and I get into Sid's act by asking questions of his Professor know-it-all character. Sometimes one of us takes a pie in the face from Milton.

Milton is the genius who holds the entire thing together. I had known him for some time, but I never realized what an expert he is at assembling the nuts and bolts of a performance. He's almost obsessive about it. He gets involved with the lighting, the sound system, the music—which is good because neither Sid nor I is that detail-oriented. Milton is also obsessive about his health. For example, he's terrified of catching a cold, Even on the hottest summer day, he'll show up wearing a topcoat or even an overcoat. He always has a towel wrapped around his neck to protect himself against drafts. All of us show-business folk have our quirks, but Milton carries his to an extreme.

If Sid and I arrive in town for our first show, say, at 9 P.M., Milton will arrive at eight that morning. He'll spend the whole day with the sound engineer and with the man who handles the lights, fiddling with the microphones and the spots until they are as close as possible to his standards of perfection—which they never are. He'll rehearse the orchestra for hours, making sure all the music is done right. Even during the show, he gets crazy if something goes wrong.

Sid does a lot of running around on the stage, doing his wonderful pantomimes and foreign-language double-talk routines with Lee Delano, his longtime straight man, who took over for Carl Reiner. Sid uses a cordless microphone, which sometimes becomes detached from the transmitter on his back when he skips around. Or he might hit a dead transmitting area on the stage. That sends Milton into a frenzy. He'll run over on the stage in the middle of Sid's act, yelling, "Sid, they can't hear you," and he'll shove his own microphone under Sid's nose until he completes the routine. It's unorthodox, but it always gets a laugh. Sid doesn't know what's going on and keeps running away from Milton.

Milton is rife with other idiosyncracies—which all of us have, but with him they're exaggerated. They are part of what makes him such a fascinating character. When he and Sid and I are scheduled to do a "Legends of Comedy" show, we usually meet at my house for a two-hour rehearsal. Except that the two-hour rehearsal gets cut down to one hour because the first hour is always taken up with a monologue by Milton about his early days in show business. If Milton gets two people together in a room, that's an audience to him, and he performs.

He talks about how his mother kept prodding him to be a performer when he was just a child. He talks about how he got a job as an extra in a Charlie Chaplin film at the age of eight. He remembers every theater he played in as a youth, and the names of every other vaudevillian on the bill. He'll say things like, "When I played the State Theater in Jersey City in 1932, a dog act opened the bill. A guy named Joe Smithson. The dogs' names were Fluffy, Rufus, and Mollie."

At Rosie's 1989 Gala for St. Jude, our "Legends of Comedy" act was the featured entertainment, but Sid was tied up in New York and Steve Allen substituted for him. At our rehearsal, Steve was probably the greatest audience Milton ever had. Sid and I had heard most of the stories before, but Steve hadn't. He listened intently for the full hour, even pulling out his pocket tape recorder, chuckling and laughing all along the way.

Milton follows the same strict pattern at all our "Legends of Comedy" shows. Before we go onstage, he walks around with his towel wrapped around his neck, apparently in a deep depression. You think he's not going to make it. But he comes to life as soon as the lights go up.

After the show's over, we might brood about what went wrong during the performance, but not Milton. He's on an all-time high. He holds court in his dressing room for the many admirers who pour in after the show. Sid, who's actually very quiet offstage, has usually left by then, but it is my custom to hang around with Milton until the fans have departed. Then, as an audience of just one, I listen to his old-days show-business stories until his energy is spent and he's ready to go out to eat or go back to the hotel.

Entertaining continues to be fun for me after all these years.

Except for one thing.

Remember when I said I started out in radio wanting to be a character actor and that that ambition has remained with me ever since? Maybe I sound like the traditional clown who wants to play Shakespeare, but I still keep remembering what that great actor Walter Huston said to me many years ago. I was playing the old Greek clockmaker in my first film, *The Unfinished Dance,* when Mr. Huston came on the set to visit with the director, Henry Koster. Walter was the father of John Huston, and both had won Academy Awards for their great 1948 film, *Treasure of the Sierra Madre.*

Mr. Huston watched me work, and then he came over and said, "Very good, boy, very good. Good stuff. You got it, boy, you got it. Just be a character, boy. Don't let it be you that sells the tickets. Let it be you that the audience remembers. The star doesn't work all the time; the character actor does."

Somehow that advice has stuck with me all these years. Is it because it was my original ambition? Or is it because I want to prove to myself that I can do drama as well as comedy? In any event, that's what led me to gray my hair and grow a moustache for the TV series *The Practice.*

As I said, it was my three beloved children who engineered that opportunity for me, and now it's one of my children, Marlo, who is making another try at helping to fulfill this lifelong longing of mine.

A couple of years ago, Marlo came to me and said, "Dad, I'm determined to come up with an idea for you and me finally to work together in a meaningful dramatic film—not half-comedy, the way *The Practice* was. I have an idea for a movie in which you play an old doctor, and I play your daughter—teamed up together."

Marlo continues to work diligently on this project. The first script she commissioned didn't pan out—the old doctor had a second life as an intelligence agent, which didn't make much sense to Marlo or to me. But she zealously keeps toiling away with another writer, and this time it may work out.

So Old Hook Nose may emerge as a character actor yet.

chapter

In the meantime, my comedy career goes on—especially as I use it to help keep money coming in for the St. Jude Children's Research Hospital. Every day brings new excitement for me as I learn more and more about St. Jude accomplishments.

How about *this* for a statistic? The hospital's five-year cure-rate for childhood leukemia is now up to nearly *seventy percent.* That has to be a miracle, especially when you remember that when we first got the hospital started, less than *one percent* of kids survived. The Hodgkin's disease cure-rate is *ninety percent.* There also have been tremendous advances in other diseases, such as neuroblastoma and Ewing's sarcoma.

Who deserves the credit for this miracle? The medical personnel, the thousands of workers—both paid and volunteer—who keep the hospital going. We have had three medical directors—initially Dr. Donald Pinkel, then Dr. Alvin Mauer, and now Dr. Joseph Simone—and it was they who have made our institution renowned all over the world. We send doctors to lecture in countries as far away as China; and nations from all five continents send doctors to take advanced training in childhood diseases with us.

In all modesty, I must take a small bow in helping to get this trend started. The story of how that came about involves an exchange of comments between President John F. Kennedy and me which I still occasionally use in my act. I knew the President and I went to see him in 1962 about sending visiting heads of state to come see our hospital in Memphis.

The President said, "What do you need with foreign politicians? You need foreign *doctors* and *scientists* to see what you're doing and to come to study with you."

I got a big chuckle out of the President when I said, "You're absolutely right and I'm wrong. And that's why you're President and I'm selling Post Toasties on television."

So, all in all, when I reflect on what I have accomplished in life, the St. Jude Children's Research Hospital always comes first. Though I have made millions of people laugh in my role as an entertainer, saving the life of even one child is just that much more important. I have an especially strong belief in the hospital because I helped found it.

I'm also very proud of the way I reared my family—with Rosie as my partner, of course. Who could have three more devoted, loving children, imbued with such an unflagging sense of family? And their talent constantly amazes me.

I'm very glad I've never forgotten to follow my father's deathbed admonition to remember my heritage. Members of ALSAC are well known everywhere as doctors, lawyers, industrialists, and politicians. But now the whole country knows them because of their fantastic deeds as the lifeblood of the greatest pediatric research center on earth.

My Number Four Accomplishment is a strange one. Though my colleagues tease me about my "sermonizing," I *did* get some serious messages across in the midst of all my clowning.

I'll never forget an incident that happened to me nearly forty years ago. It wasn't the kind of event you'd hear about in the press.

In 1952, I was invited to entertain some eighty thousand Boy Scouts at the Eastern Boy Scout Jamboree in Butler, Pennsylvania. The event took place in a huge amphitheater and it was getting dark when I took the stage. What was I going to talk about? At the last minute, I decided to cut down on my comedy and address a subject that had been bothering me for some time. That was when there was a lot of talk about juvenile delinquency and how many kids were going bad. I knew that only two percent of kids actually were bad, and looking at that sea of fresh, young faces, I felt that the other ninety-eight percent should be acknowledged.

I did a funny monologue about teenagers. Then I spoke directly to the kids. I spoke to them about the brotherhood of man. I spoke to them about democracy, how "you live in the only country in the world where the heirs are permitted to plan their own inheritance." Pretty heavy stuff from a comedian, and I didn't know how it was going over. By the time I was finished it was totally dark, and *then* I knew.

Each scout had a whistle in one hand and a flashlight in

the other, so they could find their way back to their tents and signal if they got lost. Since both hands were occupied, there was no applause. Instead, there was a spectacular demonstration of the sort I have never seen, before or since. Every kid in the place—all eighty thousand of them— blew his whistle and shone his flashlight up into the night air. It was a chilling but exhilarating demonstration that went on for at least ten minutes. I still get goose bumps when I think of it.

I think about it every time I hear President Bush speak about his thousand points of light.

At one brief moment in history, this simple entertainer, this old Lebanese storyteller, managed to provoke *eighty* thousand points of light.

Yes, and as Accomplishment Number Five (the end of the list) I did make a lot of people laugh in my lifetime.

By the way, did I tell you the one about . . .

There was this elderly man, eighty-four years old, who lived with his grown children. He didn't speak much and just moved around the house. They thought he needed psychiatric help. Just to please them, he went to see a psychiatrist.

The shrink said, "Just lie down on the couch and we'll talk. If you think of something to say, fine. If not, maybe next time." The old man lay down on the couch and fell fast asleep. It was so relaxing just being away from his nagging family. At the end of the fifty minutes, the doctor woke him up. He said, "That'll be all for today. That'll be a hundred dollars." The old man paid him and left.

He came back on Thursday, and on every Tuesday and

Thursday after that. Every time, he fell asleep on the couch and didn't say a word. Every time, he paid the doctor one hundred dollars. It would have been cheaper if he went to a hotel.

By the third week, the old man came in, sat down on the couch and jumped right up again. The doctor said, "Aha, you thought of something to say?"

The old man said, "Yeah . . . You need a partner?"

That story, dear friends, is a treacle-cutter.

acknowledgments

In sincere gratitude to these people in show business, who helped me attain my place in life.

—D.T.

My heartfelt thanks to:

John Adair

Don Adams

Steve Allen

Morey Amsterdam

Lynn Anderson

Patty Andrews

Paul Anka

Gene Autry

Pearl Bailey & Louie Bellson

Dave Barry

Tony Bennett

Jack Benny

Milton Berle

Jim Bishop

Joey Bishop

Ray Bolger

Victor Borge

Foster Brooks

Julie Budd

George Burns

Red Buttons

Pat Buttram

Sid Caesar

Sammy Cahn

Cab Calloway

Vikki Carr

Jack Carter

Nell Carter

Carmen Cavallaro
Ray Charles
Jerry Clower
Perry Como
Norm Crosby

Jim Daly
Vic Damone
Bill Dana
Billy Daniels
Billy Davis, Jr.
Sammy Davis, Jr.
Dom DeLuise
Mitch DeWood
Phil Donahue

Buddy Ebsen

Lola Falana
José Feliciano
Totie Fields
Eddie Fisher
Tennessee Ernie Ford

Danny Gans
John Gary
The Golden Girls
  Bea Arthur
  Estelle Getty
  Rue McClanahan
  Betty White
Eydie Gorme
Robert Goulet
Shecky Greene
Andy Griffith
Robert Guillaume
Rose Marie Guy

Jack Haley, Sr.
Rusty Hamer

Susan Hayward
Joey Heatherton
Bob Hope
Dolores Hope

The Ink-Spots

Kate Jackson
Harry Jarkey
Ann Jillian
Jack Jones
Shirley Jones

Casey Kasem
Alan King
Gladys Knight & The Pips

Michael Landon
Steve Lawrence
Peggy Lee
Jerry Lewis
Art Linkletter
Marjorie Lord
Gloria Loring

Norman Mamey
Barry Manilow
Tony Martin
Wink Martindale
Marilyn McCoo
Phyllis McGuire
The McGuire Sisters
Harper McKay
Ed McMahon
Liza Minnelli
Corbett Monica
Marilyn Monroe
Ricardo Montalban
Joe Moshay
Ray Moshay

Anne Murray
Jan Murray

Bob Newhart
Wayne Newton
The Nicholas Brothers

Helen O'Connell
Tony Orlando & Dawn

Patti Page
Bunny Parker
Peaches & Herb
Marguerite Piazza
Walter Popp
Elvis Presley
Ray Price
Louie Prima
Ronnie Prophet

Lou Rawls
Helen Reddy
Charley Rich
Don Rickles
Sugar Ray Robinson
Jane Russell

William Shatner
Roberta Sherwood
Dinah Shore
Frank Sinatra
Keely Smith
Kay Starr
Tom Sullivan

Marlo Thomas
Rose Marie Thomas
Terre Thomas
Tony Thomas
Diana Trask
Fred Travalena

Jerry Vale
Dick Van Patten
Ben Vereen

Jesse White
Slappy White
Andy Williams
Roger Williams
Nancy Wilson

The Young Americans
Johnny Yune

And, of course, to all of my fellow members
of ALSAC.

And to those instrumental in bringing about this publication: Phyllis Grann, Christine Pepe, Norman Brokaw, and Daniel Strone.